HORIZON®
ANCIENT GREECE

WILLIAM HARLAN HALE

ibooks
new york
www.ibooksinc.com
An Original Publication of ibooks, inc.

CONTENTS

THE HAUNTING PRESENCE

O n an April day in 1811—a year in which Europe was briefly at peace—two vessels, each on an unusual mission and each with interesting passengers aboard, fell in with each other while outward bound from the Piracus, the port of Athens. One was a chartered open boat bearing two young English architects. Charles Robert Cockerell and John Foster by name, along with a German. Baron Haller von Hallerstein, who was also an architect and, moreover, a protégé of the art patron. Crown Prince Ludwig of Bavaria. The Cockerell group had set out for the island of Aegina, some twenty miles to the south of Athens, with the object of exploring, measuring, and digging out the ruins of a classical temple on that once famed island—a temple thought to have been dedicated to Zeus, and possibly rich with fallen sculpture.

The other vessel was a British naval transport, and aboard it was no less a person than Lord Byron, fresh from making love to Mrs. Spencer Smith and other ladies in the Mediterranean area, swimming the Hellespont, and writing the first cantos of *Childe Harold's Pilgrimage*. In its hold lay a cargo of twenty cases containing marble figures hauled down off the Acropolis as a private acquisition of His Majesty's late envoy at Constantinople, Lord Elgin.

Cockerell's boat gained on the laden British craft, and when the young men came astern of it they sang out a song to announce their presence. The poet looked overside, recognized them as acquaintances, and had them invited aboard for a glass of port. After the wine, the vessels resumed their separate courses: Cockerell's sailed to Aegina, where his party soon uncovered a great trove of sculpture which Ludwig of Bavaria promptly bought for his collection in Munich: the other steered homeward with its rare freight, which ended up in the British Museum.

Though the encounter of these young visitors came by chance, it was a symbolic and prophetic one. Here were several bright spirits from the West converging upon the classical land, no longer content to learn about it at second or third hand, as their fathers had, but bent on rediscovering and experiencing it themselves, all seeking to draw some inspiration or sustenance from it. And though highly individual spirits, they were at the same time exemplars of a whole new European generation that had suddenly fallen head over heels in love with ancient Greece. The era of modern man's return to Hellas had begun— an era marked also by the hauling away of its monuments.

The return was both spiritual and physical. It was spiritual in that the romantic, restless, often revolutionary generation of 1800 had turned to far-off Athens in the belief that it would find there an embodiment of its own ideals of freedom, respect for man's individual worth, and indeed of his ability to attain something like earthly perfection. The return was physical in that first a few men, then dozens, then hundreds, and finally thousands from many lands, armed with calipers and maps, picks and shovels, and using Pausanias' ancient descriptions of long-lost sites as a Baedeker, were to undertake the most massive exhumation of a culture in all history. Classical Greece came back to life for the modern age, first through the passion of the romantics, and then by long and weary work with the spade.

It is difficult for us today to conceive, now that Greece has become a popular mecca and museum, how very little there was to see of its ancient presence a century and a half ago, when the country was still a grubby and backward fief of the Turks, neglected and depopulated by more than three centuries of Janizaries' misrule. Resurrection of the monuments of classical Rome had been going on ever since the Renaissance, and many of its greater structures had survived the preceding centuries almost intact, but most of the physical vestiges of the earlier Greece had lain submerged until the age of the master diggers, from Heinrich Schliemann in the 1870's, to Sir Arthur Evans, to those of our own day. (The variety of names in the field—Curtius and Holleaux, Dörpfeld and Blegen, Thompson and Papadimitriou—tells of the international range of the effort.)

To be sure, the Acropolis still loomed over Athens, but as a kind of rubbish heap of history, overrun in turn by Goth, Slav, Norman, Venetian, and Turk, its Parthenon converted first into a Christian church and then into a Turkish mosque (with minaret attached), its walls partly topped by Frankish towers, its Erechtheum turned into a harem, its Propylaea into a crenelated palace, and the Panathenaic Way into a parade ground for Moslems. The great sanctuary of Athena finally became an ammunition storehouse that was blown up when the Venetians bombarded it in 1687, scattering Parthenon marble all over the mount. But though there were enough stones left standing atop the Acropolis to enchant a Byron or a Chateaubriand, or to arouse the interest of Lord Elgin, the ancient city of Athens below it had almost completely disappeared. A maze of Byzantine alleys and hovels—with churches, other buildings, yards, and gardens intermixed—thickly covered the area where the spacious Agora, or market place, of Periclean times had stood. Not until the mid nineteenth century were the first excavations made on that site and not until 1931 was its systematic exhumation begun—a crowning project of the American School of Classical Studies at Athens.

Where was Olympia, the early sanctuary of Zeus that had grown into a whole city of monuments, palaestrae, treasuries, and the temple of Zeus that housed Phidias' immense gold and ivory statue of the god, which was once accounted one of the Seven Wonders of the World? What had not been destroyed by edict of the emperor Theodosius II in A.D. 426, had been shattered by earthquakes and so smothered by landslides and floods that silt and meadows now overlay it. True, a Frenchman had spotted the site in 1725, but it was not until a century and a half later that intensive digging commenced there, carried out by thorough Germans.

Apollo's shrines at mountainous Delphi and on the sacred island of Delos showed but a few traces above the surface. Centuries of avalanches followed by resettlement had helped obliterate much of Delphi, while pillage, massacre, and total abandonment had helped do the same to Delos, until the French in the late nineteenth century began their long labor of unearthing both. Once-proud Corinth lay buried under later habitations, and the great healing center of ancient Greece, the shrine of Asclepius at Epidaurus, with its marvelously designed theatre, was all but lost to sight until spades went to work in 1881.

And what of Homer's Troy, his Mycenae "rich in gold," and the ninety cities he had spoken of as thriving on the island of Crete? Since almost no traces of these had been found, students all over the world had come to the conclusion that the rich palaces and kingdoms described in Homer's poems were probably only mythical, and the Trojan War itself just a legend. Until the day in 1871, that is, when Schliemann made his first inspired strike at Troy, to be followed shortly thereafter by his uncovering of the ancient citadel of Mycenae. Within a few decades, all man's perspectives on Greece were altered and vastly lengthened. To learn that much we had thought to be fable was indeed fact—to discover, with Schliemann, that the Troy of Priam and Hector had been a real place, that there had been a Mycenae whose House of Atreus was indeed rich, meant to realize that the Greeks were not simply poetizing when they wrote of ages, golden or other, that had existed in their land long before the rise of Athens. Then a whole earlier culture that had flourished in the Aegean, centuries before Mycenae, came to light when Sir Arthur Evans and others began unearthing Minoan remains in Crete in the 1890's. The ancient Greeks had only guessed at their past; now, as spades dig deeper, we know far more about it than they ever did.

Still, for all this mighty endeavor, how much remains about Greece that we do not know! In 1952 Michael Ventris deciphered the hitherto baffling Linear B script—found first at Knossos, in Crete, and then at sites in mainland Greece—which scholars had thought to represent a pre-Greek tongue; he revealed that Linear B was actually an early form of Greek, and thus that Greek had been written many centuries earlier than anyone had supposed. But as to the spoken language of Greece, we do not know exactly how it was pronounced; we do not know what a line of Sappho or Aristophanes sounded like. The Greeks were intent on music, and in Pythagoras they produced the first scholar of sound; but though we have a few inscriptions that suggest a musical score, and have mathematical knowledge of what Greek intervals were, we are unable to reconstruct an actual piece of their music. We know that the tragedians Aeschylus, Sophocles, and Euripides among them wrote some three hundred plays; but so far, only thirty-three of these have been retrieved. We also know that well over a hundred other men in classical Greece wrote tragedy; but of their work not one play survives. The Greeks wrote of "glorious Apelles," their leading painter; but none of his art is extant—nor have we any classical Greek paintings save those on pottery.

From these vases, as well as from steles and other reliefs, we know a great deal about Greek dress, household furnishing, entertainment; we have a good idea of what a Greek dwelling as a whole looked like, although no house from the classical period has survived upward of its foundation. Though sculpture is our most glorious trove from Greece, we cannot but think of all that has been lost: the great figure of the Olympian Zeus, for instance, carted off to Constantinople by Theodosius for its gold and ivory and lost in a fire there; or Phidias' two statues of Athena that once topped the Acropolis, lost without a trace; or the friezes and pediments of innumerable temples ruined by man and nature. And whatever sculpture was made of bronze was, for the most part, melted down at some later time for gain or weaponry—save that which by merciful accident was lost during sea voyages. The surrounding sea—the "blue museum," as one writer has called it—which served Greek traders so well, has served history too by preserving some of Greece's greatest treasures safe from the hands of marauders, yielding up some of them in our day to divers and the nets of fishermen.

We know much, but wish we knew more. We are fairly certain now that there was a war at Troy, and that Troy was destroyed by men; but so many questions still persist as to just who the attackers were, or just when and why they came, that a leading classicist, M. I. Finley, recently suggested that until we learn more, "the narrative we have of the Trojan War had best be removed from the realm of history and put back into the realm of myth and poetry."

Geologically, Greece is a promontory of a land largely submerged. Archaeologically, much of it is also lost to view. Mile after mile, hour after hour, as one tours Attica or the Peloponnesus today, one is struck not so much by what one sees standing of antiquity as by what is not there to see, other than in the mind's eye. But what survives in its rarity is incomparable.

Perhaps this awareness brings us closer to the singular spell that Greece has cast—for spell it has been all along, and would be, whether Olympia or Troy had been dug out or not. Whenever before or since have a people who left so few physical survivals of their greatness exerted so mighty an influence over the ages? Everyone knows that Greece immensely stirred the imagination of the Romans, who passed the Greek legacy on to the West. What some overlook is that much of the impact was conveyed to conquering Rome at a time when Greece was already in decline, whole cities having been sacked by the invaders. Thus Alpheus of Mytilene, a Greek poet of about the time of Caesar Augustus, laments:

> Lost now are the homes of the heroes. Scarce here and there
>   a city
> From the dust lifts its head a little, where the sons of the
>   gods were born.
> And such wert thou, Mycenae, as I passed, a thing of pity—
> Even the goats of the mountain have pastures less forlorn.
> The goatherds pointed toward thee. And I heard an old man
>   say,
> "The Giant-builded City, the Golden, here it lay."

The Romans in Greece, seeking to attach themselves to a tradition more cultivated than their own, dutifully copied the art they saw there, though they had more difficulty following Greek ideas. The theologians of the Middle Ages, on the other hand, to whom physical Greece was remote and paganism anathema, were fascinated by many of its ideas and looked on ancient Aristotle as "*the* philosopher." Each successive age has found something it especially sought in classical Greece, and surely the mightiest force of Greece has been that of its image impressing itself upon each age—often becoming much transfigured in the process. One could say that Hellas, the Western world's greatest creator of myths, has over all the centuries gone on creating myths about itself in the eyes of its beholders.

For each generation has had a way of constructing its own vision of Greece, according to its own predilections. Some have turned to Greece as the embodiment of the world's lost youth; others, as that of perfected form and wisdom. Medieval versifiers imagined a knightly Troy and composed pale romances dimly based on Homer; earthy Chaucer and Boccaccio wrote somewhat more lusty versions of his tales. The Renaissance was so busy reviving Rome that it viewed Greece chiefly through Roman eyes. Another idealizing style was set when Nicolas Poussin, moved by visions of an Arcadia he had never seen, painted his idyllic canvases of Greek goddesses and heroes decorously disporting themselves in sylvan groves. (Had he actually visited Arcadia and observed how harsh and forbidding much of that fastness in the Peloponnesus is, he might have made his portrayal of it less serene.) The same sense of exquisite harmony courses through C. W. Gluck's eighteenth-century operas, which were inspired by Greek myths; while to Richard Strauss, writing his own operas in the twentieth about Iphigenía, Orestes, and Electra, ancient Greece is all angry discord and violence. Even in the same generation the impulses that drive men back to Greece may differ widely. The tender Wordsworth, secluded in his Lake Country, felt chiefly nostalgia:

> *So might I, standing on this pleasant lea . . .*
> *Have sight of Proteus rising from the sea;*
> *Or hear old Triton blow his wreathèd horn.*

The archrebel Shelley, on the other hand, felt Greek ideals to be a rallying cry for freedom and revolution, and with this in mind wrote his *Prometheus Unbound.*

It would be false to say that Greece has been all things to all men. Yet if it has been so many things to so many different men, it must be in great part because Greece was so many different things to itself. For it was a culture both uniform and diverse. We speak of Greek order; yet we are always conscious of Greek contrast. On one hand we see those drives toward clarity, balance, reason, restraint, that are reflected in Hellenic architecture and philosophy; on the other, those urges of instinct, passion, boundless ambition, and excess, that are reflected in Hellenic myth, drama, religious cult, and so often in politics. The Apollonian mean constantly confronts the Dionysian extreme; and Apollo's temple at Delphi would not have had engraved on it the cautionary words "Nothing to Excess" unless the Greeks had been so given to just that.

What makes the Greeks so endlessly absorbing to us today is that in their tensions and diverse urges we can sense so many of our own. We speak of the Greeks' democracy, and with right we regard as the first ancestor of our own republic their stirring invention of a state ruled by citizen suffrage rather than by an absolute monarch. Yet at the same time we recall that many of the best minds of Athens—none more than Plato— were disillusioned with popular government and called for a return to absolute leadership by an elite. There is nothing that has been said or felt in our own last three agonizing decades of struggle between democracy and authoritarian government that was not prefigured by what was said in the Athenian Agora 2,500 years ago.

The Greeks also experienced their own collisions between science and religion, between physical evidence and traditional belief—as what people since has not? Some of the scientists and advanced thinkers made fun of their gods (many of whom were, to be sure, pretty shabby in their behavior), and the devout in turn denounced the impious. Nonconformists, people with notions of their own, which they could not resist spreading, were sometimes silenced: thus the end of Socrates.

In a few ways, to be sure, the classical Greeks remain distant from the modern West, despite all transmissions and migrations of their spirit. Though they held that man could and should enlarge his capacities, they did not believe in progress as our centuries have taught us to do. To most Greeks the general world they lived in was just the afterglow of some better, earlier, "golden age," when gods and godlike heroes had walked on earth, and which was never to be equaled or recovered. Nor did they seriously believe in immortality and fulfillment in after-life, in the sense that most Christians do, or profess they do. They felt that glory won or honor done on earth would be sufficient fulfillment, and that such immortality as there was consisted in memory of their praiseworthy deeds among men who came after them.

Yet despite these differences, Greece remains constantly in us and around us, though we may not always be conscious of it. We are in the presence of Greece, though at some remove, when we look at innumerable court houses, banks, and porticoed mansions built in America in the Greek Revival style. Some men hold that when Roman Catholics revere the Virgin

Mary, they are unconsciously the inheritors of Greek and pre-Greek worship of a mother goddess, or that when they light candles to their patron saints they are distantly linked to ancient Greeks, who made oblations to their local deities. Plato has sometimes been called a precursor of Christ.

However all this may be, the central truth remains that there is hardly an area of aspiration known to us on which the Greek mind before us had not also exercised itself. The concept of natural law—that the physical world is not simply the plaything of dark powers, but is intelligible and can be studied in search of first principles and order—this is Greek in origin, and on it all the law and the prophets of more than two millennia of science and natural philosophy have stood. The idea of gods (or, shall we say, God) as increasingly responsible to men and solicitous of them, and of man at his best, able to walk in godliness: that too—so different from the Babylonian's submission to animal spirits and the Egyptian's to his god-kings—is Greek as well as Hebrew in origin, and has profoundly affected all our religious thinking since. And the ideal of the uttermost development of all the faculties of man, as if in praise for his creation, leading to grace of body, freedom of spirit, high discipline of mind, and the love of truth: this is the very light of Greece and, though often dimmed, it has never gone out.

—W. H. H.

WILLIAM HARLAN HALE has written many highly praised books on a variety of subjects, including *The World of Rodin 1840-1917* and *The Horizon Cookbook and Illustrated History of Eating and Drinking Through the Ages.*

RECONSTRUCTED ANCIENT GREECE

For two hundred years, historians, archaeologists, and artists have sought to reveal and illuminate the grandeur of the ancient Greek world. Today, technology has made it possible to recreate Hellenic civilization in 3-D computer-generated images, allowing us to visualize what it may have looked like at the height of its greatness. Such technology was used to create the following pictures of classical Greece.

From mainland Greece to Crete and the Greek Islands and across the Aegean Sea to the coast of modern Turkey, Greece spread the light of its civilization, in law, language, architecture, philosophy, and government. These reconstructions depict buildings and sculptures in five different cities as they would have looked anywhere from 1,800 to 2,600 years ago.

Created by a team of architects, historians, computer scientists, and 3- D animation modelers, these images are based on both archaeological discoveries and historical sources. Utilizing ancient sources, contemporary scholarship, and today's computer technology, these scholar-artists have recreated Greece's ageless beauty in all its glory.

MILETUS: North Agora Of the three agoras of ancient Miletus excavated thus far, the North Agora is probably the oldest, as its construction began with the rebuilding of the city following its destruction by the Persians in the fifth century B.C. It occupied the space of several building plots of the city's grid, on the west side of the Sacred Way. During the second and third centuries B.C., a new Doric stoa surrounding the Agora was constructed on all but the eastern side. A temple-like building, probably dedicated to the worship of the Seleucid kings, was built at the very center of its west wing.

ASSOS: Temple of Athena At Troas in Asia Minor, across the
north coastline of Lesbos, at the highest point on the acropolis of
ancient Assos, a Doric temple dedicated to the goddess Athena was
built around the middle of the sixth century B.C. It was the only

notable temple of the Doric order to appear at that time in Asia Minor. The most important peculiarity of the temple is the continuous frieze that was carved on its architrave. The frieze covered the entire length of the front architrave and some of its flanks.

KITION: Inner Harbor Ship Sheds Kition is one of the oldest cities of Cyprus, inhabited continuously from 6,000 B.C. to our day. It was a very important commercial station of the eastern Mediterranean. Excavations have brought to light a row of seven ship sheds of a military harbor dated at the end of the fifth century B.C. In the ship sheds, war vessels were maintained and kept safe when not in use. Rows of ashlar walls separated the sheds and supported the timber roofs, which were covered with red terracotta roof tiles.

KNIDUS: The Gate of the Military Harbor The construction of ancient Knidus dates from around 330-340 B.C. its walls aimed at protecting three areas crucial for the city: the Triopian peninsula, the mainland region of the city, and, of course, its military harbor.

The mouth of the military harbor was protected by a pair of towers, between which a sliding chain controlled the passage of ships.

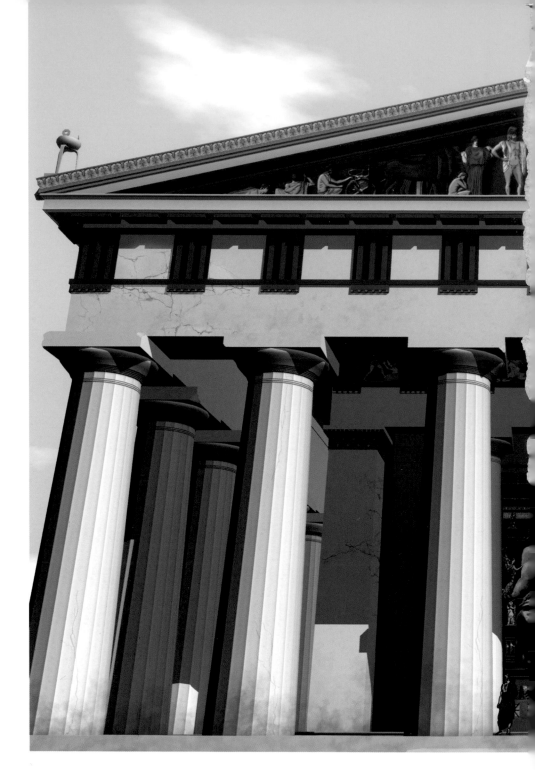

OLYMPIA: Zeus Temple The Zeus Temple of Olympia is one of the most famous Greek temples, especially because of the gold and ivory statue of Zeus made by Phidias. The construction of the temple started in 468 B.C. and was finished some ten years later. It is regarded as the standard of Doric temple architecture. The corners of the twelve metopes of the front and back inner entablature depicted the Labors of Hercules. The sculptures of the east pediment commemorated the preparation for the mythical chariot race between Pelops and Oinomaos, and the sculptures of the west pediment depicted a battle between the Lapiths and Centaurs. In 438 B.C. Phidias was called from Athens to Olympia to undertake the gold and ivory statue of Zeus, one of the Seven Wonders of the World.

MILETUS: The Delphinion The open-air sanctuary of Delphinios Apollo was built in the sixth century B.C. and was used without interruption until the third century A.D. In Hellenistic times, the sanctuary was surrounded on three sides by a two-aisled Doric stoa, or portico. During Roman times, a circular building was erected in the central area of the open-air sanctuary. The columns, as well as a large number of the inscriptions on the inside of the portico's wall, present information on the political and religious life of the city. The annual pilgrims' procession started at the Delphinion and passed through the Sacred Way towards the sanctuary of Apollo at Didyma.

MILETUS: Gate at the Harbor of Lions The Lion Harbor was situated between the Theater hill and the north part of the Humei Tepe hill and penetrated deep into the north part of the Miletus peninsula. It was the main military port of the city. Its southwest side was a center for the cult of Delphionios Apollo. The North Agora, the main agora (marketplace) of Miletus, developed on the south side of the harbor after the Persian wars. On the pier were long Doric stoas with shops and depots. The Harbor Gate was built in front of the Delphinion during the rule of Augustus (A.D. 31-14). There the Sacred Way started and crossed the whole length of the North Agora.

MILETUS: Theater The Theater of Miletus was erected in the fourth century B.C., on the southwest side of the hill of Kaletepe, the citadel of the city during classical and Hellenistic times. The remains surviving today date to the last phase of the building, from the second century A.D. It was then that the theater was at its largest size, 460 feet long, and held 15,000 spectators. In the Hellenistic period, the theater had a capacity of only 5,300 spectators and looked like a typical Greek theater. It consisted of the koilon, the slightly lower orchestra with its encircling corridor, and the stage. During the first and second Roman phases, the stage acquired a second and third floor and its width increased significantly.

MILETUS: Grattius Monument at the Harbor of Lions The Monument of Grattius was located on the eastern coast of the Harbor of Lions, near the North Agora. It was probably a votive monument offered by the Miletians in honor of a Roman civil servant or civilian who contributed significantly to the city. An inscription on its side reading C GRATTIO C. F. GAL(ERIA), as well as its architectural style, date it to the period of the Roman Flavian Dynasty (first century A.D.). It was a solid marble monument 17 feet tall , probably crowned by a marble vase.

I

THE LEANEST LAND

When on the East the sheer bright star arose
That tells of coming Dawn, the ship made landfall
And came up islandward in the dim of night.

—Homer, *the Odyssey*

Ancient Athenian sailors, threading their course homeward with a cargo of timber from Thrace or grain from beyond the Bosporus, were careful to hug the headlands and islands along the way, since they traveled without compasses or charts and were well aware of the dread storms the sea god Poseidon might send down on them if they ventured too far offshore. Yet some of the harshest waters they had to cross lay close in—none closer or more treacherous than those just off Cape Sounion at the tip of Attica itself, where winds funneled down through the narrow strait between the bony island of Euboea and Andros, another island outcrop. There the blasts often met with others whistling down from the strait of Chalcis, to the northwest, to churn up a narrow cauldron of conflicting seas. To get under the lee of Sounion—"holy Sounion," Homer called it—was every captain's need: not until he rounded it, looking up as he did so at the great temple the Athenians had built at its peak to the sea god, could he be sure that now only a short day's coasting would bring him to safe haven in the Piraeus.

As he beat his way around the bleak promontory, he passed

over a singularly dark patch of water. It is still dark today, reflecting perhaps the sudden depth below. It marks the spot below the cliff on which, according to one legend, Aegeus, a mythical king of Athens, had stood watching the ship of his son Theseus returning from Crete. Because of an oversight, it approached under black sails rather than white (the pre-arranged signal); he believed mistakenly that Theseus had per-ished in his struggle with the Cretan Minotaur, and so hurled himself headlong into the sea—the sea that thereupon became known as the Aegean.

All ancient Greece begins with myths—and, one could say, with storms as well. The expedition against Troy—the war that forms the subject of the *Iliad*—began with a contrary high wind, the norther that bottled up more than a thousand Greek ships at their assembly port of Aulis and prevented Agamemnon and his fellow chieftains from making sail for Troy. It was only when King Agamemnon, at a soothsayer's behest, sacrificed his own daughter Iphigenia on the altar to angry Artemis that the blow abated. The high wind was an ill wind too; for the deed the king performed to allay it brought about the fulfillment of an ances-tral curse upon his house: because he sacrificed their daughter, his wife Clytemnestra murdered him on his return, and their son Orestes in turn murdered her.

The *Odyssey*, in dealing with the return voyage of some of the warriors who had fought at Troy, abounds in tempests unleashed at the caprice of contentious gods. Thus, after the marooned Odysseus was helped by the nymph Calypso to escape her island on a raft, Poseidon was so bent on tormenting the hero that,

> *Brewing high thunderheads, he churned the deep*
> *With both hands on his trident—called up wind*
> *From every quarter, and sent a wall of rain*

To blot out land and sea in torrential night.
Hurricane winds now struck from the South and East
Shifting North West in a great spume of seas,
On which Odysseus' knees grew slack, his
Heart sickened, and he said within himself:
"Rag of man that I am, is this the end of me?"

Homer could hardly have composed such a passage unless the perils and excitements of the sea lay deep within his consciousness; indeed they were a part of the everyday experience of the Greeks, one of the world's first great sailor folk.

All Greece begins with its surrounding sea, the "wine-dark," turbulent waters swirling around three sides of a peninsula thrust out like a bony hand from the European main. Rarely more than thirty miles removed from the sea even when in the mountainous interior, Greece's early settlers were drawn to it despite all dangers. They called it *pontos,* which also means "passage" or "road." And road it became for them, beckoning them toward a far horizon and making the Greeks very different kind of men from the haughty lords and the serfs that peopled the river valleys of sunbaked Egypt and the Middle East. As early as the dim Mycenaean age in the second millennium before Christ—an age that Homer's sagas are now thought to reflect in part—ventures from the Peloponnesus set up trading posts as far away as Italy and Syria. At the beginning of the first millennium Greeks were settling in Asia Minor. In the eighth and seventh centuries B.C. they were establishing settlements around the shores of the western Mediterranean and sailing northeastward against the currents of the Bosporus and all the way to the Crimea. All Greece, one could say, begins with the pursuit of adventure, despite the interfering gods, and with the reward and knowledge gained thereby.

Today the image of a storm-tossed, god-tormented Greece

may seem somewhat remote. A current handbook *Tourism in Greece* advertises "balmy climate . . . enchanting islands amid sparkling waters." Byron wrote rhapsodically of Greece's "eternal summer." Painter and poet, scholar and tourist alike, have helped compound a genteel Western notion of a Hellas of balm and amplitude.

The ancient Greeks, however, saw a different kind of country: a land lean rather than rich, divided by mountains often impassable, meager of soil and water, without navigable rivers, its "sylvan groves" few and far between, discomforts great, and surrounded by seas often more malignant than benign. In such an environment life was bound to be hard-working and difficult. Homer would hardly have recognized his homeland in the courtly paintings of it done in the seventeenth century by Poussin (who had never been there); in them all waters are ample and still, goddesses are graceful presences among the copses, and no leaf stirs. Homer himself spoke of Greece as a violent land: seas are always heaving, winds and torrents are always rushing, tall trees are trembling, and gods and heroes are constantly colliding, burning with passion and intent on doing in their enemies.

Eternal summer? In the early seventh century B.C. the poet Hesiod warned:

> Beware the month of Lenaeon—foul days, all of them,
> of sharp air that would flay an ox; beware the cruel
> hoar-frosts that Boreas brings when he blows upon the
> face of the earth.

> Over Thrace the land of horses he blows, and
> breathes upon the wide sea and lifts it up. Earth also
> and her forests bellow aloud.

Ample, generous valleys? There were some, of course; but
Plato, speaking in his *Critias* of the Attic landscape, says that it
looks like "the skeleton of a body wasted by disease." Ease of
life? Herodotus, the first and perhaps the greatest Greek historian, writes in one stark sentence of the land that he had traveled well: "Hellas has always had poverty as her companion."

Even today, despite much work to reclaim and terrace its
eroded uplands, hardly one fifth of Greece is arable. The rest is
mostly tortuous ridge and pitching declivity, from the Pindus
range down through the limestone spines of Attica and the
Peloponnesus that reach out toward stony islands. There are
watered plains beside the Ionian Sea in the west, and some in
Thessaly, Attica, Boeotia, and around Corinth too; but in many
parts of the east and south the strata tend to rise abruptly from
the Aegean; and before the Greek is fairly out of sight of the sea
he is likely to find himself on a lonely height where no grain
grows, where only lean sheep graze, and where, higher up, the
only inhabitant, feeding on stunted growth, is the ubiquitous
goat, the symbol of his country's ageless poverty.

Between the heights lie isolated valleys, often fertile, without a river system worthy of the name to connect them. In such
terrain, communities tended to remain detached from those
beyond the next ridge; often communication between them by
sea around the capes was more feasible than overland. Zeus's
shrine at Olympia in the west, pleasantly sited in a vale at the
confluence of two streams, with cypress and oleander all about,
was hardly sixty miles from Sparta, as the crow flies; but to the
Spartan athlete journeying there for the Panhellenic games it
involved a trek of a week or more, winding by trail across the
Peloponnesus. A journey to Apollo's oracle at Delphi, high on
the flanks of Mount Parnassus, is today just three hours by car
from Athens, but in ancient times it was a major undertaking,

involving long days' marches along dry river beds, or across torrents in winter, followed by a slow ascent from the gorges— and, if you hailed from the southern part of Greece, it involved a trip by boat across the Gulf of Corinth as well. Yet so great was the importance attached to the Delphic oracle that there was a stream of traffic to it of individual seekers and messengers of state from all over the Greek world and sometimes from foreign kingdoms as well.

Though well-favored Olympia had its streams, most inland waters are hardly what we should consider rivers at all. They resemble nothing so much as the arroyos of the arid American Southwest—torrential with flash-floods when the rains come, but waste beds of rubble and lizards in the dry season. No wonder far-traveled Herodotus was impressed by the Nile and Euphrates when he saw them—broad rivers that actually kept flowing all the year around.

Lacking constant water coursing across his land, the Greek relied primarily on local springs, of which there was a happy abundance. Along with them was a store of myths about sacred wells and the gods who had beneficently caused them to arise. The earliest Athenians, when they chose the sheer limestone Acropolis as site for a town and citadel, could hardly have made it livable or defensible unless there had been fresh water there. And water there was, its origin according to one legend being this: In very early times Zeus's elder brother Poseidon, the sea god and earth-shaker, vied with Zeus's daughter Athena for the role of protector and patron of the city. To show his power, Poseidon struck the stones of the Acropolis with his trident, and up sprang a gushing well. Athena, for her part, cast her spell upon the stones and produced a thriving olive tree. The citizens of Athens, asked to choose between the deities, chose Athena by a majority of one vote—the winning ballot being a woman's (which was the last time that women in

Athens were allowed to vote). Vengeful Poseidon, a version of the legend tells us, then sent a flood upon Athens; but his well remained. It is known that in Mycenaean times a fountain existed deep in a seam of the rocks and supplied water for the Acropolis' dwellers. And today there are still travelers who, bending low over the fissures, insist that they hear the murmur of Poseidon's ancient waters far beneath.

And if a traveler now, as in ancient times, makes a pilgrimage to Delphi, the first welcome sight, as the dusty, hairpin road from Athens attains the heights, is that of a fountain of coldest water bursting forth from a cleft in the vertical red seams of Parnassus overhead, no matter how dry the season. This is the unfailing sacred spring, as inviting to the tourist or shepherd today, as he scoops his hands to drink of it, as it was to the petitioner even in the age of Homer.

Four millennia and more of settlement, plus the tramplings of innumerable conquests and a history of poor husbandry, have taken their toll of Greek land and resource. Denuded by woodsmen, chewed over by voracious goats, in turn fought over and abandoned when the local populations were decimated or enslaved and carried away, the upland has been eroded. Today it probably sustains far fewer cattle than it did in Homeric times. Yet the process of impoverishment began early— so early that Plato, looking back over the past of Attica, speaks of its soil in his time as only "a remnant" of what it had been, much that had once supported fine herds before the coming of great "deluges" and "ravages" having since been washed away into the sea. In Homer's tales, heroes are constantly feasting on meat; in early times a whole province of Greece was named Boeotia—"land of the cow"—for the herds that grazed on it. But such herds appear to have declined almost to the vanishing point by Periclean times. Meat was eaten only on festival days, when animals were sacrificed to the gods; otherwise, two meals

a day of barley and other grain dishes were the rule—a diet so
austere that the Persian invaders complained of it. Even today,
the rural Greek subsists on two meals a day, and a dinner of
meat is a festive occasion.

The bees of Mount Hymettus provided honey (there was no
sugar). The olive provided cooking oil (there was no butter) and,
on its subsequent pressings, oil for personal cleansing (there
was no soap) and for lamps as well, after which its lees were
used for fuel. The goat provided cheese, a little grudging milk,
and an occasional muscular haunch for the pot (if one was
ready to destroy the goat for the sake of eating the meat). Lean
sheep provided the wool that Greek wives and their maidser-
vants spun and wove into the plain oblong lengths that provided the basic year-round garment of man and woman alike.
There was some flax, and it was made into linen, another popular material for clothing. Cotton was yet hardly known, and
silk was not cultivated in Greece until long after the time of
Christ. There were a few fruits—chiefly the fig, pomegranate,
apple, and pear—but the citrus stands that now grace the western Peloponnesus did not exist then.

Grapes there were in plenty, best grown in Chalcidice and
Thrace, on the islands of Thasos, Chios, and Samos, and in
Attica; and the Greeks were a wine-drinking people. They were,
according to legend, taught the art of the vine by Dionysus, the
strange, wild god who had come down from the north and for
long was not quite accepted by the Olympians. But though
Dionysus was the patron of great revels, wine was by no means
identified with them only: it was drunk daily and somewhat
abstemiously, usually diluted with one or two parts of water, as
the only enlivening accompaniment to a generally monotonous
diet. And the Greek palate for the grape was hardly a discerning
one. A story has it that the Athenians, anxious to save their
stocks of wine during the Persian invasions by making them

unpalatable to the thirsty eastern intruders, doctored their storage jars with resin from their pine trees. This stratagem had a paradoxical result: though the Persians found the mixture not potable, when the Greeks themselves reopened the rejected amphorae, they discovered that, indeed, it was, and have been drinking *retsina,* with its strong taste of turpentine ever since. A more likely explanation is that resin was used to seal the porous clay wine jars, affecting the wine's flavor, and that the Greeks grew to like the odd taste.

Finally there were fish, with so many seas about, but the notion of ample Aegean fisheries is another literary illusion. Good fishing grounds demand strong marine vegetation; the Aegean's translucent, opalescent, stone-bottomed depths have been as bare of clouding sea-growth as Attica, throughout historic times, has been of grasslands. The result was that the fisherman was often lucky if he could haul in a handful of paltry sardines or spear an octopus for his long day's work.

One thing his country did possess: a steady climate, rather than weather that changed daily, and upon this much depended. Jutting into the sea, between cloud-hung Europe and the hard stare of Africa's sun, Greece lived under seasons that alternated but that promised half a year of almost constant warmth and light. In fall came fertilizing rains for next year's crops, in winter, torrential ones; then, as if by clockwork, in April or early May the atmosphere lifted to bring azure days that might go on uninterrupted by any cloud or rainfall for six months, until in late fall, skies thickened again, and traders and fishermen beached their boats, shepherds brought their flocks down off the heights, and ephors and councilors of state suspended wars and other expeditions until the following spring. During the long, bright summer season storms did indeed assault the coast; but such are the peculiarities of Greek atmosphere that an undimmed sun and pleasant breezes could be bathing the Acropolis while high crests of sea were driving boats into cover at the Piraeus, four miles away. And even in midwinter—Hesiod's "month of Lenaeon"—with all the winds unloosed, there might remain over Attica that extraordinary, penetrating Hellenic light.

Such a climate, so clear, firm, and hospitable throughout much of the year, left its profound impress upon the mind and ways of Greek man. He saw no fogs, as northerners do, no misty mornings of low-hanging sun mingling with gray haze and overcast. He looked up into the hills and saw instead, day after day, dry, hard, sculptural forms of nature cast into bold relief as the sun began its climb in Helios' chariot (though very few Greeks actually believed in the chariot); and then, as the orb rolled westward, he saw these forms changing in all their facets—highlights were very high, shadows were very dark, and there was little softness in between.

This sense of great clarity of form and of sharp, even violent, contrast we shall see running through all Greek consciousness and art. One first encounters it, inevitably, in the temples or remnants of temples that survive—those structures upon which the Greeks lavished their greatest care and cost, and which in the eyes of so many bespeak the very landscape itself, being so hard, spare, and lean of line, resembling Mount Pentelicon's own marble rocks in the way in which they catch the strong, contrasting, ever-changing play of sun and shade.

They were temples, moreover, open to all weathers. Though each had its walled-in, central sacerdotal chamber, windowless and dark, its greatest beauty lay in its surrounding treelike colonnade, windswept and sun-crossed like all Greece itself. Indeed, almost all the surviving Greek architecture one can see or detect today (apart from the deep tombs of Mycenae, the walled-in treasuries of Delphi, or the council chamber at Athens) was outdoor architecture—the colonnaded temple, the

portico, the hillside theatre, the roofless stadium. This in turn
tells of an outdoor people, living in close communion with sun
and landscape. The Athenian's place of business was the Agora,
originally a broad cleared field below the Acropolis; his exercise and recreation place was the gymnasium courtyard; his
walking and talking place, particularly under high summer sun
or when winds and the rains came, the covered portico, or *stoa;*
his parliament, the slope called the Pnyx. It was only in the
harshest months that he spent much time in his uncomfortable
dwellings, poorly warmed by braziers, hibernating awhile in
structures so modest that they have yielded little but rubble to
the archaeologist's spade.

In any season the Greek had time to reflect upon his unique
homeland, so exposed to the surrounding seas and thereby in
danger of conquest, so divided by inland heights and cut in two
by the Gulf of Corinth, so inchoate, and yet so strategic,
athwart the water routes from east to west, north to south. It
was a land, first of all, that called for a tough, hardy people,
able to make do with little and to supplement by their own
resources what they lacked from nature's gods. It was a land
turned outward, in need of commanding every sea around it if
it was to survive and grow, and yet one of small population.
Asia had empires at a time when Greece yet had only sparse
settlements, with local kings ruling over hamlets. Even martial
Sparta at its strongest was able to place only five thousand citizens in the field against the Persians at Plataea in the year
479 B.C.; and though great Athens and its allies mobilized
against the Persian invaders a force numbered in tens of thousands, this was still a small one to throw against one rumored
to consist of hundreds of thousands.

The Greek's greatest strength and irreducible asset, as the
world was to know, lay in intangibles—in his conception of
himself and of his relation to his gods and fellow men. Did his

physical environment play some deep part in forming these, calling forth some special genius of race? And what was it that caused men to come to the land of Greece in the first place, to become there the Hellenes of history?

There was no single race that came; there was an amalgam of several. From both east and north, early men and influences came to the land. Neolithic mounds and implements have been found at many sites from northern Thessaly down through the Peloponnesus to Knossos on Crete, and they tell of tribes with a knowledge of farming, which spread into the Aegean world from the grasslands of the ancient Near and Middle East, where, so far as we know, the art of agriculture first sprang up. By the early third millennium, Bronze Age cultures in Mesopotamia and Egypt—characterized by commerce, kingship, the skills of writing and of working in bronze—were spreading their influences to coastal Asia Minor, the Aegean islands, and primitive mainland Greece.

An exuberant and luxurious culture arose on Crete, which was peopled by a dark-haired Eastern stock. This civilization, known as Minoan after the legendary monarch Minos, was influenced by Egypt and Asia Minor, but showed a marked departure from ponderous Eastern styles in the grace and delicacy of its arts. Far inferior to the brilliant Minoan culture flourishing on Crete in this period were the Helladic culture in parts of still rudimentary agricultural mainland Greece and another, in the nearby islands, called the Cycladic. These societies are dim to our knowledge when compared to what succeeded them in the second millennium at Mycenae, Tiryns, Pylos, Orchomenos, and other sites on the mainland, where a ruling people called the Mycenaeans, who were strongly influenced by Minoan culture, established a strong and highly organized society, building proud bastions on high hills. They have left behind numerous remains—among them ornate golden cups from which they drank, their women's marvelously wrought jewelry, and even more marvelous, the traditions and tales that were later woven into the *Iliad* of Homer.

These Mycenaeans gave Greece its first age of power and brilliance. Until recently, some scholars believed them to be off-shoots of the Minoan race, but in 1952 Michael Ventris deciphered the script known as Linear B and found it to be a primordial form of Greek. Now it is believed that the Mycenaeans, who used this script, were in fact the earliest Greek-speaking peoples of the mainland. It is supposed that at the beginning of the second millennium they arrived in Greece as barbaric tribesmen, sweeping down and conquering the original inhabitants. Their incursion unsettled the whole Aegean area: vocabularies and races intermixed in the land and turbulence governed the times.

Much about their origins remains a riddle. We do know, however, that they came in close and beneficial contact with the highly civilized Minoans of Crete, and that sometime around 1400 B.C. they may have conquered that island; under their rule the palaces and culture of Crete flourished for centuries more, like the Mycenaean kingdoms on the mainland. Mycenaean traders and rovers sailed as far as Italy, Egypt, and the Syrian coast, and the Hittites in Asia Minor became aware of a Mycenaean tribe or people they called the "Ahhiyawa"—a name very like Homer's name for the inhabitants of Greece, the Achaeans. But then, amid all this stir and bustle, toward the end of the millennium a second descent from the north took place, led apparently by another and less civilized Greek-speaking tribe which had hovered long at the outskirts of the Mycenaean world, and which history was to call the Dorians. Precisely how and when these people assaulted the Mycenaeans, we do not know either; we do know that in the twelfth and eleventh centuries the lights of Mycenaean culture went out, and that in the

seizures and brutalities of the age the invaders toppled the
Mycenaean kingdoms, took their women and subjected their
peasants, but assimilated little of their high culture. After about
1100 B.C., mainland Greece reverted to a stage far more primitive than that of the preceding eras. We call the four centuries
that followed 1100 the Greek dark ages; at least, they are dark
to us.

They were dark, or at least mysterious, to the Greeks of classical times too. Men of the classical age in the fifth century
were fascinated by their origins, though they had only vague
and mythic knowledge of their ancestors. Yet they were aware
that into their making there had gone not one but several
sources of blood. They were conscious of some distinction
between a primordial folk who had lived in their land from time
immemorial and a spate of later arrivals from elsewhere who
had come to mingle with them. The proud Athenians in particular liked to insist that they themselves were descendants of
aboriginal or indigenous Pelasgians. And though modern
scholarship knows nothing about any Pelasgians as actual pre-
Hellenic ancestors, the Athenian claim is not all sheer mythmaking. For the very name of Athens, like that of its patron
goddess Athena, is paradoxically non-Greek and may hark
back to some earlier native language.

Herodotus, the first Greek student of the past, remarks on
the survival of what he calls this "barbarian language" down to
his own day, and argues that one should distinguish between
the Dorians and the Ionians (those who settled in Asia Minor) as
two main branches of the Greek people, the latter being of
Pelasgian roots. This again displays the Greeks' awareness of
diversity in their midst. This diversity was to become quite visible as Ionians raised settlements on the pleasant Asia Minor
coast, while the Dorians concentrated more and more on the
rugged Peloponnesus. The former produced the first Greek liter-

ature and philosophy, together with spirited and lively forms in art, whereas the latter stressed that strength and austerity which one associates with early Sparta and the shape of the emerging Doric temple.

This development took centuries. It was to take centuries, also, for these differences across land and sea, between tribes and tongues, to result in what can be called the Greek fusion. In the fifth century Herodotus (himself a Dorian) could write of certain general or joint qualities that had marked the Hellenes as a whole during their struggle against the oncoming Persians. These were, he said, "our common language, the altars and the sacrifices of which we all partake, the common character which we bear." And of these the last, the "common character," was to be the greatest. On a meager land, thinly peopled, divided by geography, racial origin, political differences, and often conflicting impulses a common culture was in process of creation. This was the central Greek achievement; from it, what is best in Greece springs.

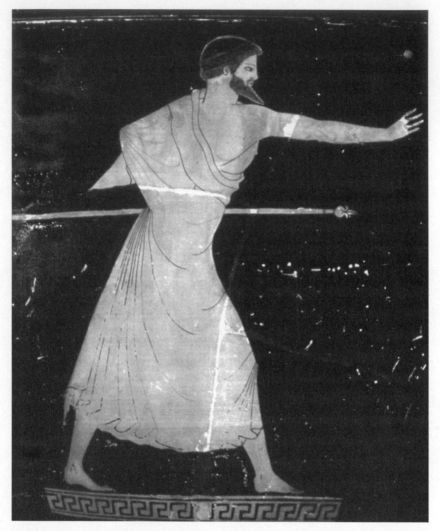

The detail of an early fifth-century vase painting above depicts Zeus, the supreme ruler of the gods. The worship of Zeus probably entered Greece during the Indo-European invasions that started early in the second millennium.

II

GODS AND ANCESTORS

Earth, the beautiful, rose up,
Broad-bosomed, she that is the steadfast base
Of all things. And fair Earth first bore
The starry Heaven, equal to herself . . .

—Hesiod, *Theogony*

The gods were there early in Greece, though not at the outset of things. "In the beginning God created the heavens and the earth," says Genesis; but the Greek preferred to see the process the other way around, believing that a dawning universe was first, rising out of primeval Chaos to bring forth its gods. Then Genesis tells us that on the sixth and culminating day "God created man in his own image"; but the Greek had different ideas about this too. Uncertain in his own mind as to what the images of his gods actually were before the origin of man, he inclined to the belief that the creation of man was probably not the act of any supreme godhead at all; rather it was an assignment given by Zeus and his peers to a demigod, Prometheus, who fashioned humans from clay and water and then went off the celestial reservation, so to speak, and brought down heavenly fire, without authorization, to assist his protégé.

The ancient Egyptians had bowed to a whole armory of animal-like gods embodying the dread spirits of nature; the Babylonians were obsessed by the terrifying presence of demons everywhere. It has been said that it was the Greek's great departure, as his centuries advanced and he built shrines to a beautiful Apollo, a wise Athena, a lovely and chaste Artemis, and a humane and ever-helpful Hermes, to be the first to erect gods in man's own image. This is not only false but it also ignores the beginnings of Greek religion and oversimplifies and distorts both the Greek's mind and his history. In classical times he did assemble a gallery of stately and more or less responsible and urbane Olympian deities; but he also retained the memory of dark, inscrutable powers that had ruled him in earlier times, and from whose spell he was never to be quite free.

A sense of the awesome, the mysterious, the numinous, remained with him even during the peak of the Periclean enlightenment: grottoes and caves were peopled by strange spirits, dread Hecate of the underworld did deeds of darkness at ghostly crossroads when the moon was down, the sea monster Triton was to be feared as Poseidon's son, and sacred snakes were to be respected. Long after the sixth-century Ionian philosopher Thales had laid the groundwork for Greek scientific thought, and even during the fifth century when Pericles was preaching democracy and Aeschylus was writing his noblest dramas in Athens, the snake—totem of many primitive peoples—was still being worshiped on the Acropolis. It is possible that even in the century of Plato human sacrifice was still practiced in the back country. In a fourth-century document called the *Minos* (a dialogue sometimes attributed to Plato) there is a reference to rumors of human sacrifices still taking place in secret places in the Arcadian hills in the Peloponnesus.

Far from being humanized deities, the early gods of Greece were all either inhuman or subhuman, in contrast with the Hebraic (and also Christian) concept of the godhead; indeed, so acute is this contrast that one stops to ask how these two traditions could ever have met and mingled. Yet mingle they did, early Christian thought owing almost as much to Greek religion and philosophy in their later, refined stages as to Hebraic theol-

ogy. At the outset, though, we have on one side the single
vision of an all-knowing god-father, creator of all things visible
and invisible, and maker of man, "the masterwork of all yet
done," as John Milton was to write. On the other side we have a
tortuous and prolix collection of Greek creation myths, beginning with some primordial Chaos out of which a semblance of
order gradually sprang.

Among the early recorders of myths, the poet Hesiod stands
out. He became so fascinated with the stories of his people that
he put them together in a kind of genealogy of some 1,000
bardic lines. (Scholars disagree on Hesiod's dates; but, unlike
Homer, he is a definitely established historical personage and
lived probably sometime around the beginning of the seventh
century.) If you go by his particular organization of mythology
in his *Theogony*, what happened was that "first Chaos came into
being, next wide-bosomed Gaea (Earth), Tartarus, and Eros
(Love). From Chaos came forth Erebus and black Night."
Another version has it that Night and Erebus between them
strangely produced Love, which in turn brought forth Light and
Day, after which, in a manner unexplained, Earth came into
being. Then Earth (personified by the aboriginal goddess Gaea)
united with Heaven (in the form of Uranus) to bring forth a race
of creatures ranging from the immense Titans to the one-eyed
Cyclopes to a trio of monsters, each possessing fifty heads and
one hundred hands. According to one fable, Uranus became
incensed at the behavior of his monster offspring and imprisoned them. This in turn aroused Gaea, who appealed for help.
The Titan Kronos answered and rose against his father and cas-
trated him; from Uranus' blood there sprang up another race of
monsters, the Giants, who in their turn were accompanied by
the fearful Erinyes, or Furies, pursuers of evildoers.

As legend has it, Kronos and his sister-goddess Rhea ruled
the universe for aeons, while a host of lesser divinities of land,

sea, and cave sprouted up beside them. Then, as the sixth of their progeny, they brought forth Zeus, whom Kronos wished to devour (he had already swallowed his first five children), having learned from a prophecy that one of his sons would unseat him. But the boy Zeus was secreted by his mother in a mountain cave on the island of Crete and thereby escaped Kronos' murderous intent; on growing to maturity, he in turn raised revolt against his sire and most of the other Titans and Giants too. Upon winning this celestial civil war, Zeus drew lots for rule of the universe between himself and his brothers Poseidon, who became lord of the sea, and Hades, who became king of the underworld, realm of the dead, while he himself became ruler of the sky. With the ancestral monsters now disposed of, all might have proceeded smoothly with the invention called man, had not Prometheus, "the forethinker," exceeded instructions and made himself man's champion. Prometheus, it appears, having first disobeyed Zeus by stealing heavenly fire in order to make man strong on earth, next proceeded to deceive the reigning god in a most humiliating fashion. Carving up a great ox that was to be sacrificed by men to the gods, he separated the good flesh from the bones, concealing the first heap under ugly entrails and hide, and the second under a handsome wrapping of fat. Then he asked Zeus to select the heap he preferred. The god chose the handsomer-looking one, only to find, when he came upon bones underneath, that he had been tricked. From then on, the old story says, men held back the best meat of the animal for themselves, and offered to the gods chiefly that part of the beast that was inedible.

In his wrath Zeus determined upon two punishments—one to be imposed upon Prometheus, and another upon man himself. For his double effrontery, the rebel demigod was chained to a rock in the Caucasus, to be visited each day by an eagle that would tear out his liver, after it had grown in again each night.

(Another reason for Zeus' vengeance against Prometheus appears in Aeschylus' *Prometheus Bound:* Zeus, like his father Kronos before him, had an inkling that a son of his own would dethrone him, and only Prometheus knew who this would be. This secret the ruler of the gods tried to extract from Prometheus by torture, without success.)

As for man, he was to undergo another form of torment. As Hesiod puts it, Zeus exclaimed, "I shall give man an evil as the price of fire: they will clasp destruction with laughter of desire." So he brought about the creation of young Pandora, beautifully garlanded and bejeweled, seductive and irresistible to men—the Eve, so to speak, of Prometheus' Adam, and the author of many of his woes. (A different version of the Pandora myth tells of her as the bringer of trouble to man not through her innate evil, but simply through her lightheadedness. Incurably inquisitive, she could not resist opening a jar that the gods had given her but had forbidden her to touch, with the result that mischief and evil flew out to spread among men everywhere.) Later, still angry at man's ways, Zeus, according to a further account, drowned the whole earth under great torrents with the aid of his brother Poseidon. Only the peak of Mount Parnassus was left showing— upon which, paradoxically, the only two humans to find refuge and so survive the deluge were Pyrrha, daughter of trouble-bringing Pandora, and Deucalion, son of rebellious Prometheus.

All told, it is hardly an elevating creation story. Neither, of course, is that of the Hebrews, with its tale of man's first dis-obedience, Cain's murder of his brother, and Yahweh's brutal extermination of all wicked mankind save Noah and his kin. Zeus, to be sure, as the incoming father god of the Greeks, is a very different presence from Yahweh, notably in his rutting activity, for he was intent upon impregnating every female whom he could lay hands upon, goddess or near goddess, from Io and Europa and Themis and Mnemosyne to Dione, Maia,

Leto, Aegina, Semele, Niobe, and his sister-wives Demeter and
Hera. The resulting offspring included Apollo, Artemis, Persephone, Hebe, Ares, Aphrodite, Hephaestus, and the Graces,
Muses, and Hours—along with Athena, who sprang from his
own brow. Yet while Yahweh in his austere and omnipotent
majesty seems to stand poles apart from lusty Zeus, the thun-
derer who was so slow-witted at times that Prometheus could
readily trick him, some correspondences between the Greek and
Hebraic stories stand forth—the equivocal role of woman and
the sending down of some great primeval, punitive flood—a dim
memory shared, in various forms, in much of the Near East.

The early Hebrews were fortunate in their own eyes, and
have perhaps remained so in ours, because they received from
Moses the God-given tablets of law. Upon that rock they
erected their system and belief, with a priesthood to support it,
and no doubt vanished in the process many tribal customs and
superstitions that had existed before. With the Greeks all was
different: there was never to be among them dogma or an
agreed theology; there was never in fact to be a professional
priesthood or caste or Mother Church or universal Olympian
ritual. There remained, instead, over the centuries a mixture of
gods high and low, divinities old and new, deities above the
earth and below it, spirits local and instant, and an accumulation of ancestral beliefs to which each Greek man either sub-
scribed or did not, according to his lights. The result, as against
the stern single-minded Hebraic belief in Yahweh, was disorder—polytheistic and often frivolous. Yet out this an impulse
was to arise in Greece that in its way paralleled the Judaic one:
to build an ethical religion in which man would be God's
responsible agent, not his slave, and in which God (or the gods)
would be responsive to man. For all their differences, this was
to set both Greek and Jew many ages apart from the sub-
servient folk of other lands around them. The savage Zeus of

legend became in Aeschylus a high moral power comparable to the God of Moses whose laws presaged the teachings of Christ.

Dense population—if not overpopulation—is the mark of the Greek spirit world, with its nymphs, centaurs, daemons, harpies, gorgons, sirens, dryads, satyrs; its Furies, Fates, and Graces (three of each); its Muses (Calliope of epic poetry, Clio of history, Erato of lyric poetry, Euterpe of flute music, Melpomene of tragedy, Thalia of comedy, Terpsichore of the dance, Polyhymnia of mimic art, and Urania of astronomy); its Hours (goddesses of the seasons varying in name and number from place to place); its ruling clan of a dozen Olympian gods and goddesses, supported by a flock of lesser ones (from Eros to Pan and Persephone) and by a few mortals become gods (the hero Heracles and the healer Asclepius), all in addition to earlier, remoter deities (Gaea and Uranus, Kronos and Rhea). This multiplicity tells of many Greek characteristics, but above all of an immense imagination, peopling with wondrous beings almost every nook and cranny of the known earth, together with the air above and the deep below. It tells also of numerous traditions ranging far over time and space and of a Greek impulse, when conquering or absorbing some town or countryside, to absorb its old gods also, rather than abolish them, as later conquerors and civilizers often did. Zeus' many "marriages" are a mythical way of expressing the union of the religion of the incoming Greeks with ancient mother goddesses or cults long present. The Argonaut Jason, on reaching the faraway harbor of Colchis in quest of the Golden Fleece, made libation to the local deities "in accordance with ancient custom," says a Greek commentator; Alexander the Great in his recorded conquests was to do the same much later.

Some of the traditions hark back to prehistoric fertility rites, magic incantations, propitiatory worship of certain beasts and of the dead; others came into Greece variously from Crete, from the Near East, from the Thracian north, with the result that inter-marriages occurred between gods and spirits that in their way mirrored the intermixture of tribes that was taking place in Greece. The worship of bull-like Zeus may have been preceded by worship of an actual bull (though most scholars now dispute this); he is generally believed to have arrived in Greece as an Indo-European thunder god; then, in Homer, he emerges as the "Father of Gods and Men" not, to be sure, endowed with a high sense of morality, but still the dispenser of rough justice. "Cow-eyed" Hera, his consort, may have been at first quite literally a sacred cow; then she became a kind of local earth mother in the wake of the earlier Gaea; and in Homer she becomes the enthroned first lady of Olympus, and an extremely difficult one too—haughty in her role as protectress of marriage, and implacably angry at Zeus' irrepressible rounds of amours.

Athena, the wise one, was supposedly born from the brow of Zeus as the embodiment of heavenly wisdom. Her chief symbol in Athens, the owl, suggests her evolution from a pre-Hellenic deity worshiped in association with birds. She seems to have been connected with the palace goddess held in high esteem among the Mycenaeans for her martial virtues and her protection of the home, her attributes having been a snake, a shield, a tree, and a bird. Much later, Homer on occasion has her take the form of a bird: "Even as she spoke, Athena left them—seeming a seahawk, in a clap of wings. . . ." (The very epithet Homer constantly uses to describe Athena, "flashing-eyed" or "bright-eyed," can also be translated as "owl-faced," again conveying a memory of an earlier incarnation.) Scholars have long asked whether the Greeks, coming down from the north, may not have brought with them a martial, Valkyrie-like figure whom they identified with the ancient native goddess, resulting in the virgin of classical times who denied herself ordinary love and marriage. In any case, Athena finally developed from a flying spirit and tutelary house goddess into the patroness of Greek culture at its greatest—later, moreover, to be identified in part with the image of *Hagia Sophia,* or Holy Wisdom, of the Eastern Christian Church. (To complete the transformation process, Western Christians were to mistranslate or misunderstand what was meant by *Hagia Sophia*—an idea, not a person—and conclude that there was a Saint Sophia.)

And who at the start was Artemis, supposed sibling of Apollo as a result of Zeus' union with the Titan daughter Leto? She was not at the outset the "queen and huntress, chaste and fair" of whom Ben Jonson speaks. In her first being, so far as we know, she was rather "the many-breasted Great Mother of Asia"—a primeval fertility queen encountered by the Greeks when they colonized Ephesus in about the year 1000 B.C., and represented in images that show her bosom erupting in multitudinous mammae, or eggs, with figures of rams, lions, hinds, griffins, and sphinxes decorating her barbaric bodice. Yet this alien deity too was taken into the Olympian pantheon and there transformed into the classical one of youthful grace and chastity—though the Greeks also entertained thoughts that she had some linkage with Hecate, underworld spirit of the evil eye.

Other deities were later arrivals in the Greek godly circle—none with greater effect than the love goddess Aphrodite, whose origins were also eastern, and the wine god Dionysus, who came down from Thrace in the north. Though Aphrodite traveled far, finally becoming the Venus of the Romans, her nature, unlike Artemis', did not change greatly in the process: her cult often promoted frank sexuality, and the Greeks of classical times used the very word *aphrodite* to denote the sex act itself. Hesiod and later poets described her rising at birth from sea foam off Cythera; and her cult flourished particularly on nearby Cyprus, an island where Greeks and Semites mingled. She seems to have been derived from the sex and fertility goddess worshiped far and wide in the Near East as Ishtar, Astarte, or Ashtoreth; Herodotus tells of such a goddess, named Mylitta, whose cult involved sacred prostitution, as did Ishtar's, and relates Aphrodite to her: "The Babylonians have one most shameful custom. Every woman born in the country must once in her life go and sit down in the precinct of Aphrodite, and there have intercourse with a stranger.... A woman who has once taken her seat [in the enclosure] is not allowed to return home till one of the strangers throws a silver coin into her lap, and takes her with him beyond the holy ground. When he throws the coin he says these words, 'I summon you in the name of goddess Mylitta.' (Aphrodite is called Mylitta by the Assyrians.)... A custom very much like this is found also in certain parts of the island of Cyprus." A comparable cult also established itself at Corinth, headquarters of Aphrodite's new-found precinct in Greece, though travelers passing through that strategic port at the junction of the Greek mainland and the Peloponnesus were usually accommodated by temple professionals.

Homer, however, while calling Aphrodite "the Cyprian," also says that she was the daughter of Zeus by Dione, one of his subwives or celestial mistresses, which places Aphrodite high in the hierarchy, despite the nature of her cult. We are also told variously that she was the spouse of the crippled and foolish Hephaestus, smith god and armorer of the Olympians, and, in a later account, that by union with Anchises of Troy she became the mother of Aeneas, who was presumed (chiefly by Vergil) to be the founder of Rome. Her partisanship for Troy against the attacking Achaeans, or Greeks, was ardent and continuous according to the *Iliad* (and this may testify further to her Asia Minor background); yet for all Aphrodite's devious and complicated history, the ancient Greeks evidently relished greatly her presence and ministrations.

The strange, daemonic, orgiastic Dionysus, so foreign in his make-up to the Olympian family when it had grown lofty and dignified, was thought by Herodotus to be of eastern, possibly Egyptian, origin. Yet it seems established now that his cult entered Greece by way of the northern mountains from Thrace, perhaps brought in by invaders, and that it mingled with local "mysteries" and fertility rites. These rites, about whose origin there has been much speculation, may trace back to a pre-Greek religion that survived in the form of secret societies. They involved initiation, rituals of purification, fasting, perhaps worship of sexual symbols, and beliefs in the magic powers of those who had risen to the highest level among the *mystai*. Though Homer knows of a Dionysian religion that may have become mixed with these ancient practices, his references to it are only incidental, and it appears to have played little part in the society he describes. Its force, with its emphasis on seeking utter freedom and escape from human limitations by momentary, total communion with the god in an ecstasy brought on by wine, music, and torchlit dancing by night, may have been felt only in later times. Still the question remains as to just when it did take strong hold in Greece—for its effects were to be immense. What we do know is that when the Dionysian cult spread southward, it was first met with considerable distaste in the more cultivated cities, whose citizens perhaps felt in it a throwback to primitive forms of worship; thus in the fifth century Euripides, in the *Bacchae,* his drama about the cult, has King Pentheus of Thebes worry about its intrusion into his realm:

> *I happened to be away, out of the city,*
> *But reports reached me of some strange mischief here,*
> *Stories of our women leaving home to frisk*
> *In mock ecstasies among the thickets on the mountain,*
> *Dancing in honor of the latest divinity,*
> *A certain Dionysus, whoever he may be!*

Whoever he was, he became a very potent god indeed—despite the disdain of what might be called the Old Society of gods and men alike—and Greek mythmakers, always anxious to provide a place for every interesting deity, claimed he was the son of Zeus and Semele. Dionysus was the deity not only of revels and abandon—attended by his company of female maenads, or "mad ones," god-possessed in their frenzy—but of festivals and spectacles in general, of poetic inspiration, and, through his ceremonies, the begetter of Greek tragedy in particular. Though few temples were ever erected to him, Aeschylus, Euripides, and Sophocles built the greatest of shrines to him when they wrote their dramas for performance at his festivals, in which celebration of human joy and fulfillment was mixed with recognition of the tragic condition of man.

For Dionysus, the reveler, the beneficent bringer of the vine, was at the same time a tragic god. In fact, he was the only truly tragic deity in the pantheon save Demeter, the corn goddess, who also knew sorrow and suffering in a way the other Olympians, disporting themselves on high, did not. The seat of the gods above the mists, which hung between their mountain top and the world of men below, was an ineffable, well-lighted place. Thus Homer describes it in the *Odyssey*: "Athena went away to Olympus where evermore they say the seat of the gods stays sure: for the winds shake it not, nor is it wetted by rain, nor approached by any snow. All around stretches the cloudless firmament, and a white glory of sunlight is diffused about its walls. There the blessed gods are happy all their days. . . ." Crop-bringing Demeter, however, was not one of these ever-happy beings. Supposedly a sister of Zeus, as well as another of his mates, she gave birth to the lovely Persephone, embodiment of the spirit of the spring. But Persephone was torn from her by Hades and carried off to the underworld, with the result that the grieving mother left Olympus and wandered about the earth, trying to recover her. During this time all crops withered and desolation lay across the land. Finally, in order to win Persephone back, Demeter had to make a truce with Hades, under which her daughter could return to earth for certain months but had to remain below for the others—the origin, in myth, of the alternation between fruitful seasons and the death brought by the drought of the Greek summer.

While the Olympians enjoyed their endless pleasures, Demeter, in her agonized pilgrimage, seemed to draw near to man and his perennial searches and sufferings. The "Eleusinian mysteries" that sprang up as a popular cult about her—recalling her visit to Eleusis in her quest—were akin to some of the rites that figured in the worship of Dionysus, who was a god of seasons and the life and death cycle too. For Dionysus, despite all his exuberance, was the vine that must be pruned back to bare stock every autumn, once the grapes were in; and thus he embodied the coming and going of all things, and particularly of man himself. As the renowned American student of mythology Edith Hamilton writes of Dionysus: "His death was terrible: he was torn to pieces, in some stories by Titans, in others by Hera's orders. He was always brought back to life; he died and rose again. It was his joyful resurrection they [the Greeks] celebrated in his theatre." The "Eleusinian mysteries," in turn, were to remain a special adjunct or cult of Greek religion throughout its lifetime, the subject of curiosity and wonder in the minds of some men, of disdain in those of others, and of veneration in very many.

No deity would seem at first glance more distant from this troubling outsider among the gods than the most noble of Olympians, shining Apollo, god of light, truth, grace, law, and order. Yet a remarkable thing occurred—and nothing could better illustrate the leaps of imagination, the talent for accommodation, and, if you will, the paradoxes of Greek religion. For three winter months every year, Apollo relinquished his high

shrine at Delphi, from which oracular word went forth to all
Greek society, to none other than Dionysus. In those months of
the revel god's occupancy, his unloosed maenads performed
their mystical fertility dances on the heights above the sacred
precincts. Thus Sophocles, after describing such a scene, has a
chorus in the *Antigone* invoke the presence of Dionysus himself:

> *Leader in dance of the fire-pulsing stars,*
> *Overseer of the voices of night,*
> *Child of Zeus, be manifest,*
> *With due companionship of maenad maids*
> *Whose cry is but your name.*

So sky god and earth god meet, and cults of lofty reason and
the magic spell and oracle mingle, in the Greek effort to reconcile all forms of worship of the unseen but immanent. Such an
impulse inevitably involves not only compromise and paradox
but leads to a certain ambiguity as well—and in the outcome
most Greek deities were to be quite ambiguous in their own
persons. Almost without exception there were no wholly
"good" Greek gods and no wholly "bad" spirits either; there
were spirits from above and below who in their own persons
mixed the good with the not-so-good and the downright hostile
and selfish and vindictive, even as men themselves often do.
And this is probably what made the Greek gods seem so much
like men, and the Greek himself seem so much like his gods.

Beautiful Aphrodite, so enchanting to men, is also malicious
and dangerous, out to enslave them. Dionysus, for all the
beneficence and inspiration that came from him, embodies the
brutalizing powers of excess. The wise Athena is at the same
time a war-making goddess. Apollo, well-beloved as the exemplar of supreme grace and the champion of lucidity and mea-
sure in all things, is on occasion heartless and mean. In their

unpredictability and caprice the Greek gods were often menaces to mankind as well as to one another. Moreover, because these deities were images or personalities which had been compounded from many sources, they were often seemingly at loggerheads with themselves.

None was more so than Apollo, who has been prized down to our own day as "the most Greek of all the gods" or "the very embodiment of the Hellenic spirit." Centuries of sculptors and painters have represented him affectionately, even adoringly, as this glorified ideal, and perhaps no more noble Grecian marble has come down to us than the heroic, mid fifth-century B.C. figure of him at Olympia. When you confront it in that bare hall of the Olympia Museum you find yourself gazing at a supreme classical image—a godly male at the peak of bodily perfection, marvelously balanced between tension and repose, bow-arm outstretched over a writhing struggle between the savage centaurs and civilized Lapiths about him, yet so calm and sure that right and reason under his governance will prevail that he sees no need to shoot an avenging arrow or enter the fray, but instead looks out above the battleground with serene and restrained majesty.

This is Apollo at his highest—Greece at its highest, if you will. Yet there were other sides to Apollo, darker ones, suggesting that the god of light and reason also had a daemonic aspect harking far back. The Pythian priestess who speaks for him from her oracular crypt under his shrine at Delphi is no reasoning woman: she is a sybil in a trance, pronouncing often incomprehensible words of mysterious import, herself possessed by Apollo. How Apollo got to Delphi—how he got to Greece, in fact—remains a fascinating mystery. He was definitely a non-Hellenic god. Some scholars have argued that he came with other gods from the north, possibly from the lands of the obscure Hyperboreans; others, that he was of eastern, perhaps Anatolian descent, since on the Asia Minor coast the Greeks may have encountered an Apollo-like god of Hittite origin named Apulunas (the fact that this greatest of Greek gods sided with the Trojans of Asia Minor against the oncoming Achaeans of the West also testifies to an Eastern background); still others, like Gilbert Murray, believe that he may have been a compound of both.

Greek mythology tells us little about Apollo's origins; it simply holds that he, like Artemis, was born of Zeus and Leto. But the fact that he was particularly worshiped both on the island of Delos, his supposed birthplace in the mid-Aegean, and on the heights of Delphi along the passes from the north, suggests a multiple origin. Perhaps he himself was the amalgam of several gods and layers of being and feeling, able in the end at Delphi to make marriage, so to speak, with the contrasting Dionysus just because he too encompassed so much. Aeschylus suggests as much when he refers to Apollo—Apollo, not Dionysus—as "the ivied, the Bacchic, the prophet," and Euripides speaks of "Paean Apollo of the tuneful lyre."

Long before the time when Aeschylus and Euripides wrote, however, a very slow yet mighty process had been going on, in which Greek man civilized and humanized his gods, and in which one could say that the gods helped humanize the Greeks in turn. Like other men, the early Greek had begun life in lonely fear, anxious to propitiate the unknown; then he had populated all nature with spirits, thereby making the surrounding world less threatening, since he could now meet and mingle with them as familiars; finally he imagined these spirits to be more and more like himself, his gods being akin to men in their motives and passions and differing from them only in their superior powers and in their one special attribute—immortality. Some gods even came down to earth to sire mortals, while on the other hand a few mortals rose to join the Olympians. Yet both the gods and men alike were subject to the inscrutable providence of *moira,* or ultimate fate. So there was a constant interplay—one might even say an intimacy—between Greek men and their gods, the deities being fallible, and man at his noblest being almost godlike.

Almost, but not quite: the heart of much of the highest of Greek writing tells of the dark fate that may overtake a man who presumes too much, even when he thinks he has obtained some promise from the gods or some compact with them, as Agamemnon had. A "holy fear" should still pervade all mortals. As Pindar writes: "There is one race of men, one race of gods; both have breath of life from a single mother. But sundered power holds us divided." Icarus must not attempt, as he did, to soar too high: to come too near to the heat of heaven invites disaster.

Greek godmaking and mythmaking received their early culmination in Homer, who was to be the great organizer and expositor through his poetry of the splendid presences on Mount Olympus, both lifting them out of the Titanic hierarchy of terror that had gone before and bringing at least some of them close to man. Hesiod, in his *Theogony,* was to go further, by enlivening and humanizing them. The vision remained a glorious fantasy, to be sure, but how did it come about? One of the great students of the emergence of Greek thought and feeling, the German philosopher Friedrich Nietzsche, remarked that the Greeks—whom he saw as not "classically" composed at all, but as emotionally extremely intense—must have been so painfully alive to the terrors and horrors of existence that in order to make life possible at all, they set up this gleaming Olympian dream. However that may be, having set it up, they proceeded to emulate it.

The mightiest of Homeric heroes was Achilles, who is shown here in a fifth-century vase painting. Achilles's powers were so great that the Greeks were unable to conquer Troy without his aid.

III

THE AGE OF HEROES

Sing, MOUNTAIN GODDESS, *sing through me*
That anger which most ruinously
Inflamed Achilles, Peleus' son,
And which, before the tale was done,
Had glutted Hell with champions—bold,
Stern spirits by the thousandfold;
Ravens and dogs their corpses ate.

Homer, "Invocation of the Muse," *the Iliad*
(translated by Robert Graves)

One night, according to an ancient tale, the ever-amorous Zeus visited Alcmene, bride of the Theban general Amphitryon who was then away fighting, and, having disguised himself as her husband, bedded with her and spawned a child who grew up to be Heracles (in later, Roman usage of his name, Hercules), the mightiest of mortals. This man, or rather this superman, whose strength was enormous though his mental powers were somewhat limited, accomplished a series of stupendous feats or labors, most of them in order to expiate a monstrous crime he had committed in a fit of madness. Raised in Thebes and having helped the Thebans against their enemies, he was given in marriage their princess Megara, who bore him three sons. But Zeus' wife Hera, always resentful of the god's extramarital exploits, caused Heracles to become insane and kill Megara and their children. Recovering his mind, he sought out the Delphic oracle and was told that by Zeus' order he must perform any twelve punitive labors that his cousin King Eurystheus might dictate.

Placing himself at the oracle's bidding into the service of Eurystheus, who was king of Argos (of Mycenae, according to some versions of the tale), he slew the marauding Nemean lion and the feared nine-headed Hydra; he cleansed the vast stables of King Augeas at Elis in a single day by diverting two rivers to flush them; he brought back from a far western island the cattle of the horrible three-bodied Geryon, erecting, as he did so, two mountainous rocks at the Mediterranean's end—the Pillars of Heracles; he also brought back from the ends of the earth the golden apples of the Hesperides, and on that same venture, moreover, freed long-suffering Prometheus from the shackles that bound him to a high mountain of the Caucasus.

This was not all. He spent a year tracking down the stag with golden horns, sacred to Artemis, and brought it back to Argos. He trapped a great boar lowering on Mount Erymanthus. He drove off the swarm of monstrous birds that had plagued the people of Stymphalus. He sailed to Crete to seize for his master the great snorting bull that Poseidon had given to King Minos. He vanquished the man-eating mares of King Diomedes of Thrace. He brought home to Greece the girdle of Hippolyta, queen of the Amazons. He descended into the lower world to seize barehanded its three-headed watchdog Cerberus, and while he was there rescued his fellow hero Theseus from the oblivion below.

These twelve labors were not the only adventures of Heracles. As formidable indoors as outdoors, he was also capable of possessing in one night some fifty women—the daughters of King Thespius. Perhaps most remarkable of all, he vanquished in a wrestling encounter the death spirit Thanatos (some versions say it was Hades himself) on another quest to the world of the shades, this time to bring back his friend Admetus' recently lost wife Alcestis. These and other deeds made Heracles believe himself the equal of the gods, which in many respects he manifestly was: his arrows had greatly helped the Olympians put down the primeval Giants. But in other respects he was not their equal. "Cow-eyed" Hera, Zeus' official consort, had always been filled with hatred of her mate's children by others, and had several times tried to destroy Heracles, on occasion by vipers, on occasion by sending fits of madness down upon him. Indeed, as we have seen, Heracles was under such a spell when he murdered his wife and children. Not knowing his own immense strength and, furthermore, easily angered, he was likely to kill when he did not really mean to do so. Thus, when provoked, he killed the centaur Nessus who was ferrying him and his new bride Deianira across a river. Nessus, dying, gave her some of his own blood, telling her it would serve as a charm to keep the hero from loving other women. Later, when Deianira found Heracles straying, she smeared some of the blood on a shirt which he thereupon donned only to fall into horrible orment. After learning what she had unwittingly done, Deianira killed herself; and Heracles, unable to bear the torture, immoated himself on a tall pyre.

So even the greatest of heroes must die. Achilles, the greatest of the heroes who came after him, remarks in the *Iliad*:

> For not even the strength of Heracles fled away from
>   destruction,
> Although he was dearest of all to lord Zeus, son of Kronos,
> But his fate beat him under, and the wearisome anger of
>   Hera.

Let Heracles, unlike other heroes, was raised from death and made god. Some stories say he was wafted upward in a cloud from his funeral pyre; others that he was borne aloft in Athena's four-horse chariot and guided by swift-footed Hermes to the portals of Olympus. The hero Odysseus, who on his long voyage home visited the shades to seek advice from the spirit of the blind prophet Tiresias, saw there the wraithlike figures of many departed kings and warriors and the *eidolon,* or phantom, of Heracles as well; but Heracles himself, Odysseus adds, is

> *Feasting amid the gods, reclining soft*
> *With Hebe of the ravishing pale ankles,*
> *Daughter of Zeus and Hera, shod in gold.*

This gargantuan, ancestral tale, compounded of many elements and accretions over early centuries, seems far removed from the light and reason of classical Greece. Yet despite all its crudities, it remains one of the greatest of tales, conveying on one hand the richness of Greek mythmaking imagination and on the other the scope of Greek feeling about the capabilities as well as the faults of man. It tells, in particular, of the Greeks' absorption with the heroic ideal and their veneration of it, even while aware of the inscrutable fate that overtakes the all-too-human hero.

The Greeks did venerate Heracles over many centuries, erecting altars to him and making a cult of the man who for his deserts had become a deity. The frieze of Zeus' temple at Olympia was given over entirely to sculptures celebrating Heracles' labors. The idea came to prevail that the work of this primeval giant—roistering, foolhardy, and often barbarous—exemplified man's power to overcome inhuman obstacles and his desires to ride abroad redressing wrongs. Nevertheless, in the sophisticated fifth century, many Greeks were to look with disdain on some of their old legends. Herodotus, who was not only the Greeks' first historian but their first student of comparative mythology as well, wrote at one point: "The Greeks tell many tales without due investigation," and scoffed at what he called a "silly fable" about Heracles among the Egyptians. What he was trying to show was that there had been two Heracles—one the Greek hero and the other an Egyptian god—and that the

Greeks had mixed up the stories. The dramatist Euripides, who was also critical of much that was handed down in Greek legendry, made Heracles a blunderer, almost a buffoon, in his *Alcestis;* yet he was so taken with his presence that he also made him into a great tragic hero in his *Heracles.* And Sophocles, similarly engaged, devoted *The Women of Trachis* to the final episode in Heracles' life—the story of the robe poisoned with Nessus' blood and of the destiny that comes upon those who think they are all-powerful.

Every society, from the savage ones on up, creates its myths; the anthropologist Bronislaw Malinowski has argued that these are not mere storytellers' yarns retold for their entertaining interest, but arise out of some act of belief and live as statements of some "primeval, greater, and more relevant reality." The far-reaching analyst Carl Jung has looked upon myths as expressions of the "collective unconscious"—fantasies arising in the primitive psyche as it awakens with its desires and passions, but which are often repressed below the conscious level until they finally emerge as wish-fulfilling tales. Thus there are the recurrent fables of some great quest into the unknown; of the winning of great treasures, talismans, or magic weapons; of descent into the underworld to wrestle with the monster and perhaps bring back the beloved. However one may choose to interpret their origins, there are fascinating correspondences between such tales as they emerge in cultures far apart in time and place.

The Sumerians of Mesopotamia, for instance, told of a legendary king, Gilgamesh of the city of Uruk, which flourished in the fourth millennium B.C. Gilgamesh fought with giants, lions, and a monstrous bull, and made a descent into the underworld to contend with Death itself. In Greek mythology, not only Heracles but also Dionysus, Theseus, Orpheus, Odysseus, and Aeneas of Troy were to visit the realm of the dead. Furthermore,

Mesopotamian cuneiform tablets, recording a very ancient tradition, tell of the imprisonment of a fertility goddess in the
underworld—a story strikingly similar to the Greek legend of
the detention of Persephone in Hades. The story of the
foundling and of the divine or semidivine king also appears in
Eastern as well as Greek lore. What is perhaps most significant
in the mythmaking process is the cult of the hero and its relationship to the cult of the dead—nowhere more pronounced and
prevalent than in Greece, where there was an ancestral belief
among its people that doers of great deeds exerted some
extraordinary power from the grave.

In the Greek mind, hero worship (often actual worship of a
mortal hero in his tomb) was combined with worship of the
gods, and this, in turn, reflected a sense of some earlier, heroic
age when men had been greater, loftier, and closer to the gods
than they were in times present. No doubt this accounts in part
for the wondrous proliferation and persistence of Greek myths
about humans, which were in effect a part of religion. The great
Greek problem was to try to resolve the coexistence of gods and
men and to explain, or at least to indicate, the presence of the
divine in man. What better solution, then, than to relate man to
his gods by actual blood ties, and to dream back to a splendid
race that we might call Founding Fathers—and mothers, too—all
descended from the loins of great Zeus himself.

Many kings, dynasties, noble families, and emerging cities
encouraged this process, anxious to claim for themselves a lineage of godly origin, and many imaginative bards were on
hand to aid it. Thus King Minos of primeval Crete was made out
to be the son of Zeus, who had appeared in the form of a bull to
Europa, daughter of the king of Sidon. From Minos' union with
Pasïphaë came Catreus, the father of Aërope; she slept with
King Atreus of Mycenae (also supposedly a descendant of Zeus)
to become the ancestor of that tragic house. Perseus, who

became king of Tiryns, near Mycenae, after fetching the head of the Gorgon Medusa, was described as the offspring of Zeus and another princess, Danaë. Helen of Sparta, Menelaus' spouse and the cause of so much mischief and bloodshed at Troy, was said to be the result of Zeus' mating with the mortal Leda, whom he had visited in the guise of a swan. Athens prided itself on having had as its first great hero the brave king Theseus, vanquisher of the Minotaur and the son of the city's founder Aegeus—though some claimed he was the son of Poseidon, Zeus' brother. And in Thebes genealogists and bards worked out a scheme by which the royal Theban line went back to Cadmus, born of Zeus and Io (whom Zeus had conveniently turned into a heifer in order to deceive ever-prying Hera)—a lineage that produced a veritable *Almanach de Gotha* of heroes and other royal figures, among them Creon, Jocasta, Oedipus, and Antigone. Even the great god Dionysus was included, for (according to the Thebans) he was born of the never-flagging Zeus and Cadmus' daughter Semele, and as such was the grandson of their own King Cadmus.

All this fabric of imagination about gods and men interbreeding helped to establish in Greece a particular form of ancestor worship. The kings of Mycenae were laid to rest in spacious tombs and surrounded (not unlike the Pharaohs of Egypt) by their treasure and instruments of daily living, with the thought evidently in mind that they would continue to use them. True, Homer speaks of the departed spirits among the shades as "strengthless." Yet though among the mythical heroes only Heracles rose to Olympus, glorious Achilles (son of Thetis, a sea nymph, and great-grandson of Zeus) was said to enjoy immortality on earth, off on an island in the Euxine, or the Black Sea, and there he became the subject of particular worship. Local cults sprang up: at Athens, of Theseus; at Colonus, of Oedipus of the Theban line; at Sparta, of beautiful and ill-starred Helen; on the island of Lesbos, of Orpheus, the fabulous musician (appropriately, son of a Muse)—his cult eventually produced an agglomeration of poetry and ritual that came to be part of a cult of Dionysus that was known as Orphic religion.

What the Greeks believed about their past heroes varied not only from place to place but from generation to generation. Many heroes, like many lesser gods, were revered as ancestral spirits simply in one locality, the next having its own. As one family rose and another fell, the genealogies of heroes changed too. Through early centuries the multiplication and alteration of tales was probably immense and chaotic, and it was not until the emergence of Homer—presumably at some time between the years 800 B.C. and 700 B.C.—that a bard came forth who was both a great recorder of myths and one who could impose some order on them. With him, both the heroes and the Olympians become organized in relationships, and a rough *ethos,* or scheme, of values is cast over them all and their actions. Thereafter, the vast body of saga about great ancestral deeds, compounded of folklore, travelers' yarns, and tales devised to glorify this or that dynasty or town, begins to coalesce into a national legacy of heroic poetry and moral teaching. Much later, in the fifth century, Pindar is found trying to distinguish between myths that are based on historical evidence and those that are based on imagination; and Euripides, who was often called "the destroyer of illusions," re-examines the great tales too, rejecting some but making use of others as subjects for his dramas to illustrate the tragic issues confronting man.

After the four or more "dark" centuries following the extinction of Mycenaean civilization, during which the knowledge of writing was apparently lost, the written word reappears; but the telling of old tales remains for a long time an art of reciting them, not of writing them down—and each recitation, since there was no text, contained its own possibilities of invention.

There are parallels between eighth-century Greece, emerging slowly from the dark, and early medieval Europe, emerging from long submersion more than two millennia later. In both, the civilization that survives is centered in isolated, crudely built strongholds, with few comforts, separated by lonely and dangerous valleys; their lords, for the most part, are unlettered, and communications difficult and rare. But there is the welcome arrival of some traveling bard or minstrel, bringing to those within their rubble walls some information or remembrance of the outside world as he sings for his supper. The *jongleurs,* harp in hand, intoned the song of brave Roland, and the *Minnesänger* of the dragon-killing Siegfried of the Nibelungen. Bravery and monsters were the stock in trade of the storyteller of ancient Greece too, and he could ring wondrous changes on such subjects.

He told, for instance, in one of the oldest sagas handed down, of the fabulous voyage of the Argonauts—notable because many Greeks seem to have thought of it as one of their first major overseas expeditions, preceding that to Troy by a generation or more, and also because it included in it so many illustrious figures. A precise list of those who accompanied Jason on the good ship *Argo* to the Black Sea was never established, innumerable Greek families claiming, as they climbed to high estate in later centuries, to have had some ancestor aboard, as if it were a kind of *Mayflower.* But Pindar and later poets, culling the legends, agreed that Jason's vessel had undoubtedly carried such figures as Peleus, the father of Achilles; the inseparable twin sons of Zeus and Leda, Castor and Pollux; the archmusician Orpheus; and for a while the mighty hero Heracles himself was aboard, along with a band of the noblest youths of Greece.

It seems that once upon a time a prince of Thebes named Phrixus was about to be sacrificed on the altar for the sake of

procuring crops. (The legend of the ruler who was put to ceremonial death to ensure a good harvest is of great antiquity and
appears in many cultures, recalling a time when such sacrifices
actually took place.) However, a miraculous ram with a fleece
of gold appeared and wafted Phrixus away to the remote lands
of the wild Colchians beyond the Hellespont, where the precious fleece came into the possession of the Colchian king.
Later young Jason, heir to a kingdom in northern Thessaly that
had been usurped by a blood relative was told that he could
have his patrimony if he brought back the Golden Fleece. The
bravest of Achaeans joined Jason in this adventurous quest and
on the way they met with immense perils. Though they dallied
pleasantly enough for a while with the women of Lemnos, after
which Heracles parted company with them, they were set upon
by the mighty-clawed, flying Harpies, "the hounds of almighty
Zeus"—this in spite of the fact that Zeus' mate Hera, and Athena
too, were warm partisans of Jason. Escaping these monsters,
the Argonauts had to pass through a narrow strait (the
Bosporus) that was guarded by the Clashing Rocks, or Symple-
gades—vast boulders that rolled together and smashed every
vessel that tried to pass between them. Barely getting clear,
they eventually came to the land of the warrior Amazons and
escaped them too. Finally, after passing close by the Caucasus
and seeing Prometheus in agony bound on a peak, they reached
Colchis, only to be faced with further danger. For the Colchian
king Aeetes, angry at this intrusion into his realm, told Jason
that he could have the fleece only if first he himself harnessed
two fierce fire-breathing bulls to a yoke, plowed a great field,
and sowed it with the magic teeth of a dragon. From each
dragon's tooth a fully armed warrior would spring up, who
must be immediately cut down.

Jason knew he could not possibly perform such a feat, and
that the unloosed dragon-seed warriors could well overcome

his company. But on Olympus, Hera and Athena connived and persuaded Aphrodite to have her son Eros shoot one of his love-bringing arrows at the heart of the king's daughter Medea, causing her to conceive a passion for Jason and therefore seek to help him out of his predicament. This Eros did, and with good result, for Medea, as it happened, was a princess possessed of great powers of magic and spells, which she now applied in Jason's behalf.

To make a long story short (which, however, was never the aim of a Greek bard, his listeners evidently liking a good tale to go on and on), Medea gave Jason both ointments and strata-gems by which to overcome the suicidal task imposed on him by her father. These he used successfully, yoking the bulls and downing the seed-warriors, only to find that the astonished King Aeetes would not keep his side of the bargain. Medea then charmed to sleep the serpent guarding the fleece, after which the lovers made what we could call a classic getaway—fleece safely aboard, broad sails straining toward Greece, Jason prom-ising to wed Medea, and King Aeetes, impotent in wrath, left standing on the shore.

Yet this was not quite the end of the tale. It was said that Medea, in her passion to escape with great Jason, either slew her pursuing and avenging brother or caused him to be slain. What happened to her and Jason when they returned to Greece with their treasure remained obscure to many story tellers. But as the legend grew over the centuries, some additions suggested that the bewitching Medea had herself been a human monster, and Jason, for his part, a good deal less than honorable. Just when these accretions arose, no one can tell; but when Euripi-des came to write his *Medea*, the returning Jason had become both a cowardly avenger and a faithless lover: cowardly in that he turned to ever-helpful Medea to rid him of the treacherous usurper Pelias; and faithless in that after siring two children by her, he jilted her and planned to wed the king of Corinth's daughter instead. Medea, for her part, became not only the murderess of Pelias but of Jason's bride and, in her frenzy, of the two sons she had borne to Jason as well.

Though Jason emerges from this story a very tarnished hero, and everyone in it from the gods on down behaves amorally and deceitfully, there is yet present in it, as in the tale of Heracles, that fascination with past fame, daring deed, and far place—particularly the daring deed in a far place—that marks all Greek epic poetry making. For poetry it was, created by certain powerful imaginations to inspire others. The theme of wonderment, of the quest of the faraway, of fabulous and glorious adventure once lived, runs through and inspirits all of it. And not all the tales told of ancestors were brutal, either; some were most poignant. Heroes descended into the underworld on brave missions to rescue the dead: Heracles, to find Alcestis; Theseus of Athens, to try to bring back Persephone; and Orpheus, armed only with his lyre, to bring back his beloved bride Eurydice. Orpheus, the archsinger and musician, schooled by Apollo, so moved Hades with his melodies that the king of the underworld gave up Eurydice on condition that Orpheus would not look back on her, as she followed him from the world of the shades, until they had both reached the light of day. But Orpheus, always the lover, could not forbear, as they ascended, to cast his eyes on Eurydice, and so she was forever lost to him.

Then, too, there were early morality fables of bold men who, apparently forgetting the fate that had overtaken the archrebel Prometheus, behaved toward the gods in ways arrogant or importunate, and who as a result received interminable punishment. Though not all these men were heroes in the Promethean sense of helping man, the theme of revolt against the gods evidently fascinated the Greek mind, and the early Greek imagination devised exquisite forms of torture for those mortals who had overstepped the line. This was so, particularly in the cases of Tantalus and Sisyphus, two legendary kings who ran afoul of Olympus.

Tantalus, reputedly a son of Zeus, and ruler of Sipylos in Lydia, was and remains a baffling figure. Favored by the Olympians to the point where they came to dine at his palace, he was so seized by some obscure motivation that he served them a ghastly banquet of which the main dish was the flesh of his own son Pelops, whom he had caused to be killed for the occasion. One explanation, to which Robert Graves as a leading modern student of Greek mythology subscribes, is that Tantalus found that he did not have enough food for the gods' dinner, and so, either to test Zeus' omniscience or just to show his goodwill, he sliced up and offered his son. Another has it that Tantalus' fell purpose was to make the gods unwittingly become cannibals. In any case, for this monstrous deceit he was condemned to stand forever in Hades in water up to his neck, athirst and deprived of nourishment: whenever he stooped to drink, the water disappeared; whenever he reached upward to grasp the branches, laden with fruit, which hung overhead, a wind tantalizingly wafted the grapes and figs out of his reach.

The character of Sisyphus, a king of Corinth and son of the wind god Aeolus, is more understandable—though his fate was no less agonizing. His crime was simply that he gave away an amorous secret of ever-lusting Zeus to a friend, the river god Asopus. When Asopus came to Sisyphus, lamenting that his lovely daughter Aegina had disappeared, Sisyphus replied that he had seen her borne off by an immense eagle (that is, Zeus in the shape of one) to an offshore island, and gave him directions for pursuit. In return for this information, Asopus supplied Corinth with an ever-running spring. But for thus revealing Zeus' love nest, Sisyphus paid a heavy penalty: he was doomed to remain in Hades and endlessly roll a rock up to the top of a hill from which, each time he had placed it there, it rolled down again.

Remote and strange as these two tales seem, their sequels lead us into the midst of a familiar company—the heroes of Homer. For the gods resurrected Tantalus' butchered son Pelops, who, in turn, sired Atreus, founder of the tragic dynasty (the House of Atreus) that produced Agamemnon and Menelaus. Fair Aegina, for her part, whom Sisyphus had observed at the wrong moment, in due course had a son by Zeus, and it was that son's son, Peleus, who mated with the nymph Thetis to bring forth the hero Achilles.

With Homer we emerge from shadowy realms into a sudden, brilliant, immediate presence. Homer has been called variously the first articulate European, the author of the bible of the Greeks, and, by Dante, "the sovereign poet"—all of which he was. Perhaps what most of all strikes a reader on first looking into Homer is his immense vividness and concreteness. He is not spinning a tale of highly improbable persons in an abstract landscape, outside of time and known space; he is narrating one particular episode in one particular war at Troy in which many heroes participated (all listed in Book II of the *Iliad* together with their cities of origin, the strength of their cohorts, and the number of their respective ships). He follows this tale with another detailed account of the adventures and struggles of one of the victors on his voyage to regain his home and kingdom in Ithaca. To be sure, Homer does not say just when all this took place or what happened before and after; yet he speaks with such detail and absorption about the customs and accoutrements of his heroes—their methods of rule, their dress, their food, their weaponry, their siegecraft, their manual skills, their codes of conduct toward both men and women—that he evidently regards it integral to his story to recall and evoke some past society and environment in which his heroes lived.

This he does with unending delight—from descriptions of Achilles' tent and shining armor to menus of banquets and summaries of speeches made at councils of war. And this he accompanies with searching characterizations of all that was most human in his heroes: the sulking egotism of great Achilles; the indecisiveness of not-so-great Agamemnon, a poor leader of men; the saving guile of Odysseus; the bluff bravery of Hector; the garrulousness of Nestor, a kind of Homeric Polonius; the fatuousness of Helen's lover, Paris; the irresponsibility of Helen herself; the tired yet manly dignity of aged Priam, the Trojan patriarch; the artfulness of Penelope, spinning her endless web and (at least supposedly) standing off her army of suitors during her twenty years' wait for her husband's return; the boyishness of her son Telemachus; so keen to play the man; the matronly sturdiness of Eurycleia, guarding Odysseus' treasure room; the still but imperturbable faithfulness of Eumaeus, his devoted swineherd.

But what was that past society of heroes of which Homer tells? Did it ever exist as he describes it? First of all one must confront that question, Did Homer himself ever exist as a person? Herodotus thought that he had, and placed his life and work some four centuries before his own—which would put Homer somewhere in the ninth century before Christ. Though Greek sculpture represents him as a venerable, bearded bard ("deep-browed," John Keats was to describe him in his splendid sonnet written on first looking into the Elizabethan George Chapman's translation of Homer), nothing actually is known of the identity of the man, save that the language or dialect of the *Iliad* and *Odyssey* suggested that he was of Ionian origin. Mythical biographies were made up about him—he was variously said to have been a son of the Muse Calliope, or a son of the stream Meles that passed through the city of Smyrna, or a descendant of Orpheus—but the very word "Homer" was not a personal name at all but a term widely used to designate a fellowship or group.

Later scholars, however, were less and less convinced of Herodotus' identification; instead, they began to think more and more of Homer not as a person but as a tradition, and of the epics called Homer's as the sheer accumulation of stories recited by several centuries of fraternities of minstrels. And a particular Homer had of course left nothing in writing to prove individuality of authorship: the earliest texts of the *Iliad* and *Odyssey* appear to have been assembled in Athens in the sixth century, possibly by order of the Athenian ruler Pisistratus in order to establish an agreed version to govern reciters at public festivals. By that time innumerable variants and interpolations must have entered into what had come down by word of mouth. What is important is not the changes—since no one knows what may have gone before—but the fact that the Homeric tales persisted in the Greek mind, while other tales gradually evaporated or at least were never brought together as a kind of canon. Homer's poems, recited endlessly by minstrels in a society that remained unlettered for centuries, became, in effect, Greek religion. Herodotus remarks that it was Homer who first fixed for the Greeks the genealogy of their gods and assigned them their titles and functions. Homer was also telling tales with some remote foundation in fact, as against pure fantasy. In humanizing or, up to a point, civilizing the gods, he was also providing a body of precept and example for generation after generation. The singsong of his repeated epithets and images— the "wine-dark sea," the "rosy-fingered dawn," the "flashing-eyed Athena," the "Odysseus of many wiles," the "silver-footed Thetis"—are the almost ritual lines used by bards as a refrain when going on with their story, night after night; but the heave and bulk of a great chronicle was always there, both brutal and humane. No doubt many further changes entered into the texts in subsequent centuries, by the hands of copyists and editors; for the oldest manuscripts that we presently possess are medieval ones, supplemented by a few ancient papyrus fragments.

Our own era has seen an impulse to return to the concept that there actually was a poet named Homer. In view of the marked differences in style, imagery, and construction between the epics, there may even have been two poets: one the compiler-author of the *Iliad;* the other of the *Odyssey.* The *Iliad* is all action, tense, swift, bold, built about one central theme—the wrath of Achilles before Troy (brought on by the fact that he was deprived of his prize, the captive girl Briseis); the *Odyssey* moves from episode to episode, as its hero does from place to place, in what often seems like a marvelous, spacious dream of adventure and revenge. The ancients felt this distinction as we do, Aristotle remarking that the *Iliad* was simple and disastrous, the *Odyssey* complicated and moral, while the Roman commentator Pliny thought that there was far more "magic" in the *Odyssey.* It does have the quality of a fairy tale, as against the brusque and bloody *Iliad.* Hellenistic scholars who had lingered over the notion of a single Homer regarded the *Iliad* as a work of the poet's maturity but the *Odyssey* as one of his garrulous old age.

Modern belief in the historical existence of a Homer (or, if need be, two Homers) rests chiefly on the sheer literary values of the poems. They are so superior to other early Greek tales that have survived, in terms of unity, coherence, imagery, plausibility of characters, and ethics (roughhewn as these were), as to suggest the controlling presence of an individual of very great creative powers who gave them the shape we know. And one Homer or two, in view of all the contrasts between *Iliad* and *Odyssey?* This problem may remain insoluble—if indeed it is a problem. If we did not know from records that there had been a playwright named Shakespeare, it would be difficult to conceive that works so utterly contrasting as *King Lear* and *A Midsummer Night's Dream* could have been written by one and the same hand.

Yet now we come to the other question. Homer tells vividly of a long-remembered past: But what does he really know about that past as an actuality, and to what extent is he in effect describing instead the age in which he himself moved, poetizing and projecting his images far back in time? Some knowledge had evidently come down to him in the eighth century, of an earlier civilization of which Mycenae was a center, but the knowledge was dim. Mycenae's splendor by his time had been effaced from all but legend, and was to remain so until the brilliant archaeologist Schliemann brought it back to light in the late nineteenth century, discovering the Bronze Age culture that had flourished there and revealing many remarkable correspondences between Homeric descriptions and Mycenaean artifacts. Yet despite these correspondences, in many ways Homer and history meet only to part again. The weapons he describes resemble the bronze ones of the Mycenaeans, but his anachronisms are legion: he speaks of temples, whereas the ancestors of the Greeks appear to have built none; he tells of Archaeans cremating their dead, whereas in the heroic age, of which he purports to speak, they buried them.

He tells of one great ten-year war against Troy, but for all Schliemann's and later scholars' studies, we still have no historical proof of it. There may well have been not one but several wars or raids against Troy in the Mycenaean age, but the notion of a ten-year siege, in an era of small kingdoms that were often hardly more than country households, is probably sheer fantasy. Herodotus, though he accepted the traditional story that the Achaeans, "for the sake of a single Lacedaemonian girl, collected a vast armament, invaded Asia, and destroyed the kingdom of Priam," thought that the idea of their fighting for ten years for the sake of a woman was foolish. But this problem of duration never troubled Homer; on the contrary, he assumes it as the dramatic background for his superb opening, plunging at once into what proves to be the climax of the war—the wrath of Achilles amid chieftains Greek and Trojan, made savage by nine years of frustration and slaughter.

These chieftains, as we get to know them, are tribal leaders in a world not yet made up of states, but of clans. Their kingdoms consist of a palace or citadel and a few villages surrounding it. Their wealth lies in stock-breeding and in their land, owned by the family or clan, which they cultivate themselves: thus King Odysseus boasts that he can drive a furrow as straight as any man. They drop their plowshares to lead their fiefmen or serfs in war (little is said in Homer of the supporting hosts, large as they are made out to be; all drama concentrates on individual combat between heroes). They have slaves—particularly female ones, procured on this raid or that—and of these, like Agamemnon's Chriseis and Achilles' Briseis, they make concubines, their wives having nothing to say in the matter. Their wives, in turn, are not only mistresses of the household but are probably also accomplished in various crafts—witness Penelope, who by devising a shroud became the most famous weaver of antiquity. Their so-called palaces are mostly of rough brick set upon stone foundations. Their arts consist chiefly in the hammering of metals for armor and ornament; both Achaean men and women, as Homer describes them, wore jewelry. Their morals, finally, find their strength in codes of manly friendship, in a religious respect for the duties of hospitality, and above all, in a dedication to the idea of heroic excellence, or *arete*.

To what extent Homer in all this is describing a remote, heroic age of which he had only intimations, as against that which he had himself seen and known, remains a matter of some debate. But when he moves from supposed remembrance of things past to portrayal of mind and manner and belief, we stand with him on timeless ground—indeed, on the fundamental ground of Greece. For he is speaking, in every book of the *Iliad* and *Odyssey,* of the necessity of valor, even though it is very likely to lead to one's own destruction. He is saying that a man should fill his life with brave deeds; that the only weakness is cowardice, or the failure to seek heroic goals; and that a hero's main duty is toward himself, for by finding honor he will attain near-godly glory.

The Homeric hero is often selfish, blind, and brutal—none more so than Achilles, whether sulking in his tent or monstrously maltreating the body of his slain foe Hector—but he is also chivalric, loyal to his oath, his blood tie, and his friend (in Achilles' case, Patroclus). To be sure, he is a good deal more chivalric than the gods, who in the way the Homeric imagination organizes them, become in effect the senior partners of one or the other contending sides before Troy, and very prone to chicanery, deceit, and unsportsmanlike intervention in behalf of their favorites. Thus the whole abduction of Helen by Paris, we are told, was contrived by the ever-mischievous Aphrodite— who also lifts her weakling favorite out of battle at the moment when he is about to be properly speared by avenging Menelaus. Apollo, Artemis, Ares (with whom Aphrodite was discovered in bed in one episode of the *Odyssey,* thus giving rise to much Homeric laughter) are on the side of the Trojans; Hera, Athena, Poseidon, and Aphrodite's awkward husband Hephaestus are on the side of the Achaeans; and though Zeus tries to adjudicate and bring about some order on Olympus, in a memorable scene in Book XIV of the *Iliad* his consort Hera wantonly seduces him in order to keep him from supporting the Trojan cause.

The gods live on—even though obscure Fate rules them, too,

as Zeus learns in the *Iliad* when he finds his son Sarpedon is doomed—but the heroes must die; and the greater the heroism, probably the earlier the death. Achilles knows this, and when the gods offer him long life and mediocrity on one hand, or glory and an early death on the other, he makes the inevitable choice. His proudest foe, Priam's son Hector, knows it too, sensing that his days are numbered as are those of Troy itself. And in one of the most poignant scenes in the *Iliad,* when his tender wife Andromache comes to him, accompanied by a nursemaid with their infant son in arms, to remind him that Achilles has already killed her father and all her seven brothers and to plead with him that for her sake and the child's he abstain from further combat after all his past victories, his reply, again, is the only possible one: "I have learned to be valiant and to fight always among the foremost ranks of the Trojans, winning for my own self great glory, and for my father." Not to be in the forefront would be unthinkable, though Troy must fall.

In a touch that shows a poet at his peak, Homer then has Hector reach out to take in his arms the little boy—who, however, screams in terror at the sight of his father's helmet with its fierce horsehair plume. At this unsettling outburst, the parents smile; then Hector removes his helmet, places it on the ground, kisses his son, and prays to Zeus and the other gods to grant that this boy may be superior to himself.

Soon thereafter Hector is slain by Achilles, who, however, knows that his own death is near, having been told by his mother Thetis (who may have had it from Zeus): "For you will not be with me long, but already death and powerful destiny stand closely above you." So the Trojan Hector, who is as superior to most of the gods in valor as his wife Andromache is superior to the goddesses in character, succumbs to a rival who is at once the most brilliant, the most brutal, and in the end the most knightly of men. Achilles, however, gloriously caparisoned with Hephaestus' armor, fights on, knowing that Apollo and Paris both have the secret of his vulnerable heel.

The gods themselves pale beside such presences as these, as Homer models his heroes with his images of flashing helmet or swiftfoot or well-greaved shanks or wily wisdom stalking for prey or the grace of honor. Indeed, though far more powerful than men, the gods seem less good than men. They are not moral by human standards: they show little pity, little magnanimity, and often little wisdom. They plan the ruin of a great city. They contrive against men and each other. They induce madness in a hero. They indulge in foul play or poor sportsmanship, as when rescuing the wife-stealing Paris by wafting him away from the Achaeans' avenging shafts. The heroes of Homer are men; the villains, always ready for mischief or a bargain, are gods. Perhaps this is what makes Homer the most heroic and humane of poets, and the preceptor of Greek man's own dignity.

An early end overtakes most of his heroes—as, indeed, an early end was to overtake the brief splendor of Greece. But Hector remarks eloquently—as a new translation by the American poet Richmond Lattimore renders it, seeking to recapture Homer's stately, dactylic rhythms:

And some day one of the men to come will say, as he sees it,
One who in his benched ship sails on the wine-blue water:
"This is the mound of a man who died long ago in battle,
Who was one of the bravest, and glorious Hector killed him."
So will he speak some day, and my glory will not be forgotten.

Or, in the older version used by generations of readers of the Loeb Classical Library, "And some one shall some day say even of men that are yet to be, as he saileth in his many-benched ship over the wine-dark sea: 'This is a barrow of a man that died in olden days, whom on a time in the midst of his prowess glorious Hector slew.' So shall some man say, and my glory shall never die."

And so it was to be.

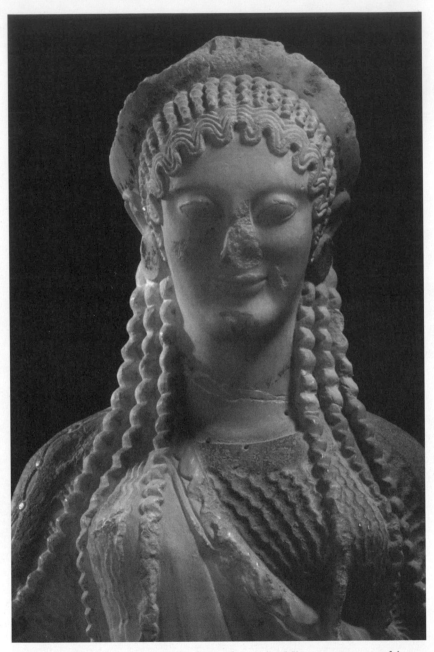

Ionian civilization developed along the Asia Minor coast, reaching a peak of prosperity and artistic influence in the sixth century. At that time a sculptor, probably from the island of Chios, carved this statue of a girl, which was placed as a votive offering on the Athenian Acropolis.

IV

THE GREEK ERUPTION

We are as leaves in jeweled springtime growing
That open to the sunlight's quickening rays;
So joy we in our span of youth, unknowing
If God shall bring us good or evil days.

—Mimnermus of Colophon

If a great Trojan War actually occurred somewhat as Homer described it, one way of thinking of it is to regard it as Greece's first disastrous civil war. For before the walls of Troy Greek-speaking warriors from the peninsula battled warriors of the Asia Minor coast who worshiped the same gods and many of whom also spoke Greek. In the outcome Troy was totally destroyed and the decimated victors returned to their homes (if indeed they did return) to find their thrones or wives pre-empted, their kingdoms in disarray, and dark times ahead. When Odysseus visits Hades on his long voyage home, he encounters, among the shades of many heroes of either side, that of his commander-in-chief, Agamemnon of Mycenae, slain on his return by Aegisthus, lover of Agamemnon's wife Clytemnestra, along with the king's remaining men. Odysseus himself regains his own palace at Ithaca alone (all his followers perished along the way), reaching it after ten years of travel and travail only to find it overrun and despoiled by his wife Penelope's suitors.

Was there actually any such voyage as the fabulous one described in the *Odyssey?* To this day we have no clue. We know that the Mycenaeans had fallen heir to the Mediterranean trade routes of the great Cretan sea empire after its sudden destruction around 1400 B.C. But sometime in the twelfth century the Mycenaean kingdoms in turn fell prey to Dorian invaders, who came from the north. These warriors were content to settle the land and left the sea lanes to others, notably the Phoenicians, who set sail for far places perhaps as early as the tenth century. But as to tales of early travels, we remain in the realm of sheer myth and wild surmise. In legend the Argonauts explored the Black Sea, but we know little concrete of such a venture. In Homer's tale Odysseus ranges over a vast area of seas, islands, straits, and currents in his efforts to get home; various listeners or readers of the epic at various times have thought that his wanderings represented a voyage eastward beyond the Bosporus or westward as far as the Strait of Gibraltar. But we know nothing provable about this either. What we do know is that there is so much fascinating detail in Homer's telling that for fully two and a half millennia students of it have been bent on identifying with actual sites the strange places he mentions in bardic terms as visited by his hero. This just may have been history's most perennial guessing game, and if so, it is sovereign testimony to Homer's lasting spell; yet so many tantalizing geographical and navigational correspondences are embedded in the poem that some surmises about Odysseus' route may well be true.

The ancient Greeks believed wholeheartedly in the existence of Odysseus—the great schemer who after Troy's fall became Hellas' greatest sailor—and in the actuality of his voyages. Thus Hesiod, perhaps less than a century after Homer, places some of Odysseus' adventures specifically in or around Italy. Herodotus identified the land where the Lotus Eaters gave Odysseus' crew their opiate of honey-sweet flowers with western Libya, on the North African coast. Thucydides and most ancient writers thought that the menacing sea monsters Scylla and Charybdis, between which Odysseus had to pass, referred to the Strait of Messina, with its dangerous rocks and currents. Tradition, in the wake of the old historians, has identified the seat of King Aeolus (the keeper of the winds who gave Odysseus' departing men a sack containing the worst of them, instructing them not to open it—which of course they did) with the Lipari Islands north of Sicily. Later the Roman Vergil in his *Aeneid* placed the cave of the one-eyed Cyclops Polyphemus in Sicily; and centuries later Dante in the *Inferno* describes his meeting Odysseus in Hell and has the hero recall the enchantress Circe with the words, "She who twelve months near Gaeta detained me"— Gaeta being a town north of Naples and close to the high promontory called Monte Circeo.

Over the centuries many travelers and scholars, noting Homer's comments on winds, currents, number of days traveled, and land seen, became convinced that Odysseus' farthest voyage of all—that which Circe advised him to make to the banks of the "Ocean stream," there to enter Hades and learn from the prophet Tiresias how to get safely home—referred to an actual expedition to the Strait of Gibraltar, the western limit of the Mediterranean world. Still, there were some who felt that possibly he had erred into the Black Sea between *its* straits, in the wake of Jason; others thought the Pillars of Heracles were simply a figment of the imagination.

What is relevant is that there lay in the Greek consciousness, as expressed by Homer, a tradition of belief in very early Mediterranean travel and exploration. The stories told of the Pillars of Heracles may have been transmitted by Phoenician seamen who had ventured out westward in advance of the Greeks and thus had contributed to the legend and folklore of Heracles. Homer, when he speaks of the "stream" (possibly a current?) of "Ocean" (the Atlantic?) is telling, many observers have thought, of something he might have learned from the Phoenicians—for a constant current flows in from the ocean through the Gibraltar straits to replenish the waters of the otherwise landlocked Mediterranean, evaporating under each summer's sun. We do know that if there was a historical Odysseus, he had obviously to sail west from Troy to get home. On this long voyage Odysseus encounters no other sail of any sort. Like a Columbus, he moves into regions previously unvisited and comes back freighted with lore.

Down to this day there are travelers, often in small boats, with the text of Homer beside them in the stern sheets along with sailing charts and pilot guides, who set out to retrace Odysseus' route, as Samuel Eliot Morison of Harvard did that of Columbus. One spirited British scholar-sailor, Ernle Bradford, has done just this. In his book *Ulysses Found* he identifies the home of the nymph Calypso, where Odysseus dallied for seven years, with Malta; the cave of Polyphemus, with a particular one just north of Trapani on the Sicilian west coast; the harbor of the gigantic, cannibal Laestrygones, who destroyed all Odysseus' ships but one, with Bonifacio on Corsica; and the rocks from which the Sirens sang, with the Galli Islands in the Gulf of Salerno of World War II fame. (Indeed Bradford, standing watch one night on a destroyer covering the Allied landings there, almost thought he heard the Sirens sing to him as he passed the Galli. At least he heard—or thought he heard—some low and almost human music coming from there. His shipmates smiled, thinking him gone dotty, but the captain steered in close just to see if anyone was on the rocks: no one. "There are plenty of rocky caverns and fissures just above sea level in the Galli Islands," writes Bradford, musing, "and such places are great originators of moaning sounds, whispers, and far-off wailing voices. But there was no wind on that night, and the sea unruffled." Imagination can play strange tricks on classicists as on others.)

Unlike Columbus' expedition, Odysseus' was involuntary. For he was, of course, simply seeking to get home to his kingdom of Ithaca, generally identified today with the island of that name off the western coast of Greece. For this purpose he had to round the southern Peloponnesian capes, but a strong offshore wind blew him out to sea and into the westerly unknown; and there-with his ten-year wanderings began. That westbound wind, the propellant of Odysseus, bears a striking resemblance to the one that many centuries later drove Saint Paul helplessly from Crete to shipwreck on the island of Malta; and anyone even in our own time who has skirted the southern Greek headlands under sail is familiar with the "Greco," or "Greek wind," particularly troublesome as it drives a boat westward off Cape Matapan.

At length, after his final and longest adventure—his thralldom to Calypso—Odysseus leaves her island and sails for seventeen days on a raft and (Poseidon having wrecked it in vengeance for Odysseus' blinding of the god's son Polyphemus) then for two days on a log, to be cast up on the land of the Phaeacians, which may have been Corfu, an island about sixty miles north of Ithaca. King Alcinous, hearing the tale of Odysseus' woes, aids him to make a swift descent onto his own kingdom—and to the greatest recognition scenes in all literature. These are the moments when Odysseus reveals himself to the faithful swineherd Eumaeus; when Telemachus throws his arms about the shaggy stranger, realizing from his bearing that this is indeed his noble father; when the old watchdog Argus wags his tail in greeting; when the servant Eurycleia, washing a stranger's feet, sees a scar she remembers from years ago; when Penelope, still wishing a final test of identity, orders Eurycleia to move outside the bridal chamber the bed that her own Odysseus had built, only to have him exclaim that this couldn't be, for didn't she remember that one of the legs of the bed had been a living tree growing in their chamber? (this was just what she wanted to hear); and when his aged father Laertes, plowing in the fields, hears him enumerate the vines and fruit trees the father had once given the son to tend. All these episodes are so immediate and compelling in their humanity that one can readily understand why the Greeks always felt so close to Odysseus, no matter how far he had sailed away on strange adventures. So do we still. For to read about him is to be on his side, so to speak, against all the forces arrayed against him (which is not necessarily so when one reads about Achilles or Hector, where one's loyalties may be equivocal or divided), and to feel in him the presence not only of an antique hero but of a very palpable man, sorely beset.

The poet, to be sure, is out to evoke just such a reaction from his audience; this he does through a long preparation, setting forth the loom of Odysseus' eventual return, and through his masterful use of the device of poetic irony. We know all along that the unlikely stranger who lands on Ithaca to seek restitution is in fact its rightful king, but the doubters and the suitors with whom he is to deal do not. Our foreknowledge of the outcome is at least equal to that of the gods (who have behaved all along in their usual contentious and meddlesome fashion); but all depends on the sureness of Odysseus' avenging bow-arm at the climactic moment.

As we close the pages of Homer, we come up inevitably to the actualities of Greek history. Was there in fact one great Trojan War, or were there sporadic raids extending over many years, or even generations, which some sovereign poetic imagination fused into one concerted drama of strife? And what happened to the rich civilization of the Homeric warriors? The discoveries of present-day archaeologists indicate that the Mycenaean kingdoms entered a time of troubles shortly before 1200 B.C. and were completely destroyed later, in the twelfth century. This is about the time the Dorians invaded Greece, and we may conclude that these Greek-speaking but illiterate tribes from the north found an easy prey in the decadent and possibly war-weakened kingdoms. The lights of Mycenaean Greece went out, and many a goodly state disappeared in that long night which was followed, four centuries later, by a new dawn in which Greece reawakened, bursting with energy. Then, in a matter of a few decades, the Greeks moved into the light of history—not only that, but into the forefront of history.

Traditionally Greek history begins in the year 776 B.C., for it was from then that the Hellenes began to count time: they believed that the quadrennial Olympic games in honor of Zeus were founded in that year, and from then on great deeds and events were to be located in memory by a word or an inscription denoting in what particular Olympiad they had occurred. And Olympia provided more than a calendar. It marked the start of the Panhellenic impulse—an urge to bring Greek-speaking and Greek-thinking men from their scattered towns and hamlets together on a common ground. Some had already begun to converge on the high mount at Delphi to hear Apollo's oracle—as mentioned by Homer—but in the eighth century Delphi was probably only one of many local shrines, not becoming a Panhellenic one until the seventh.

The early seventh century brings another significant scrap of information, too. In 683 B.C. the leading families of Athens had taken to electing one of their members to serve as archon, or chief of state, for a one-year term. This was the culmination of a long process in which the old monarchy coming down from Theseus' time was transformed into an aristocratic republic.

By this time a remarkable process of Greek state-making,

expansion, and colonization had begun. But this had been preceded by several centuries of very gradual migration of Greek
tribes into the eastern Aegean, a movement of which we have
only the dimmest outlines. People who were later to call themselves Aeolians had begun wandering to the Asia Minor coast
before the year 1000, possibly seeking new lands as refuge from
the encroaching Dorians. They settled, for instance, on the
island of Lesbos (where there are evidences of an earlier culture
as well). Perhaps not long after, the Ionians had commenced
moving to the far mainland as well, to be followed by the Dorians who began penetrating the Aegean islands and southern
Asia Minor sometime after the year 900 B.C. Scholars today are
inclined to doubt the supposed ethnic differences between
"Aeolians" and "Ionians" and to hold that these terms were
invented only when the process of systematic writing of Greek
chronicles and histories began, centuries later. The "Ionians,"
for instance, hailing presumably from the northern Peloponnesus and Attica, may have been a mixed folk who developed
the culture we call "Ionian" only after they had crossed the sea.

By the eighth century this process of dispersion, previously
cloaked in mystery, begins to take on some recognizable form.
So-called Ionians, in their probings along the Asia Minor coast,
had seized a settlement that was to become known as Miletus—
a place possibly of Minoan origin, and then inhabited by what
Homer calls the "barbarous-tongued" Carians, who had fought
on the side of Troy. Now beginning in the seventh century,
Miletus (its citizens supposedly descendants of Ionian men and
the Carian women they had taken to wife after having slaughtered their husbands) sprouted dozens of offshoots of its own,
some as far away as southern Russia.

Other Ionian refugees had traveled to what was to become
proud Ephesus, mingling there with an Asiatic tribe who worshiped a primeval mother goddess whom the newcomers

blended with their own Artemis. ("Great is Diana of the Ephesians," was the protesting cry that went up many centuries later among its people when Saint Paul arrived seeking to convert them to the faith of Christ.) Aeolians, meanwhile, had set up five cities on fair, volcanic Lesbos, rich with vines and orchards, and produced there by the end of the seventh century a distinctive culture of much grace and charm—and the most famous of the Lesbians, the poetess Sappho. Aggressive Dorians, still energetic after subduing most of peninsular Greece, had organized Rhodes, the southernmost of the Asia Minor offshore islands, and established three independent cities there. Rhodes, to be sure, was not to shine in the immediate generations ahead with a light comparable to that of Lesbos or Ephesus or rich and many-talented Miletus, but its time was to come: in the era of Alexander the Great and after, it would emerge as one of the great Mediterranean trading centers.

And this was only the beginning. By mid eighth century, colonists from Euboea, the long island strip just to the north of Attica, were setting off to found settlements in Thrace—to the north—and in Italy, where Cumae and the offshore island of Ischia were probably the first sites (Cumae in turn established Neapolis, present-day Naples). Soon after, Naxos on Sicily was founded (named, some say, for the Aegean island of Naxos), and also Syracuse, a Corinthian colony that was to have an illustrious future. At about the same time Greeks began moving toward the Hellespont and in the following centuries they entered the Black Sea and founded numerous colonies on its shores. By the end of the sixth century the entire Mediterranean was encircled by Greek offshoots—ranging from Thrace and Asia Minor to Syria, Egypt, Libya, Spain, southern France, and Italy. In areas like Syria and Egypt, where they encountered old, established local cultures, the Greeks had trading posts; elsewhere they founded replicas of their own city-states.

In some of these far-shore settlements culture and wealth grew fast—much faster even than on the parent peninsula itself. The geographer-historian Strabo, writing at the beginning of the Christian era, described one episode of this astonishing spread to southern Italy and Sicily: "Archias, sailing from Corinth, founded Syracuse about the same time that Naxos and Megara were established. They say that when Myscellus and Archias went to Delphi to consult the oracle, the god asked whether they preferred wealth or health. Archias chose wealth and Myscellus health, and the oracle then assigned Syracuse to the former and Croton to the latter." Thus Strabo conveys something of the gist of an original Greek process, which might roughly be summed up as this:

A given Greek city, having attained a certain degree of stability, is still subject to some degree of restlessness, perhaps because of expanding population or inadequacy of resource, or both. Some of its younger spirits conceive the idea of setting up beyond the seas a new town with more space or resource that will be related to the old, yet not beholden to it. They then choose a distinguished citizen as their *oikistes,* or city-founder, and consult the oracle as to whether this undertaking will be beneficial to all concerned. Finally, having been encouraged by Delphi, they proceed, carrying with them sacred fire from their old city shrine to ignite a new one; from then on they regard themselves as bound to the parent city by no ties other than those of filial friendship.

The motives of the Greek settlers were quite unlike those of the triumphant Caesars, seeking to acquire tributaries to be subject to Rome, or of the conquistadors, out for glory and gold for Spain. It was, instead of a true colonization, more in the nature of emigration; *apoikia* was a word Greeks used to define it, meaning an "away-home"—a thought no doubt comparable to that which stirred many settlers of North America. Impulses toward commercial exploitation played a strong part, but so did urges for new land; and the city fathers at home were wise enough to see that their emigrant sons had best be left to pursue their own fortunes—with some parental guidance.

Such a vast extension in relatively so short a time by so small a people (some scholars believe there were no more than 200,000 Dorian, Ionian, Aeolian, and other Greeks living in 700 B.C.) leaves one still asking, How did they do it? One answer is that they embodied a new force at large in a surrounding vacuum. That vacuum was one of power and culture both. At the time when Greece came back to life seeking fresh horizons the ancient kingdoms of the East had either crumbled or were falling into decay. The Hittite empire in Asia Minor had long disappeared. The Phrygian kingdom that in part succeeded it was destroyed in about 700 B.C. The Lydian kingdom that in turn succeeded *that* was only just taking form under Gyges, and had not yet produced the Croesus who would threaten Ionian settlements along the coast. Egypt's glory had faded, and its dynasties lived in torpor, to be conquered in the early seventh century by the Assyrians. The Phoenicians had their share of Mediterranean trade; but not until they founded Carthage did they seriously menace the Greeks. Farther off to the east, the Persian realm had hardly begun to assert itself from its mountains. The Macedonians were still backward, northern hillmen. In Italy, the Etruscans had indeed made themselves known to the Greeks, and were carrying on a lively trade with them. But the Romans—a people still under Etruscan influence—were all but unknown.

In a sense, then, the Mediterranean world of the eighth and seventh centuries was singularly open. As the classicist H. D. F. Kitto writes, "The ironies of history are many and bitter, but at least this must be put to the credit of the gods, that they arranged for the Greeks to have the eastern Mediterranean almost to themselves long enough to work out what was almost a laboratory experiment to test how far, and in what conditions, human nature is capable of creating and sustaining a civilization."

The ideas the Greeks carried with them were those of self-determination and individuality; and their "peculiar institution," the *polis,* or city-state, both embodied and furthered these notions, encouraging men as they set off to a far shore to be as self-reliant and independent abroad as their fathers were at home. Vigorous competition between daughter cities, diversity in their mores and make-up, vitality in their sense of freedom, and the pursuit of excellence—all this was of the essence of the Greeks' uniqueness and success wherever they went in those centuries, for all the troubles it was to cause them in later ones.

The Greeks, the more they met and traded with the *barbaroi,* tended to look down on them. (The time was still far off when the Greeks, in the irony of history, were to be absorbed in the vastest of ancient empires, that of the "barbarian" Romans, to whom they had taught so much.) Only the Greeks, they knew, had brought forth the polis, and by this they meant a sovereign city or independent small state, but also something more: the word "polis" denotes not only a place but its people—a community acting together to govern itself under the idea that public affairs are the affairs of all its citizens. To be sure, this idea did not spring forth full-born, Athena-like, from the Greek brow. In the eighth and seventh centuries Greek city-states were ruled by aristocrats who ran them with little concern for the general interest. But the polis concept, once implanted, was rapidly to grow, creating a way of life that was diametrically opposite to that of the hierarchic Eastern and Mycenaean kingdoms, with their absolute despots. The Pharaohs were actually worshiped as gods and had abject subjects; the Greeks (though they had slaves too) were out to breed citizens. Later Aristotle was to remark, looking back over the origin and nature of the polis, that "while it grows for the sake of mere life, it exists for the sake of the good life."

A local form of government had come into being as a practical necessity in the chaotic times after the decline and fall of the Mycenaean kingdoms and during the tenuous growth of Greek settlements beyond the seas. What was remarkable was what the Greeks made of it, and how obstinately they were to stick to it. With survival uncertain, men in their isolated valleys had huddled for protection around some hilltop stronghold or citadel maintained by a vigorous local clan. These clans, each claiming descent from some ancestral hero or ruler, had gradually taken over the functions of decayed kingships by appointing some man or men from their own number to rule in their behalf. Sometimes they still styled these magistrates "kings" (Sparta, throughout its history as an independent city-state, had two such "kings" ruling concurrently); but actual, hereditary kingship in Greece had all but disappeared by the close of the eighth century, and all power lay in the hands of the local aristocracy and its representatives.

These feudal squires, or "first families,"—so we gather from the seventh-century poetry that tells of them—were a stout breed of men, greatly savoring the good life of war, love, and wine. They were also a jealous breed, intent on retaining sovereignty over their small specks of land. And how small some of these were: Boeotia alone, hardly the size of the smallest American state, brought forth all of twelve separate, independent city-states; the island of Ceos, only fifteen miles long and eight across, three; and all told, the number of self-governing Greek city-states was to reach a peak of perhaps fifteen hundred.

One might have thought that in time, as civil order revived in Greece along with a new sense of the community of all the

Hellenes, this fragmented scheme of things would have been superseded by a drive toward over-all organization. Not at all. And here we come closest to what was both the genius and the eventual tragedy of the Greeks. They had found in the individual commune, in the self-determining locality, what seemed to them the most natural, workable, and responsive form of political life or polity—particularly as they developed the schemes of a council and of a public meeting of all citizens to hear and debate what their leaders had proposed. And though in the eighth century Sparta conquered and annexed the whole neighboring region of Messenia, and Athens expanded through Attica and later extended its influence and hegemony far beyond, the Greeks never became reconciled to any scheme stronger than that of a loose federation—certainly not to the idea of union. This was to serve them ill during the wars against Persia, when many reluctant or isolationist city-states either stood aside or gave in to the invader, not because they liked Xerxes and Darius more, but because their sense of common cause with Athens was less; and it was to prove suicidal in the end when Athens and Sparta, each proud, each vigorous, each aided by allies, but unable altogether to conceive of any general overriding Greek interest, went to war against each other in the late fifth century, to the second ruin of their land.

Yet even after that catastrophe of disunion, in the fourth century the two leading political philosophers of Greece were to go on arguing the case of the small, autonomous state, Plato in the *Republic* placing the ideal number of its citizens at 5,040 and Aristotle in his *Politics* arguing that a polis should be small enough so that all of its citizens could know each other by sight. What underlay all this thinking was a belief that every citizen should play some direct part in governance, which in turn implied a belief in the rule of law. As Pericles of Athens said, "Laws are all the rules approved and enacted by the majority in assembly, whereby they declare what ought and what ought not to be done." And the Greek mind, heady with this unprecedented idea, had doubts as to how the voice of the majority could effectively be delegated. Must not every individual citizen be permitted to stand up in the assembly and speak for himself? Even at the time of Greece's fifth-century strength there were probably no more than three city-states (Athens, Syracuse, and Acragas) with more than 20,000 citizens—the term "citizen" in the Greek context referring to those adult males who by reason of property, local birth, and other standing were eligible to vote and hold office. The citizens were only a fraction of the total population: thus while Sparta in its prime may have had 300,000 souls in its five communes and countryside, there were never more than 4,000 who could be called citizens.

The Greek respect for law, and particularly for law as enacted by will of the polis, was not of sudden birth. Centuries were needed to resolve such questions as. Whose law? For whom? One law for rich and another for poor? and How to go about changing the law, once it had been set forth? The Greeks generally held that in the beginning, justice came from the gods, who punished transgressors against divine will (a paradox in later eyes, to be sure, since the gods themselves were thought to be so lawless). The early warrior-kings, ruling by fiat and caprice very much as the gods did, had naturally found it to their advantage to claim divine sanction for their acts. As man-made laws emerged, derived from ancient custom and religious observance, the Greeks felt that these laws stood under some divine protection and that their early lawgivers—such as Lycurgus of Sparta and Solon of Athens—had been directly inspired by the gods. As Demosthenes was to say to the Athenians in a celebrated address in the sophisticated fourth century: "The whole life of men, O Athenians, whether they inhabit a great city or a small one, is

governed by nature and by laws. Of these, nature is a thing irregular, unequal, and peculiar to the individual possessor; laws are
regular, common, and the same for all. Nature, if it be depraved,
has often vicious desires; therefore you will find people of that
sort falling into error. Laws desire what is just and honorable and
useful; they seek for this, and, when it is found, it is set forth as
a general ordinance, the same and alike for all; and that is law,
which all men ought to obey for many reasons, and especially
because every law is an invention and gift of the gods."

Yet it was by no means true, in the period when the aristocrats took over from the kings, that laws were "the same for all."
The poet Hesiod, writing sometime around the beginning of the
seventh century, spoke of "bribe-devouring judges" and complained that the ruling families tended to hand down judgments
in their own favor. With the rebirth of literacy, a process began
of codifying the laws that hitherto had come down orally, and of
carving them on tablets (the oldest of these to survive being a
city ordinance set up at Dreros on Crete perhaps in the mid seventh century); but for decades what was written down was feudal landlord's law, and it was administered by magistrates of
that class. The code of the Athenian Draco, set forth in about the
year 621, was particularly harsh in that it reaffirmed the right of
a creditor to personally enslave a debtor for nonpayment, and
even made petty pilfering punishable by death. A later biographer, Plutarch, wrote, "Those that were convicted of idleness
were to die, and those that stole a cabbage or an apple to suffer
even as villains that committed sacrilege or murder. . . . Draco's
laws were written not with ink but blood."

Meanwhile, though, a new force was rising in the land, fired
by the oppressiveness of the hilltop lords, the leanness of life
below, and the glimpse of better possibilities in the law. In
Attica a massive protest arose among impoverished farmers,
tenants, and small proprietors against the great, against the size

of their holdings, and against their power to seize any person who, in a time of such scarce money, had not been able to meet his mortgage or his sharecrop payments on time. It was all very well to speak of the virtues of a community life and of self-dedication to the service of a polis. But so long as so many men remained with little land, or without land, or with their very persons pledged to some ancestral baron, wasn't this a sham?

Very many Greeks thought it was, and the late seventh century and the sixth were to see a class struggle that reached the dimensions of a social revolution. Aristotle recalled of this period that "the poor, with their wives and children, were enslaved to the rich," and had no political rights; and it was emancipation that they now demanded, turning in their turbulence to quite another type of man who might further them—the popular leader, seizing power from the nobles without any authority save his own. These men—a Pheidon of Argos, a Periander of Corinth, a Polycrates of Samos, a Gelon of Syracuse—were those whom the Greeks called *tyrannoi,* meaning self-appointed despots ruling supposedly in the people's interest; indeed, many of them did so, but enough ruled in their own interests to give the word "tyrant" the unpleasant meaning attached to it today.

Athens was to have its tyrant too in the person of Pisistratus, a most likable, benevolent, intelligent patrician who had placed himself at the head of the popular party, even as a "traitor to his class," and who shrewdly advanced the peasantry, chastened the landlord nobles, calmed civil strife, strengthened the power of Athens, and launched public works—above all, the building of the first great temples on the Acropolis. That he was able to do so much was, ironically, in part the result of the work of a man who had been put into office before him by apprehensive nobles to write reforms that would head off just such a tyrant as he.

That man, Solon, elected archon by his peers in 594 B.C. with

extraordinary powers to revise their code, is one of the most
appealing figures in all Greek history—as well as the first of the
great Athenians. Of high birth, well-earned substance, wide
travel, literary temperament, and profound humanity, he used
the mandate given him to propose reforms that, while they did
not satisfy all the radicals, astonished what we would call the
old guard with their sweep and range. While he did not go along
with the demands of the extremists that land should be redis-
tributed, he did abolish slavery for debt and furthermore abol-
ished all existing debts involving land and rent payments, and
he decreed that those Athenians who had been enslaved because
of such debts should go free. The result was an immediate
reduction in landlord power. Moreover, he wrote provisions
designed to protect the poor against rule by the rich by setting
up the right of appeal in court and that of a third party to seek
justice in behalf of some accused person who might be unable to
defend himself. No wonder that these reforms were celebrated
by a public feast in the Agora when Solon pronounced them, for
the foundations of Greek democracy and Athenian greatness
were laid on that very day early in the sixth century—even
though Greeks had not yet coined the term *demokratia* and
though Solon's reforms were in the first instance to be administered by Pisistratus, a dictator related to him by blood.

Though later Greeks were to think that he had been inspired
by the gods. Solon himself, ever urbane, felt he had been ruled
by earthly good sense; he wrote in verse:

> *Such power I gave the people as might do,*
> *Abridged not what they had, now lavished new,*
> *Those that were great in wealth and high in place*
> *My counsel likewise kept from all disgrace.*
> *Before them both I held my shield of might.*
> *And let not either touch the other's right.*

Having accomplished this, he thereupon left Athens for a decade so that the polis would have time to try out his proposals without being embarrassed by his presence.

If Solon needed to enlarge his inspiration, he had the opportunity when visiting the cities of Ionia beyond the Aegean, then flourishing with commerce and arts far in advance of Athens' own, and whose literature and taste he knew well. For in prosperous Miletus, and in many other Greek settlements along the Asia Minor coast, mixtures of new blood with old, and contact with the Near East and Egypt had produced not only physical but intellectual enrichment and a life marked by lively curiosity, free self-expression, and a degree of oriental sensuousness. The art of personal, lyrical, or elegiac poetry arose, with the distinctive "measures" or rhythms in which to write it—never greater than when ever-amorous Sappho, a contemporary of Solon across the sea, wrote what is perhaps her most famous single line,

'Ηράμαν μὲν ἔγω σάθεν, 'Ἀτθι, πάλαι ποτά
(I loved thee once, Atthis, long ago.)

She would also compose so savage a stanza on some woman who had perhaps rejected her as this one:

Death shall be death forever unto thee,
Lady, with no remembrance of thy name
Then or thereafter; for thou gatherest not
The roses of Pieria, loving gold
Above the Muses. Even in Hades' House
Wander thou shalt unmarked, flitting forlorn
Among the shadowy, averted dead.

The worldly Ionians, by turns sunny and skeptical in disposition, and less concerned with the ancient menacing gods than

with the intelligent enjoyment of a fleeting life, could well
savor such a stanza as that by Mimnermus of Colophon which
in translation heads this chapter. Or, relaxing in a way that
their generic foes in Greece proper, the austere Dorians of the
Peloponnesus, never could, they no doubt relished such a
drinking song as this, by another accomplished poet of Lesbos,
Alcaeus:

> *Zeus rains: a storm comes in its might*
> *From heav'n, and freezes rivers tight . . .*
>
> *Put down the storm! Pile up the fire.*
> *Mix the sweet wine to your desire,*
>   *And round your forehead set*
>   *A dainty coronet.*
>
> *To woe the heart must not give in.*
> *In grief's no help. One medicine,*
>   *My friend, alone is fit—*
>   *Wine—, and get drunk on it.*

Meanwhile there were more serious spirits in Ionia, who
having some acquaintance with Babylonian astronomy and
ancient Egyptian priestly wisdom, had then struck out to try to
explain the nature of things without recourse to myth and the
supernatural. Were they original in their efforts to pierce the
riddle of the universe? The idea that the Ionian Greeks owed
much of their dawning interest in science and philosophy to
Babylonian and Egyptian sources, has until recently been
widely accepted; but now some scholars discount this, believing that the unique scientific spirit of the Ionians was self-
generated. A very new kind of thought sprang up in Ionia in the
sixth century, particularly in the city of Miletus—the first

Athens of Greece—where Western studies of the nature of things began.

Many stories have been told over many centuries about Thales of that city, the pioneer figure who always appears early in the first chapter of textbooks on the history of philosophy, and most of these tales are probably apocryphal. He is said variously to have been a shrewd Milesian trader who made a killing out of cornering the olive presses that served the market; to have been a stargazer who accurately predicted an eclipse of the sun that took place in the year 585 B.C.; to have been an engineer who served as adviser to Croesus and who diverted the river Halys from its course. Renowned as one of the Seven Wise Men of Greece, Thales was as adventurous in thinking about the physical world as Solon was in thinking about the welfare of man.

The old creation stories of the world's rising out of Night or Chaos, with primeval gods and goddesses then mating to shape it, were simply not adequate answers to Thales' inquiring spirit. What *was* the origin and nature of the physical world—leaving the gods aside? Amid its manifold appearances, its riot of diversity, was there not some central physical scheme or substance from which everything had sprung? Thales pondered, and came forth with the surprising thought that the "world-stuff" was water, from which he thought all things had arisen and to which they would in the end return. This was a leap of the imagination that many later thinkers were to regard as challenging but naïve, but which today we do not regard as quite so naïve, with its first intimations of evolution and of the central role of hydrogen, a basic element from which other substances can be compounded. Gods were immanent in all things, Thales seems to have felt, but there was still some fundamental law or unity of nature greater than the gods; and his follower Anaximander, though disagreeing with Thales' water theory, went on—in another imaginative leap—to argue that "originally man was born from animals of another species," and that he was "like a fish, in the beginning."

Here, as Greece entered into the sixth century, was revolutionary thought—to remain revolutionary, indeed, until the priests and presbyters of the West finally yielded to Charles Darwin two and a half millennia later. But there was even more to this Greek eruption than the pursuit of natural science, poetry, and social polity. There was also a revolution in art, in this case influenced distinctly by the Orient. Egyptian heroic statuary, as known for instance to the early school of Hellenic marble carvers whose work has been found on Delos, inspired the first characteristic Greek free-standing sculpture—the tall, idealized figure of an athletic male, foursquare, left foot forward, arms firmly at his side like his Egyptian prototype. From the East also came new techniques of working in decorative metals and ivory, and the inspiration for a fanciful style of pottery painting which employed many oriental motifs. In architecture the Greeks turned from mere crude building and began to develop the distinctive styles that the world has treasured ever since.

The Mycenaeans had built no temples, only crude fortress palaces and well-engineered subterranean tombs; what followed for centuries consisted of rude wood beams with clay or wattle sidings raised over stone footings. At some point the idea arose of extending the porch or colonnade (in the beginning fashioned of tree trunks or hewn timber) to surround a sanctuary and support its roof; and, once the idea had arisen, as in the early temple of Hera at Olympia, it led to gradual replacement of timber by stone, first in the form of monoliths, then in that of fluted drums once the original supports decayed. (Pausanias, visiting Olympia in the second century after Christ, saw one of the original oak supports of Hera's temple still standing.) In discovering the potential grace and magnificence of their own marble and limestone, the Greeks in one sense discovered themselves.

Their architecture arose from bold experiment in building and the use of native materials; their sculpture from searching thought as to grace and balance; their philosophy from inquiry independent of the gods; their style—from themselves. Conqueror had mixed with conquered; slavery was the fate of some, the idea of freedom the hope of others; the Orient helped inspire not only a Thales but a Pythagoras, the combination mathematician, musician, and mystic, who moved from Samos to southern Italy to set up his philosophic school there. This springtime of Hellas can perhaps be felt most closely in the mysterious so-called archaic smile that dominates its sculpture, as if these youthful beings and their mates had knowledge of some great though possibly short-lived fate to come. Their physical surroundings were long to remain lean and harsh, but not their intellectual ones: thus the men who designed the new temple at Corinth in the mid sixth century applied to it a most sophisticated refinement—the use of a slight correction, entasis, to swell their columns in mid-height to offset what otherwise might have been an optical impression from the ground of concavity or weakness of shape. And though the philosopher Pythagoras set up a cult surrounded by many a primitive taboo and mystic rite, and was called by his devotees a son of Apollo if not an embodiment of Apollo himself, he was the Greek who proposed the theorem that schoolboys have been asked to learn ever since, namely that the square on the hypotenuse of a right-angled triangle equals the sum of the squares on the other two sides. What is so important about that? two millennia's schoolboys have no doubt asked themselves when told to resolve it. What is important is that formulating this theorem demanded a stirring development of the human intellect. The emergence of Greece came about in large part because so many of its men were ready to make such demands on themselves.

The small bronze spearman, above, shield in hand, is dressed for battle. Over his short chiton he wears a decorated cuirass, and greaves cover his legs.

V

THE RIVAL CITIES

Go tell the Spartans, thou who passest by. That here obedient to their laws we lie.

—Simonides of Ceos: epitaph to the Spartan dead at Thermopylae

To sum up, I say that Athens is the school of Hellas.

—Pericles: funeral oration for the Athenian dead

What passes for Sparta today is a grubby, dusty provincial town of some 11,000 souls tucked away in the upland valley of the thin-flowing Eurotas, and neither the oleander blooming along the riverbank nor the reeds and rushes that sway handsomely with the wind can overcome, when you visit it, a general impression of torpor, oblivion, and gloom. The valley itself is not one of Greece's more favored ones. The surrounding heights are near and hard, yet not dramatic; the bottom lands are fertile, but dull: you miss the soaring mountainscape of Delphi, the splendid setting of Athens overlooking the spanking sea, the elegance of Epidaurus, poised between its well-shaped slope and pleasant water, and the enchantment of the curving vale of Olympia. You find yourself asking why, if the Greeks were so imaginative, a particularly vigorous tribe of them—the Dorian conquerors of the Peloponnesus—should have picked this landlocked, ordinary spot as the seat of their kingdom, when there was so much else to beckon them—sites as splendid as Mycenae, looming on its crags high over coastal plains and strategic bays. One answer is that there were many kinds of

Greeks, and that imagination was the least of the qualities that distinguished those who became the Spartans of history—a breed that eventually became as dour and ingrown as Sparta's landscape.

Thucydides, an Athenian, was to write of the city that engaged his own in mortal combat: "If Sparta were laid waste and there remained nothing but the temples and the foundations of public buildings, posterity, I think, would find it difficult to believe that the power of this town corresponded to its fame." In the end Sparta was to be destroyed—not so much by others as by its own shortcomings—and if hardly a foundation stone survived, that was primarily because the Spartans had laid so few. While other cities built, Sparta drilled; what its people in fact constructed was little more than an armed camp surrounded by outposts and dependent villages, and sustained by a military code. Yet it was this barracks of a state that led almost all the Greek peninsula when Athens was still only a second-rate power, and that in the end succeeded in bringing down its rival from a zenith of Periclean brilliance and glory into humiliation and shame.

Athens and Sparta are not even one hundred fifty miles apart, separated by Attica's western slopes and the narrow isthmus of Corinth that leads down into the province of Argolis, but in their primes they moved at the opposite poles of Greek being and met chiefly to collide. There are few greater paradoxes in history: here were two communities of men settled on the same south-European outcrop, related by origin, speaking the same language, worshiping the same gods, linked by tales of common ancestral heroes, and equally proud of their Hellenic superiority over the *barbaroi,* or lesser breeds without the law; yet they were so diametrically different in their ways of living and thinking as to make each in effect the reverse of the other—though also, in another sense, the complement.

Fifth-century Athens stood at the cosmopolitan crossroads of the Greek world, bustling with trade, its Piraeus port lined with ships, its streets crowded with visitors from Asia Minor, Sicily, Egypt. Sparta sat in the hinterland as a self-sufficient commune of manorial soldier-lords who frowned upon trade, and foreigners too. It was as if Athens looked forward, and Sparta back. Athens, ever ready to try the new, for instance adopted from the Lydian kings of Asia Minor their seventh-century invention of currency of fixed weights as a convenient medium of exchange; and the drachma, probably first minted in Solon's day and later stamped with the Athenian owl, greatly helped expedite commerce. Gradually these became to Mediterranean trade what the British pound sterling was to become to world trade more than two millennia later: a stable unit in terms of which many-sided commitments could be made. Yet the Spartans, even through the fifth century, stuck obstinately to unwieldy, primitive iron bars as their only instrument of barter—a symbol of their suspicion not only of exchange but of any kind of change.

The Athenians prided themselves on their costly, richly painted and decorated temples, stoas, and gymnasiums; the Spartans, on their disinterest in outward show. The busy Athenians, when an outside challenge or danger reared, raised conscript armies led by amateur generals, each elected to serve for a year; the Spartiates—that is to say, the master class who controlled Sparta, descendants of the Dorian tribesmen who had won the land—were themselves a standing army, each soldier-citizen being permitted to do little more than dedicate his life to the profession of sword and spear. These prototypes of Prussians were the most skilled and devoted soldiery of the age, as King Xerxes of Persia was to learn when he attacked the Greeks early in the fifth century. Herodotus recalls that a deposed and renegade king of Sparta, Demaratus by name, who had placed himself in the service of the Persians, warned Xerxes that the Spartans, small as they were in number, would put up a phenomenal resistance against him: "when they fight singly, [they] are as good men as any in the world, and when they fight in a body, [they] are the bravest of all." And so they were to be, when three hundred of them faced the entire Persian host at the pass of Thermopylae in the year 480 B.C., dying to the last man. The glory of the Athenian-led sea victory over Xerxes' fleet at Salamis in the same year was no greater than that of this self-sacrifice.

Although so bold in battle, the Spartans nevertheless remained fearful and recessive at home. Athens proceeded from early kingship through oligarchy and rule by tyrants to the world's first democracy. Sparta, though it managed to combine the rule of kings with oligarchs, went no further than that; on the contrary, while Athens was feeling its way forward, Sparta stuck fast in the extremes of oligarchy. In Athens a series of reforms, inspired by Solon's, broadened the franchise and steadily increased popular participation in government over the resistance of Athens' own class of eupatrids—the nobility, literally "the well-born"—but in Sparta nothing of the sort took place. In Athens, in due course, a tradesman or a blacksmith, provided he was of old local lineage and good repute, could not only vote but was encouraged to hold public office. In Sparta the very small elite minority withheld all political rights from the subjects whom they had conquered and whom they reduced to the state of either *perioikoi* (voteless freemen) or helots (bondsmen and agricultural serfs). While Athenians listened in the Agora to popular orators and reformers such as Cleisthenes in the late sixth century, the Spartans set up the unattractive system of Europe's first secret police, the *krypteia*. Under this system young Spartiates were yearly commissioned to put to the sword any helots they suspected of disaffection. The fears of their governing clans were only too well founded, since the Spartiates had set themselves so aloof from the subject populace that there was a constant danger of insurrection: Sparta's brave arms were first of all pointed against social upheaval at home.

Such Spartan preoccupation with maintaining discipline and class distinction was bound to lead to rigidity and even desiccation, while Athens by contrast experimented and expanded. This, Thucydides himself was to point out in a searching passage early in his history of the climactic struggle between the two states that broke out in 431 B.C. Shortly before the clash, as the rivals are girding and there is uncertainty in the Spartan camp as to whether the moment is ripe for assaulting Attica, Thucydides has a Corinthian spokesman friendly to the Spartans deliver them a lecture on their faults. "The Athenians," he says, "are addicted to innovation, and their designs are characterized by swiftness alike in conception and execution; you have a genius for keeping what you have got, accompanied by a total want of invention, and when forced to act you never go far enough. Again, they are adventurous beyond their power, and daring beyond their judgment, and in danger they are sanguine; your wont is to attempt less than is justified by your power.... Further, there is promptitude on their side against procrastination on yours; they are never at home, you are never away from it: for they hope by their absence to extend their acquisitions, you fear by your advance to endanger what you have left behind."

"A total want of invention": biting words, and true. Athens produced in statecraft a Solon, a Themistocles, a Pericles; in drama an Aeschylus, a Sophocles, a Euripides, an Aristophanes; in sculpture a Phidias, a Praxiteles; in architecture a Mnesicles, one of the builders of its new Acropolis; in history a Thucydides; in philosophy a Socrates, a Plato; whereas Sparta in its prime produced soldiers. Brave as they were, they were almost literally dumb; if in their "laconic" style of speech they cultivated brevity and silence, it was, as has been remarked, because they had little or nothing to say.

Athens' readiness to pursue a new idea can be seen prophetically developing throughout the sixth century—the era that established its character, as the fifth century was to bring about its leadership. Of Solon's innovations in his still simple and agricultural polis of the first decade of the sixth century, none was more telling than his scheme to introduce manufactures (chiefly smithing, pottery making, woodworking); and since Athens was wanting in craftsmen, he proposed that his fellow citizens invite many such men from abroad. Not only that, but he offered them full citizenship as an incentive to their coming. His countrymen agreed, even though this meant diluting their own franchise with the votes of foreigners and of the lower classes, and their reward was trade and prosperity.

If this was a milestone in Athenian economic growth, a comparable one in culture was the effort by Solon's long-ruling successor Pisistratus, in and out of power from the 560's to the 530's, to make Athens the spiritual center of the Attic communes that were grouped around it. Some of his work took the form of developing the first religious Panathenaic games in about 566 B.C.; then, of bringing to Athens the annual festivals to the nature god Dionysus that had been held in the countryside for decades past, with their choral chants and dances. Finally, as there grew out of these festivals the rudimentary art of the drama, the first public contest for a tragic play was set up in Athens in the year 534 B.C.—and with this event the history of the Greek theatre begins.

Military, too—for all its amateur methods under arms—sixth-century Athens showed verve and strategic insight when about 570 B.C. it seized from the neighboring city-state of Megara the offshore island of Salamis, which dominated the western approaches to the Piraeus and thus threatened Athens' seagoing trade. By this shrewd stroke Athens made itself mistress of all its nearby waters, and soon a strong naval power was in the making.

Then just before the close of the century Athens took a revolutionary stride politically and socially in the reforms instituted by Cleisthenes, who identified himself with popular aspirations, as Solon and Pisistratus had. Not a great sage like Solon, not a benevolent tyrant like Pisistratus, Cleisthenes was an insurgent leader who, in the last decade of the sixth century, proved himself a superlative organizer of a liberal state.

Ironically, he had come to power with the aid of Sparta, in the course of a revolt of leading Athenian eupatrid families against the sons and heirs of Pisistratus, who had behaved privately in an unseemly fashion and publicly in an all too partisan one. Sparta had several designs in aiding the rebellion: one was to make Greece safe for oligarchy, and another was to gain a hold over Athenian affairs—which Sparta did by requiring Athenian aristocrats, as the price for its help, to join its own Peloponnesian League. Sparta miscalculated badly: Cleisthenes, emerging on top as a popular leader in this tortuous struggle, at once swung Athens into the opposite direction from oligarchy. It is with him that the city's working democracy actually begins.

For Solon, while curbing the exclusive power of the old nobles, had left many of their institutions more or less intact— chiefly their senate, the Council of the Areopagus, restricted to leading men who had once been archons of the state, and endowed with supreme authority to oversee the people and their officials. But he had created, below this, the Council of Four Hundred, which was known as the *boule*. This was carefully apportioned so that equivalent numbers of men would come from each of the four traditional Ionian tribes of free citizens. A second breakdown of the populace, based on a ladder of income—from the *pentacosiomedimni,* or affluent "five-hundred-bushel men," down to the *thetes,* those of small resource—determined who was eligible to hold office. Then, a general assembly, or *ekklesia,* of free citizens elected officials annually, but its choice was limited in that the highest—the archons and military commanders—could be chosen only from the top class; and the thetes were not eligible to hold any office at all, although they took part in the voting.

Cleisthenes, in his sweeping innovations of 507 B.C. or thereabouts, changed all this. First, he threw out the old structure of four tribes, dissolved several hundred clans led by entrenched families, and set up a new division of ten Athenian tribes, each of which included residents of the city, the coast, and the Attic countryside. At the same time he almost doubled the size of the electorate by further extending the right of citizenship. Then he took sovereign power from the old Council and vested it in the Assembly, to which all officeholders high and low were to be directly responsible. The Council, or *boule,* was to continue as a body preparing business for action by the Assembly, but its membership was now based on the ten tribes (each providing fifty men) without reference to income class; moreover, it was not to consider itself a superior representative branch of government but simply a high executive committee reporting to the Assembly of some twenty to thirty thousand citizens, which now was the legislature.

Eventually any citizen, whatever his station, was to be eligible for any public office; and it came to be expected that every citizen would serve at some time or another in at least one. This was achieved by a system of election by lot and the annual rotation of most major public offices, with a ban on re-election until many other men had had their chance to serve in turn; so that anyone might find himself chosen one of next year's magistrates or jurors or tax collectors or councilors. Then, if he had been picked for the Council from the roster of citizens, he might also suddenly find himself its presiding officer for a day: for the Council chose from its number, also by lot and turn, a different president for each day's session. Since the Council met some three hundred days a year, this meant that in a decade three thousand Athenians had sat in the highest chair—one that in view of the turbulence of Athenian politics was very often the hot seat.

The effect of this scheme of things, as it developed over the half century from Cleisthenes to Pericles, was to distribute first-hand experience of government among more and more people, with less and less reference to class. There was no bureaucracy, no hereditary caste of governors. To be sure, it was thought to be to the good that men of prominent lineage, wealth, and station devote themselves particularly to public life, they having the leisure and the means to do so, while others must think of earning a living. (Pericles later paid wages so that the poorer citizens could leave their daily labors to assist the state.) The idea of professionalism at the top became abhorrent to very many Athenians as they savored, even if only briefly, the challenges and pleasures of sharing in government. In theory every citizen was capable of filling any office for which he might be chosen—or, under this revolving system, he would soon learn how to be, for if he failed, there were serious penalties. Even Athens' ten yearly generals, the *strategoi*, were elected annually from the entire body of citizens, although in practice experienced military leaders were given preference again and again. The historian Thucydides was to find himself a general in the war with Sparta and was exiled for his failure to hold the city

of Amphipolis. And Pericles himself, greatest of Greek statesmen, was to be heavily fined by the Assembly for what its
strategists regarded as his miscalculations in the same war.

For those citizens not tapped by the lot, there was the drama
of participation in the Assembly. It met outdoors, usually four
times every month, on the slope known as the Pnyx, opposite the
Acropolis, its session commencing at dawn with the sacrifice of a
pig to Zeus. The order of business had already been prepared by
the Council in its roofed chamber at one side of the Agora, where
it had been reviewing legislative proposals and carrying on state
affairs pending the Assembly's next meeting. Hard by the Council's building was the Tholos, the circular headquarters of the
chief administrators, who were prepared to be called upon at any
moment. The sun rises, the pig is killed, prayers are offered, the
agenda is presented—and then, as like as not, disorder threatens.
Though only some two or three thousand of the eligible assem-
blymen actually appear (most of those from outlying districts do
not find the time to come), the mass is large enough to be difficult to handle. While there are no organized political parties as
such, men of different factions seek to outshout, browbeat, and
insult each other, to the whistles and foot stamping of a crowd
that not only likes candor but relishes vituperation. Only when
his time runs out on the water clock is the speaker stopped. By
the late fifth century only a highly skilled orator—the professional of persuasion—can prevail above such a boisterous crowd
as this one. Enter, finally, the demagogue.

So broad and bold and unpredictable a frame of rule
inevitably did not sit well with the proudest old families. Class
antagonism was to plague Athens throughout its history. The
scheme also contained within itself obvious dangers of corruption, foolhardiness, incompetence in high office: all this, too, was
to be visited upon Athens. Yet there were many of the gentry
who swallowed their prejudices or memories and plunged in gen-

erously to help make the new system work: and in so doing, they lent to it the kind of grace that in America we associate with Jeffersonian democracy, of which the Athenian one was the distant model. Moreover, the exuberant participation of so many different kinds of men in their newly discovered self-government lent to the Athenians as a whole a style theretofore unknown.

Far removed from this stands the bleak, fixed world of Sparta. Although it may seem repugnant to us now and out of accord with all that we admire most in ancient Greece, we are repeatedly brought up against the fact that the Athenians themselves were by no means united in distaste for it. On the contrary, numbers of them—and in particular many of their chief philosophers—were strongly drawn to it, preferring it to the system of Athens. Socrates, ever the skeptic about Athens' ways and waywardness, may have been speaking half in jest when he remarked of the Spartans' "laconic" speech that it was really a sort of disguise: "But they conceal their wisdom . . . and pretend to be fools, so that their superiority over the rest of Greece may not be known to lie in wisdom, but seem to consist in fighting and courage. Their idea is that if their real excellence became known, everyone would set to work to become wise." Plato, however, was in earnest when in mapping his scheme for an ideal state in the *Republic* he modeled it largely on Sparta.

The Athenians pursued liberty, but there remained among many of them a fear—a partly justified fear, as it turned out—that too much liberty, or rather too little restraint, might lead to popular license. Among their eupatrids in particular there was a contrary impulse toward order, stability, hierarchy—and whatever else Sparta lacked, it most certainly had that. Dull or not, it had *eunomia,* or "the state of being well-lawed," which in turn was the embodiment of a rigorous ideal that required of everyone total, uncritical devotion to the state. Therefore Plato admired it, impatient at democracy's disorder and dreaming of a dedicated rule by only the best and most highly trained. Athens, he wrote, "is full of liberty and free speech and every one in it is allowed to do what he likes. This being allowed, it obviously follows that each man can plan his own life as he pleases." But it was just this that he found displeasing, enthralled as he was by the Spartan scheme of a firmly led band of brothers living like a garrison, eating at common mess tables, and thinking their thoughts in common.

With the Athenian Xenophon, Plato's contemporary and like him a pupil of Socrates, the attraction for Sparta became positively rapturous. Far-traveled and widely employed as a soldier of fortune (he went into both the Spartan and the Persian service, leading the famous march of the Ten Thousand to the Black Sea that he described in the *Anabasis*), he finally settled in Sparta and wrote a panegyric that not only acclaimed its system for its authoritarian virtues but agreed with the Spartans that it was divinely inspired. Much later still, the biographer Plutarch, a Greek who entered the Roman service in the first century A.D., was to produce in the life of the ancient Spartan lawgiver Lycurgus his own paean to the system that had humbled the Athenian state. "In general," he wrote approvingly, "Lycurgus made the citizens accustomed to have neither the will nor the ability to lead a private life; but, like the bees, always to be organic parts of their community, to cling together around the leader, and, in an ecstasy of enthusiasm and selfless ambition, to belong wholly to their country."

This admiration for things Spartan on the part of some of the most distinguished men of Greece often outdid what some Athenians had to say in praise of their own. This was not the case with Pericles, the guiding spirit of his city's democratic party as well as of the polis as a whole during the high fifth-century era that bears his name. Always eloquent about Athens, he was to be at his proudest in the great funeral oration he gave in 431 in honor of the first Athenians to die in the great war with Sparta. Enumerating the virtues and blessings of his fellow citizens, he dwelled especially on their civil freedom and went on to say (as Thucydides reports it): "The freedom which we enjoy in our government extends also to our ordinary [i.e., private] life. There, far from exercising a jealous surveillance over each other, we do not feel called upon to be angry with our neighbor for doing what he likes, or even to indulge in those injurious looks which cannot fail to be offensive, although they inflict no positive penalty." In such an open society, a Plato or an Aristotle was to be free to call for a closed one. Conversely no Spartan of record had the wit or the daring to call for an open one. Athens was to betray its principles by resorting to banishment and assassination; but Sparta never even learned those principles. As the great Athenian orator Demosthenes in the fourth century remarked. "You are not allowed to praise the laws of Athens or of any other state; far from it, you have to praise what conforms with their institutions." All the contrast between the libertarian and the totalitarian spirit that has come down through history rings in such words as these.

The class divisions of Athens, its chronic upheavals, the corruption that finally overcame it, explain much of the Athenians' attraction toward Sparta; but there was more. Undoubtedly Sparta's emergence as a teaching state, bent on forming its citizens' characters into a cohesive mold, absorbed many of those taken up with the training of youth—narrow though its training was. Athens was long to wrestle with this problem of order versus individuality. It may well have been an awareness of the fascination for Sparta on the part of the Athenians that caused Pericles in his oration for the Athenian dead to claim for his own city (as against Sparta) the role of being "the school of Hellas." Significantly, the primary argument on which he based his claim was the following: "I doubt if the world can produce a man, who where he has only himself to depend upon, is equal to so many emergencies, and graced by so happy a versatility as the Athenian."

However, as many an Athenian no doubt sensed, versatility alone was not enough to make a full man. The iron of order was needed too. Here we can detect a contrast of personality between the two main stems of the Greek race as it developed— on one hand the Ionians of Attica and Asia Minor, adventurous, imaginative, high-spirited, and on the other the Dorians of the Peloponnesus, sturdy, austere, conservative. There was an urge on the part of the livelier breed to strengthen itself with some of the steadying virtues of the other. The Spartan was one of the least pleasing of Dorians, when compared for instance to the many-sided Corinthians, his kin who dwelled closer to Athens; but he was certainly the most vigorous and, moreover, bred of the purest Dorian stock. The traveling bard Pindar of Thebes, who early in the fifth century wrote poems in praise of the best people of practically every city-state that harbored him— Athens, Syracuse, Aegina, Abdera, Corinth, and Sparta—liked to celebrate the ancient Dorians as the "fair-haired Danaeans" of the heroic age, and many Greek listeners seem to have regarded the Spartan as the embodiment of some superior strain from the North. (However, the myth that Greece owed its glory to Aryan blood, so attractive to Nordic racists, sprang up only when Germanic scholars went to work.) However, there was recognition among Ionian Greeks of a grave and potent Dorian (or Doric) style, which expressed itself most forcefully in thick-columned temples like that of Hera at Olympia—a style very different from the slender grace of Ionian buildings. The Athenians themselves were to adopt the Doric style for the Parthenon, the greatest shrine of their Acropolis.

Though Sparta itself was visibly a cultural desert during

Greece's greatest centuries, there was a sense both north and south of the Gulf of Corinth that at some time in the past it had flowered in the arts no less than in war—indeed, that it had experienced its own "golden age." This, too, may have added to its lure. Finds such as gold and silver jewelry of the seventh century, well-carved work in ivory, and pottery tell of an early time of Spartan imagination as well as luxury. We also know that although all the arts save martial music (in the Doric mode) were discouraged in the Sparta of its martial prime, in earlier times the city had been as receptive to the lyre and the bard as other Greek cities were. Thus early in the seventh century, perhaps in response to advice from the oracle at Delphi, the Spartans imported the lyric poet and musician Terpander from the faraway Aeolian isle of Lesbos, presumably to stage a contest in choral singing. Terpander, so far as we can learn from this dimly recorded period, was a considerable innovator in music. He was often regarded by the Greeks as the inventor of the lyre of seven strings, as well as the creator of the drinking song—a form without a future in the puritan Sparta to come.

Only a few fragments of his verses or songs survive: thus

> *Let us pour a libation*
> *To Memory's daughters,*
> *The Muses, and to the Muses'*
> *Leader, Leto's son.*

Soon after Terpander, the Spartans also gave harbor and audience to the amorous and romantic poet Alcman of Lydia, east of the Aegean, who in one of his surviving fragments wrote significantly, "The skillful playing of the lyre has equal rank with the sword," and then tuned his instrument to sing such a song as this:

No more, O maiden voices, sweet as honey, soft as love is,
No more my limbs sustain me.
A halcyon on the wing
Flying o'er the foam-flowers, in the halcyon coveys,
Would I were, and knew not the care,
The sea-blue bird of spring!

or this, one of the loveliest lyrical fragments of all Greek time:

The far peaks sleep, the great ravines,
The foothills, and the streams.
Asleep are trees, and hivèd bees,
The mountain beasts, and all that dark earth teems,
The glooming sea, the monsters in their deeps:
And every bird, its wide wings folded, sleeps.

With poetry and music and ornament, early Sparta appears to have developed very much as other Greek states did; then either late in the seventh century or early in the sixth an extraordinary change of course and character came over it. In the eighth, it had a working kingship and had enriched itself by conquering the neighboring Messenians in the fertile southwest; a few more steps of growth might have found it extending itself to become a trading power in the Aegean. But then came Lycurgus, the divinely inspired lawgiver who reformed luxurious Sparta and gave it a new code or constitution. Or so the Spartans later said, claiming that Lycurgus had received his edicts directly from the Delphic Apollo, god of law—somewhat as Moses had received his tablets from the great God of the Hebrews.

There is no historical proof that there ever was an individual named Lycurgus, any more than there is that there was a man named Moses. But there is abundant evidence that the change in Sparta's life brought about in his name was immense, even though myth and mystery surround the process. Tyrtaeus, a late seventh-century chronicler, tells in a surviving fragment of an approach made by the Spartans to Apollo's oracle at Delphi and reports what they were told: "For thus the lord of the silver bow, far-working Apollo, the golden-haired, gave response from his rich shrine: There shall govern the Council [of Sparta] the Kings, honored of the gods, to whose care is entrusted the lovely city of Sparta, and the Elders ripe in years, and after them the men of the people, giving obedience in turn to just decrees. . . ." Later, in the fifth century, Herodotus, although he was usually anxious to get through the veils of legend to the core of truth, repeated another traditional Lacedaemonian tale: "Lycurgus, a man of distinction among the Spartans, had gone to Delphi, to visit the oracle. Scarcely had he entered into the inner fane, when the priestess exclaimed aloud:

'O thou great Lycurgus, that com'st to my beautiful dwelling,
Dear to Zeus, and to all who sit in the halls of Olympus,
Whether to hail thee a god I know not, or only a mortal,
But my hope is strong that a god thou wilt prove, Lycurgus.' "

Thereupon, having been so extraordinarily praised from on high (for it was of course Apollo who was speaking through the mouth of the priestess), he was presented with Sparta's "entire system of laws."

All this has every earmark of a piece of shrewd invention by the Spartans to strengthen the acceptance of their harsh new system by giving it an air of divine command. As the American scholar Moses Hadas observes: "The only reasonable deduction from the mass of conflicting evidence is that Lycurgus was not the inventor of the Spartan constitution, and that his name (which probably represented an ancient wolf god) was deliber-

ately associated with the new legislation to enhance its credit."
But of the particularly close ties that existed between the Delphic oracle and Sparta there is no doubt. As Dr. Hadas remarks,
"Delphi was always against Athens and democracy"; and
Thucydides himself wrote that at the start of the Peloponnesian
War the oracle proclaimed that it would take Sparta's side.
Spartan officials were constantly on the move to the holy
precinct to obtain the latest advice on how to administer their
state. At certain times on moonless nights the ephors, or over-
seers, of Sparta would search the sky, and if they saw a shoot-
ing star they would suspend their kings from office until they
could get fresh counsel from Delphi.

The fact that there were two kings, and that the ephors could
suspend them at will, shows up the "reformed" Spartan system
of government in all its incongruity. The kings, hereditary and
two in number, were probably survivals of the circumstance
that Sparta and its surrounding countryside had originally been
conquered by separate tribes of Dorians. That so odd an
arrangement was allowed to continue no doubt reflected an
urge on the part of the leading families to have each king check
the other, while they in turn through their elected ephors would
check both. The kings, moreover, had been reduced to chiefly
ceremonial status: they presided at processions, held certain
priestly offices, and occupied the first seats at banquets, where
they were entitled to a double portion of every viand served.
However, when Sparta made war, one king went into the field
as commander, his military powers then becoming absolute,
while the other remained at home, watching him—no doubt
jealously—from a distance.

Along with the ephors—the high magistrates of the city—
there stood a council, or *gerousia,* of well-born elders who
advised the dual kings and served as a high court. This council
was literally a body of old men, since no one was admitted to

this office until he had reached the age of sixty. Below them, in turn, came an assembly, or *apella,* of all Spartiate male citizens of the age of thirty and over. This was theoretically a public meeting empowered to vote on every issue confronting the state, but in practice it was hamstrung by having no right of initiative or debate. It was, as we would say, simply a "rubber-stamp" legislature like those maintained in totalitarian powers in later eras to lend applause to decisions already made; and one Spartan statute provided that if the councilors found a vote of the Assembly wrongheaded or "crooked," they could simply throw it out.

Below the electorate of 3,000 or 4,000 Spartiates lay a voiceless helot population over forty-six times greater in number. But above the whole creaking structure stood the five annually elected ephors (one for each old Spartan commune), who together acted as a directorate that oversaw the state in general and its kings in particular. Although most Greeks praised the Spartan state for its *eunomia,* actually no scheme of government more cumbersome or guaranteed to produce eventual paralysis could have been devised; and this precisely was to be the outcome.

Lycurgan "reform" also meant that hitherto common lands were divided into lots that were made hereditary, passing from Spartiate father to son. Their holders were forbidden to engage in trade or any commercial enterprise, all their support coming from the labor of serfs. Boys were taken from their homes at the age of seven to be trained in state schools for martial pursuits (with a little reading and writing thrown in), while girls of nubile age were prepared for marriage and motherhood by drilling nude in outdoor exercises (without the necessity of learning to read and write). Sickly infants were exposed—that is, ordered to be taken to a nearby mountainside and abandoned to slow death or the swift jaws of wolves. Youths were unmercifully hazed by being required to do servile attendance on their elders and to endure hunger and deprivation as tests for manhood. They were required to mess and bunk with other males until well on into their married life, visiting their wives only furtively.

Considerable sexual freedom was, to be sure, one of the few liberties granted in this disciplinary state, but in the first instance much of it was directed homosexually. It was understood that a young Spartiate would enter into a liaison with some elder friend or mentor of the armed squirearchy; then if he chose to play the field with discus-throwing girls who appeared in the arena as unclothed as himself—well and good. If children then resulted before marriage, no damage whatever was done to the girl's reputation—unless the offspring were weak or faulty and thus unworthy of the fatherland. Those who have studied the mores of the late Nazi Germany may be struck by certain correspondences.

If despite all this many Athenians romanticized Sparta, there have been reverse impulses in times since to romanticize the Athenians and to think of their state as somewhat more ideal than it actually was, democratically speaking. The splendors of the great age that lay ahead for Athens were prefaced by certain limitations. For all its spreading of political rights, Athenian democracy, while allowing more freedom than Sparta, did not mean that the great majority of adult males or anything like a majority were to obtain the franchise. Pericles, in fact, when leading the city in the mid fifth century, was to reduce the number of voters. Athens ratio of enrolled citizens to total population may have been one to seven or eight—more than double that of Sparta; it was hardly a full democracy, if indeed there is such a thing. Several categories of men remained excluded: chiefly those who were employed by others (on the ground that, being so employed, they were not their own masters and free to lend their time to public service); resident foreigners, some of whose families had been established in Athens for generations (with an exception for those who had been granted citizenship by Solon's or Cleisthenes dispensations); and, finally, the mass of slaves.

Just how many of the latter there were in Athens in a given generation can only be conjectured. One leading authority, A. W. Gomme, estimates that toward the end of the fifth century, when the full-grown Athenian state extended over some 1,000 square miles of Attica, their number may have reached 115,000 out of a total population of possibly 315,000 (of which, again possibly, some 43,000 by then were citizens). Of the slave population, perhaps a half were in domestic service, while the other half worked on the fields, in industries, and in the marble quarries of Mount Pentelicon or the silver mines of Laurium.

The Athenian slave was, to be sure, a different person from the one we think of when we use the term in the context of the West's seizure of black Africans on the Guinea coast. He was likely to be a fellow Greek or near Greek who had fallen into bondage by taint of birth or capture in war or default in payment of debt. Every Greek state—like the kingdoms of the East—followed this method of obtaining cheap, unfortunate, subjugated, and often highly talented manpower. Ironically it was Solon's own reform of abolishing bondage for debt at home that caused Athenians to seek slaves abroad by raiding the lands of the *harbaroi*. A few rich, landed families accumulated as many as a thousand; a middle-class household might have up to a dozen—Plato, we are told, had five, and Aristotle, thirteen. There are records of highly gifted slaves who served their masters as children's tutors, architectural draftsmen, business assistants or even associates, and educated intimates of the family. Since many a master worked hard too at trade or other enterprise, the system was relatively more decent than at

Sparta, where the master did no work at all except with the sword; but it rarely occurred to the best Athenians to free their slaves as Aristotle was to do, and as Thomas Jefferson at Monticello did more than two millennia later.

Occasional amnesties were granted by the state—particularly when in an emergency Athens needed to swell its army or navy. (Slaves were not normally permitted to bear arms.) Such an instance arose in 490 B.C., a pivotal year in Greek history, when the mightiest attacking force yet known to Hellenes descended upon Euboea, the island strip just off the Attic coast. The generals of King Darius of Persia had come with possibly as many as 30,000 men, to burn its key city of Eretria, cross over to the mainland, and encamp at Marathon on the approach to Athens. Many nearby Greek states would not help fight off so formidable an invader, and the Spartans were slow to respond to Athens' appeal for aid (it was the time of the full moon, and they said they must complete their religious observances of it before taking to the field). Desperate for support, the Athenian commander Miltiades enlisted a considerable number of slaves as supporting infantry, and marched them along with his trained hoplites straight to Marathon.

The Persian assault upon mainland Greece was complex in origin. Its basis lay in three circumstances. The first was the decay of old empires in the Middle East; the second the fragility of the little Greek settlements and states that had arisen on the Asia Minor coast; the third, the awakening of a vigorous breed of tribesmen in the rough Iranian inland to the possibilities of extending themselves over richer country than their own. The Assyrian realm, long the chief power in the Near East, had sunk by the seventh century into torpor; the Babylonians and the Medes had revolted against it; and eventually the Persians gained control of the entire realm, while the kingdom of Lydia in Asia Minor—once an Assyrian tributary—rose in power. Lydia had shown itself hospitable to the Greek settlements strung along the Asia Minor shore; and Croesus, the fabulously wealthy king who ruled Lydia in the mid sixth century, had been anxious to ally himself to Greek ideas and institutions. This had taken him to the point of consulting the oracle at Delphi, which was to prove his undoing. Fearful of the rise and approach of Persian power from the East under King Cyrus, he asked Delphi for advice and received the counsel that if he crossed the river Halys, which lay between him and Cyrus' Persians, he would destroy an empire. The oracle however omitted to say which empire. Importunately he crossed the river and in doing so, did in battle destroy an empire—his own.

Profiting from Delphi's mischief, the Persians took over Lydia in about 546 B.C., and for the first time, Lydia's neighbors to the west, the Greeks, confronted a major expansionist power. Yet Lydia was only a minor element in Persia's emerging grand design: first the subjugation of all the Middle East, then expansion northward to the Caucasus, southward through Syria to Egypt, and eastward all the way to India. Far from being hostile to the Asiatic, or Ionian, Greeks, the Persians, like Croesus before them, felt considerable kinship with them and respect for their cultural attainments in such towns as Ephesus and Miletus, and many Ionians in turn willingly entered Persian service.

But the rule of satraps, even when benevolent, was bound to come into collision with the Greek political awakening, especially as the idea of self-rule spread from town to town and from island to island. A brilliantly gifted Persian ruler, Darius I, coming into power about 520 B.C., had set about reorganizing his empire into provinces and building new roads and canals. In 512 B.C. he extended his realm even into Europe, crossing the Bosporus to subjugate wild Thrace along the Black Sea coast, and then reaching west to Macedonia and north to the Danube. Shock and apprehension came over the Hellenes; and the bravest of these were the Ionians who in several Asia Minor cities revolted against the satraps, the Milesians going so far as to attack and sack the Persian-held city of Sardis, with help from Athens and Eretria.

In this sense the Greeks themselves instigated the Persian wars. For Darius, returning from his far triumphs, found himself with a domestic revolt on his hands that seemed to call for punitive action. And act he did, first crushing Miletus and the other rebellious cities and islands, and then sailing a great expedition westward to chastise the Greek mainland conspirators, of whom, we are told, he knew only dimly. "The Athenians," he is said to have remarked contemptuously, "who are they?" He was soon to learn.

The military task seemed simple. It was, after having reduced Eretria, to land upon the Attic coast and then proceed to invest presumptuous Athens, which lay thinly garrisoned and hemmed in between mountains and sea, protected only by the Acropolis heights. All might have gone well for Darius' commanders (aided by Sparta's deference to the full moon) save that Miltiades of Athens, a tactician of the first magnitude, elected not to await attack at the city's gates, but to deliver a counterattack of his own out of the hills upon the Persians who were forming up on their landing area at flat seaside Marathon, over twenty miles away. With only about 10,000 armed men at hand (Plataea alone, among Greek sister states, sent a contingent in time to be of help), his scheme was a master stroke, relying on the Greeks' familiarity with their own terrain, their aroused individual patriotism, their skill at man-to-man combat, and their readiness to charge in at the double against the flanks of a far superior host, throwing it off balance. As Herodotus writes, "The Persians, therefore, when they saw the Greeks coming on at speed, made ready to receive them, although it seemed to them that the Athenians were bereft of their senses, and bent upon their own destruction; for they saw a mere handful of men coming on at a run without either horsemen or archers. Such was the opinion of the barbarians; but the Athenians in close array fell upon them, and fought in a manner worthy of being recorded. They were the first of the Greeks, so far as I know, who introduced the custom of charging the enemy at a run, and they were likewise the first who dared to look upon the Median garb, and to face men clad in that fashion. Until this time the very name of the Medes had been a terror to the Greeks to hear.

"The two armies fought together on the plain of Marathon for a length of time; and in the mid battle, where the Persians themselves and the Sacae had their place, the barbarians were victorious, and broke and pursued the Greeks into the inner country; but on the two wings the Athenians and the Plataeans defeated the enemy. Having so done, they suffered the routed barbarians to fly at their ease, and joining the two wings in one, fell upon those who had broken their own center, and fought and conquered them. These likewise fled, and now the Athenians hung upon the runaways and cut them down, chasing them all the way to the shore, on reaching which they laid hold of the ships and called aloud for fire."

The tardy Spartans, once the moon waned, arrived on the field too late to assist, and congratulated the victors. The day was Athens'—and so, it now seemed, was the Greek future. Among the many who found honor on the field that day was a rising Athenian leader, Themistocles, who was then perhaps only thirty, and a promising playwright, Aeschylus, about thirty-five. Phenomenal lives and works lay ahead of both.

Themistocles, supposedly of foreign origin on his mother's side, had made his first mark before Marathon, putting forth as a very young archon the challenging proposition that Athens had not been giving anywhere near enough attention to its fleet: its future, he claimed, lay on the sea, and it must build a force of triremes second to none, and fortify its harbors. Hard, unscrupulous, and later treacherous, he was nevertheless a spacious inspirer of a whole new Athenian military policy, and the years after Marathon proved him right. The Persians, having failed to humble Athens, might well come back; no conceivable land army alone could contain them if this time they came with all their force; but defensive walls would help, and a powerful navy could hack at their troop transports and supply ships on the wide Aegean. This was precisely what happened when Darius' successor, Xerxes, arrived in 480 B.C. with a much vaster armament for a second assault; though hugely outnumbered Greek troops died sacrificially at Thermopylae and Athens itself was sacked, the great Greek sea victory at Salamis decided the issue.

This time the Persian host, advancing by ship and foot from Asia Minor and Macedonia, was in Greek eyes all but numberless. There were Medes, Bactrians, Hyrcanians, Phoenicians, Thracians, Cissians, Egyptians, Ethiopians, Cypriotes, in the mass. Herodotus, in one of his most dramatic passages, says that some forty-six different peoples and tribes were included, and a computation of his highly imaginative listing comes out at a figure of 1,700,000 fighting men, in addition to sailors of the fleet and fresh contingents that joined as the horde advanced toward Attica. This wildly improbable estimate has been reduced by modern students such as J. B. Bury to a figure of 180,000 supported by possibly 800 triremes—still a stupendous force to hurl against so lean a land in men and wealth as Greece. There has rarely been a greater force so poorly led against a much inferior one.

The polyglot host swarmed down over the northern Hellenic plains, state after state surrendering to it. But this time there was no matter of a full moon, and Athenian and Spartan and other leaders of marrow, knowing what was coming, met in conference and determined to try to hold off the horde at the pass of Thermopylae between the coastal hills and the sea—the gateway to Attica and thus to Athens. The honor of leadership went to King Leonidas of Sparta, who died along with his 300 picked Spartans rather than yield the pass, while betrayal led the Persians around his flank, to decimate several thousand troops gathered in support behind it. This threatened Athens with mortal danger, and Themistocles, rather than face a holocaust there, persuaded the Athenians to evacuate their capital, save for a small sacrificial garrison on the Acropolis, and to fall back upon the island of Salamis, where he had managed to concentrate a force of almost 400 triremes belonging to Athens and its allies.

The Spartans, being non-sailors and only too aware of Xerxes' vast fleet, argued that all defenders should draw back into the Peloponnesus itself. But Themistocles, the apostle of sea power, would have none of this, and argued against them that the Persian armada should be lured into the close waters off Salamis just west of the Piraeus, where the Greeks would have the advantage of fighting "in a narrow sea with few ships against many." As Herodotus has it, he added that "if things turn out as I anticipate, and we beat them by sea, then we shall have kept your Isthmus free from the barbarians, and they will have advanced no further than Attica, but from thence have fled back in disorder; and we shall, moreover, have saved Megara, Aegina, and Salamis itself, where an oracle has said that we are to overcome our enemies." Themistocles' summons prevailed, and the Greek captains delivered a smashing blow at the point he chose, while Xerxes reportedly sat on a nearby hillside watching his navy—his major means of retreat—being reduced to broken timber. The Persians fought bravely, the historian adds, and "each did his utmost through fear of Xerxes, for each thought that the king's eye was upon himself." But they were not equal to the Greek seamen.

Thus shaken, the main concern of many Persians was how to get home. Another land battle took place in 479 B.C. at Plataea in Boeotia, north of the Attic border, at which the Spartan king Pausanias highly distinguished himself and won the field, and upon which the army of the greatest empire dispersed and made its way eastward as best it could in what remained of its fleet.

There was now honor enough in Greece for all. Athens had been destroyed in substance—its temples toppled, its houses fired, its treasures looted—yet it was raised in spirit. Sparta had been confirmed in its extraordinary valor. A solemn pride came over both states. Yet it was Athens that responded most vigorously to it, rebuilding its templed city, constructing walls, and enlarging its fleet, making the Aegean waters safe for Athenian traders wherever they went. Moreover, island after island in the Aegean, fearful of a third assault by the massive Persians, turned for support to Athens, with its strong defenses and well-led ships. So the league that became known as that of Delos was founded, Delos being the sacred island of Apollo in mid Aegean and a symbol of the new-found unity of men ranging from Attica to Ionia. Though not a stronghold, it was to be the center of administration of fleets and funds for mutual defense. Indeed, a spirit not only of pride but of something approaching exaltation came over Athens as great creative energies were unleashed. Aeschylus, its poet who had fought both at Marathon and Plataea, was to embody this in his own symbolic way in a famous passage at the climax of his Orestes trilogy written about the year 458 B.C. He is telling of the final moment when the hero, pursued by the Furies, is granted trial and reprieve by Athena on the hill of Ares above the city, after which the avenging Furies are turned into benevolent

Eumenides, helpers to new law and enlightenment. In a joyous invocation at the close of the *Eumenides*, the final play of the trilogy, the chorus chants:

> χαίρετε χαίρετ᾽ ἐν αἰσιμίαισι πλούτου.
> χαίρετ᾽ ἀστικὸς λεώς,
> ἵκταρ ἥμενοι Διός,
> παρθένου φίλας φίλοι
> σωφρονοῦντες ἐν χρόνῳ.
> Παλλάδος δ᾽ ὑπὸ πτεροῖς
> ὄντας ἅζεται πατήρ.

> *Joy to you, joy of your justly appointed riches,*
> *Joy to all the people, blest*
> *With the Virgin's love, who sits*
> *Next beside her Father's throne.*
> *Wisdom ye have learned at last.*
> *Folded under Pallas' wing,*
> *Yours at last the grace of Zeus.*

Athenian youths—and many since—were to learn these lines by heart. Sparta, however, for all its victories, was not capable of such a speech as this, which so confidently foresaw a glorious future. Indeed, strong as it stood, it was highly suspicious of the Athenian alliance, which it was not invited to join. It preferred to go its own way, in any case. The two ways were tragically to collide.

The musician above plays the lyre, the favorite instrument of the ancient Greeks. The lyre was said to be invented by Hermes, who gave it to Apollo, and it became Apollo's chief attribute. With it, he represented all that was rational in the Greek spirit—adherence to harmony and respect for order—as well as gaiety and artistic sensitivity.

VI

APOLLO AND DIONYSUS

Now shall my song remember Apollo, Lord of the Bow.
At whom the Immortals tremble, what time they see him go . . .

—Hymn to the Delian Apollo

But I am Dionysus, Lord of the Revel—he
Whom Zeus begot on Cadmus' child, His own beloved Semele. . . .

—Hymn to Dionysus

Measured against the Apollonian idea, the Dionysian one reveals
itself as the eternal and basic wellspring of art. . . . Yet wherever
the Dionysian powers arise in their impetuousness, Apollo also,
wrapped in his cloud, descends upon us.

—Friedrich Nietzsche, *The Birth of Tragedy*

The story is told that the philosopher Pythagoras, walking one day through the streets of the Greek settlement of Croton on the boot of Italy, passed a blacksmith's booth and was attracted by the diverse tones produced by different hammers striking the anvil. Pausing, he observed that the hammers ringing out at different pitch were of different weights, and that there seemed to be some regularity of scale between the notes. Might there not be some arithmetic progression governing the intervals of music?

He thereupon conducted an experiment—one of the first in the history of western science. Familiar with Greece's chief musical instrument, the seven-stringed lyre, he matched up two strings of equal length, thickness, and tuning, and found that when he "stopped," or clamped, one at its halfway point and

plucked it, the string he had shortened by a half sang at precisely an octave higher than the other string. Similarly, if he
"stopped" it at two thirds of its length, the shortened string
sounded the fifth note of the octave above the first string. If he
"stopped" it at three-quarter length, it sounded four notes
higher than the first. He had found that there were numerical
ratios between what we call the "concordant" intervals of scale
(2:1, 3:2, and 4:3, to take the above). In terms of physics, he had
shown that the vibration of two similar strings varies in inverse
proportion to their length.

If some of this sounds abstruse and technical to the layman,
it was not to Pythagoras and his disciples. On the contrary: in
their eyes the recognition that music had a mathematical basis
was one of transcendent import. For when considered together
with other studies Pythagoras had been making in his absorption with number and form, it seemed to light up man's com-
prehension of the entire physical world around him, and of his
own inner world of being as well. Greek art, architecture, ethics,
religion, all were to be profoundly influenced by the numerical
theories of the many-sided genius of sixth-century Croton.

That a discovery in music could exert so wide an impact
upon Greek life was due in part to music's own role in that life,
which was large and pervasive—perhaps more so than the role
of music in any succeeding culture, even the Vienna of Haydn,
Mozart, and Beethoven. Unhappily, we do not know with any
certainty how it sounded. We do possess a few surviving fragments of ancient musical notation, with letters used to indicate
the tones at which the given syllables of a chant were to be
sung; but these letters cast no light on what the notes actually
were in terms of any scale we know, and we have no idea of
what Greek pitch actually was—that is, how a lyre's strings were
tuned or a wind instrument such as the flutelike aulos was
voiced. What we do know is that the Greeks, quite apart from

Pythagoras, had arrived at a highly developed system of harmonic series, or modes (one could call them "moods" more
accurately than "keys"), and, moreover, that music making was
an everyday activity among all classes. By "music" the early
Greek also meant the dance and chanted poetry which were
accompanied by the lyre or cithara or aulos. No wedding feast,
no funeral rite, no harvest festival, no banquet or public ceremonial seems to have been complete without a gay or solemn
music. We hear of the art very early, when in the *Iliad* a delega-
tion of Agamemnon's men visit Achilles in his tent before Troy
and find him singing lays of other heroes before him to the
accompaniment of a lyre. By the time of the Panathenaic and
Pythian games, devoted like those at Olympia to the celebration
of spirit and body both, we find prizes being offered for performances on instruments and in song. Music became—partly
as a result of Pythagoras' teachings—a subject of basic education; so great was the recognition of its importance that Plato,
ever the puritan and moralist, laid down precepts as to which
modes were to be taught to strengthen character, and which
were not.

These modes, and the notion that each had its own ethical
and emotional content, have fascinated and perplexed musicol-
ogists ever since, especially since no scholar can with any
assurance reconstruct them on a western instrument. The
Dorian mode was regarded as somber, virile, and warlike; the
Lydian, lyric and plaintive; the Phrygian, passionate and unbridled; there were perhaps ten other modes, and all included
quarter notes and other intervals that we associate with oriental
music. Only the mind's ear can reconstruct in imagination the
rise and fall of such music, its beat no doubt determined by
stressed syllables of chant or movement of dancers, and its
singers or players performing in monody without harmonic
supports.

Immediate and stirring as music evidently was to the Greek, Pythagoras' study of it was part of a far greater search, namely that of the awakened Greek mind for central, governing principles that would reveal an underlying order amid the everyday diversities of nature. We have seen that Thales of Miletus thought he had found such a ruling principle or substance in water. His successor, the evolution-minded Anaximander, sensed a basic force in what he vaguely called "the Boundless." Another Ionian successor, Anaximenes, felt that the primordial unifying substance was air; still another, Heraclitus of Ephesus, identified it with fire, and further argued that the essence of all things lay in change: "Everything flows," he is said to have declared, "and nothing remains the same." All this, of course, was the sheerest guesswork—the imaginative young Greek mind striking out in many directions, ardently hunting for a more intelligible world than that provided by the random gods and their creation legends. Pythagoras, not satisfied with these explanations, turned from speculation to precise calculation. And his conclusion, based on what he had measured and counted, was that the root of all things was number.

He had found that musical relations can be explained by number. Ratio and symmetry could also be seen at the heart of many other manifestations around him: in the marvelous geometry of plants, in the relations of triangles, in the properties of individual numbers and series of numbers. Pythagoras, the first Greek scientist, was also the first man to pursue mathematics for its own sake rather than just as a practical aid. He became fascinated by the series or patterns that showed up when he represented given numbers by arrangements of rows of dots or pebbles. (This, as Bertrand Russell points out in his *Wisdom of the West*, "is a method of reckoning which in some form or other survived for a long time. The Latin word [for] 'calculation' means 'a handling of pebbles.' ") Most fascinating was the number ten, which Pythagoras expressed thus:

Here, in what he called the *tetraktys,* was a perfect triangular series (note that it is the sum of its first four integers: 1 + 2 + 3 + 4 = 10), and one whose pattern, moreover, was infinitely expandable. In the eyes of Pythagoras' followers the *tetraktys* had such transcendent properties that it became a mystical symbol by which they swore. Other numbers, when laid out geometrically by the same "pebble" method, were either "square" or "oblong." Some (4, 9, 16, etc.) were "square" in that they were the sum of successive odd numbers:

Others (like 6, 12, 20, etc.) were "oblong," being the sum of successive even numbers:

Still others, like the number five and its multiples, were asymmetrical and "irrational," and were often expressed by the Pythagoreans in the form of the pentagram, or five-pointed star, which became a cabalistic symbol in the Middle Ages.

What is interesting in this to the mathematically inclined is that a series of integers (1 + 2 + 3 + 4) yields triangular numbers, while that of odd integers (1 + 3 + 5) yields square numbers, and that of even integers (2 + 4 + 6) yields oblong numbers. And while modern number theory has of course gone far beyond Pythagoras, it still uses his concept of the symmetrical numbers that satisfied his sense of order and progression as against the "irrational" ones that did not.

Ratio, consonance, rhythm, then, seemed to govern all things. To grasp the world about him, man must first find the number or proportion in things. Only when this is found can he truly distinguish the basic from the apparent, the permanent from the passing. Physical matter comes and goes and changes, and is perceived by the senses; but the forms, or "numbers," that underlie it are eternal, and these are perceived by the reasoning mind. The mind discovers the perfect, or the "ideal," and this is the only "real"; for that which is made known to the senses is transitory and imperfect. With this mighty leap of thought Pythagoras opens the way of Greek philosophy and prepares it for Plato, who (also beginning from mathematics) was to argue further the difference between the universal and the particular, between reality (which is one) and appearances (which are many), between what "is" and the objects of sense which are always "becoming" something else. Plato went on to argue that the highest reality is the Idea of The Good—which in turn, as we shall see, led to a new concept of a godhead.

Pythagoras' fifth-century followers were not ready to venture that further leap. Yet in their way they prepared for it. In their minds the result of their perception of the "real" through numbers and forms was a recognition of the entire world's unity or *harmonia*. At the highest level this was that harmonious "music of the spheres" which, they said, we failed to hear only because "the sound is with us right from birth and has thus no contrasting silence to show it up." The heavenly bodies, they claimed, gave out tones or vibrations at related intervals as they swung in orbit, and indeed every object "sang" or emitted some force of its own. (Was this some premonition of Newton's gravitational theory, or of ideas of radiation? Pythagoras is full of premonitions—he thought, for instance, twenty centuries before Magellan's ship finally proved it, that the world was round.)

While feeling his way toward the concept of some divine rule or Word or *logos* immanent in the numbers and proportions he saw about him, Pythagoras turned and peered deeply into the qualities of man himself. If man and nature were to be thought of as in concord, were not our individual beings ruled by number and *harmonia* also? What was the soul itself but a system of proportion? He asked the question, and his followers came forth with an answer. The soul, they argued, was made up of three parts as if on a scale—instinct and feeling (which we share with the animals) and reason (which is ours alone, and immortal). What was morality other than an effort to achieve balance and symmetry, and to pursue the just mean between extremes? Was not the healthy man (or, we would today say, the "well-adjusted" man) the one who was in a state of *harmonia*—quite literally "in tune"?

What was "well-adjusted" or well-proportioned or harmonious, then, was the ideal. It was also the most "real." It followed that whatever form or image a man himself created, that which had the most perfect proportions was the truest. In sculpture an ideal human shape carved in marble was "truer"—that is, more universal and relevant to the nature of man—than a representation that dwelt on the particular individuality of some one man, with all his imperfections or blemishes or departures from the ideal. In architecture a temple was most "true" (and this also in the literal, builder's sense of the word) when it stood in a just balance between vertical and horizontal, between thrust and support, between lift and weight, mass and interval. True proportion led to grace and beauty; indeed, the whole basis of beauty lay in proportion.

This was a thought many creative Greeks had been entertaining well before Pythagoras time, expressing it in their own works. In every work of art, it was believed, there should be a harmonious ratio or relationship among all the elements: in architecture, for instance, so many units of length for so many of width or height. In Greek sculpture too, as it developed from its archaic forms, there was a similar search for ideal numerical ratios, the theory being that a figure not only required over-all balance and symmetry but a measurable relationship of each part to the rest. Polycleitus, one of Greece's greatest fifth-century sculptors (whose work, unhappily, we know only from Roman copies) was to be explicit about this, writing in a manual for students that "beauty consists in the proportions not of the elements but of the parts, that is to say, of finger to finger and of all the fingers to the palm and wrist, and of these to the forearm, and of the forearm to the upper arm, and of all parts to each other"; and he set out to codify certain rules of proportion—such as the height of a full figure equals seven and a half heads. This delight in discovering the "number," or inner order of things, was to continue and become central to the Greek legacy.

If we have been taken up here with highly intellectual concepts, it is because we are dealing with a people who discovered themselves in love with intellect as the way to truth, and found reality in abstraction. The very word *philosophia*, "the love of wisdom," may have been coined by Pythagoras; and this love, as Plato was to see it, led to knowledge of The Good—or God. There was one great god who best symbolized this Greek passion for the harmonious and true. Soon Greece was being beautified, on temple pediments like that at Olympia, with sculptures of Apollo, Pythagoras' patron and presumptive forebear. The divinity was carved in his cold majesty as the most perfect of gods, being in the shape of the most perfectly beautiful of men. And why was he the most beautiful? Because he embodied certain ideal laws of proportion, and thus the divine beauty of mathematics.

Yet Pythagoras' patron Apollo, as we have seen, was not only the lofty and luminous god of Greek reason and law. He was also a god of occult rite and eastern mystery and of the possessed priestesses at the oracle of Delphi which he shared with his supposed opposite, the unbridled and earthy Dionysus. And Pythagoras, the enlightened Apollonian, was like his patron half a Dionysian too, wedded to strange cult. Nothing illustrates more the contrasts and tensions in the Greek mind than the coexistence in it of the twin godhead images of Apollo, a god of reason, and Dionysus, a god of instinct and the irrational (indeed Apollo and Dionysus, when we come down to it, may well have been two sides of the same primordial image and thus, in the deep layers of Greek consciousness, one god divided). Again, nothing is more symptomatic of Greece than the presence on its earth of a Pythagoras, who in his person combined the varying strains of both, as geometer, mathematician, logician, magician, mystic, cult leader, healer, and soothsayer all in one.

Of the influences that shaped him we know little that is certain, though it seems clear that he absorbed a vast range of currents stirring in the Mediterranean world. (Like Thales before him and Socrates after him, he left not one word in writing; he simply talked, and his followers passed on his thinking.) Tradition has it that he was reared on the Aegean island of Samos, that he studied and traveled widely in Asia Minor and Egypt, and that he then quit his homeland as a man of about forty—

perhaps in the year 530 B.C.—to escape the oppressive tyranny
of Polycrates and settled in Italian Croton, one of the many
Greek daughter cities that had been established in the west. He
appears to have come into direct contact with the Milesian
thinkers of the school of Thales, as well as with Egyptian priest-
stargazers and with the mystical sects of Orpheus then flourishing in mainland Greece and southern Italy; for echoes of each
resound in his life's work.

Orphism, taking its name from the "divine musician," was a
religious movement about whose origin, practices, and very
nature there remains much obscurity as well as controversy. It
may have sprung from eastern antecedents; it may have been
not an organized cult at all, but simply a body of beliefs shared
widely by people in the seventh and sixth centuries in the most
diverse Greek places. However it may have arisen, its essence
was a belief in the immortality of souls, in their transmigration,
in personal redemption or purification through strict codes of
abstinence, and in participation in rites or "mysteries" which
the votary was not allowed to disclose. Some Orphic tales told
that long before Homer's time Orpheus, a priest of Apollo, was
killed by followers of Dionysus—from which the conclusion has
been drawn that Orphism was an effort to redeem the
Dionysian cult from this evil done. Others told of a proto-
Dionysus himself being killed by Titans, to be resurrected as the
Dionysus of the Olympians. Revelation from inspired texts supposedly received from Orpheus, as well as illumination through
inspired healers, or *shamans,* in states of trance, figured in the
worship, which centered not only about Dionysus as a symbol
of rebirth but also about Apollo as a god of purification, or
katharsis. (Again it can be seen how Dionysus and Apollo mix
in the mists of early cult.) Now Pythagoras, when setting himself up as a teacher at Croton, seems to have brought with him
not only an Ionian absorption with science and a mass of

Egyptian priestly lore but much of Orphic faith and practice as well: for what he did was establish a religious brotherhood very much along Orphic lines, with himself its high priest.

This Pythagorean community was in a sense a monastic order, in which dedicated young postulants took vows of silence, abstinence, and retreat while they served a three- to five-year novitiate to prepare themselves for becoming *eso-terici*—the initiates who would be admitted to the esoteric or secret knowledge of the Master. The community was open to women too, who were admitted under the same vows. Instruction emphasized mathematics and geometry. The doctrine of an afterlife was preached, but in the context of a belief in the transmigration of souls (therefore no eating of meat; the animal might have harbored the soul of some human predecessor). Together with philosophical enlightenment, purification was the goal of the Pythagorean fellowship, and this *katharsis* was believed to lie in the recognition of *harmonia*.

Property was held in common, but this communistic society was at the same time markedly aristocratic, as members of leading educated families joined it. The fellowship was politically assertive too; under Pythagoras' leadership it tried to take over and run the city-state of Croton according to its ideals. For this it was persecuted by the local popular party; and as the order spread to other cities, its devotees were attacked or run out of town. They especially worshiped (as who of intelligence in the Greek world did not) the noble Apollo, but this hardly surpassed their veneration of Pythagoras himself, the white-robed master of vast and mysterious learning, of whose pronouncements or revelations they said in hushed tones ;γα;α';γν;γτ;αγ;γο;γ8 ;α';αα;νλ;γφ;γα—"He himself has spoken."

So compounded of contrasts, the sage of Croton is a central figure and symbol of Greek being, itself so divided between the rational and the irrational, between logic and instinct, between the scientific and the magical, between the state of self-possession and that of being possessed; and, one can continue, between symmetry and diversity, between order and abandonment, between the recognition of limits and the pursuit of the limit-less, between restraint and vaulting ambition, or *hubris*. Pythagoras in all his wisdom could achieve no resolution or *harmonia* of all these diverse elements present both in himself and in those around him, any more than could Plato and Aris-totle, who came after him. What was greatest in him and in Greece was the recognition of these conflicts for what they were and the belief that by grappling with them man might achieve a better order in his life.

The Greek arts most visibly embodied the contrasts. In those of form (architecture, sculpture, ceramics, vase painting), where men were the molders of supposedly enduring objects, it was natural for the Greek to lean to logic and make his shapes reflect ideals of harmony, perfection, and permanence. Here, one could say, the spirit of Apollo-Pythagoras was at work. But in another high art of Greece, the drama, in which the "clay" was human, another spirit—or another side of the Greek spirit—was paramount: the Dionysian. The stage play itself—a form unknown until the Greeks invented it—arose from magical and primitive rites connected with the worship of Dionysus. A sense of order, to be sure, was present even in the earliest Greek pub-lic performances designed to marry ancient ritual with the recital of lyric or epic poetry. But it was a different sort of order than that of the cold Apollo. A dynamic new structure emerged when a protagonist—supported by a chorus commenting, as if in the audience's behalf, on a stirring narration—was supple-mented by a second and, then, a third speaker. As this prototype of drama evolved, it took on both a serious religious aspect that led to tragedy and a boisterous lewdness that led to comedy. In

either case the concern was with the ever-changing and prob-
lematic condition of individual man—in tragedy, with his
hubris, violent passions, and ill chance; in comedy, with his
vulgarities and follies.

Yet, though Greek fine arts and drama may often seem far
apart in the languages they speak—on one hand a Phidias carving man in gleaming perfection, on the other a Sophocles
exploring his individuality and dolor—the extremes do meet.
Though Greek drama deals with lawlessness, excess, and seemingly fortuitous circumstance, its tragic playwrights see some
moral order behind all that. Perhaps the playgoer in the great
Theatre of Dionysus at Athens, sharing the righteous wrath of
Orestes that led him to kill his murderous mother Clytemnestra
or pitying the innocent Oedipus for his unwitting parricide and
incest with his mother Jocasta, found it hard to comprehend the
justice of the fate meted out to these unhappy heroes. But an
underlying law and design there must be, the dramatists said,
even though it might be inscrutable. As if to emphasize the very
shape of the design, they expressed their intimations of it in
mighty symmetries or cycles of action and reaction, of guilt
and consequence—in the Orestes plays a crime is punished by
an avenging crime that in turn must be punished. So,
immutable law and logic—Shall we say "number"?—govern
each individual, who is only an offspring or shadow of the universal: and with this we once again move back from Dionysus
to Pythagoras in his pure white robe and to Apollo.

Dionysus is also present in the Greek fine arts (he is always
nearby wherever Apollo is), for the arts are not all serenity and
sublimation by any means. The very siting of the temples of
Delphi amid vertiginous cliffs and wild gorges suggests a linkage that Greek men felt between the reasoned and orderly and
the tumultuous energies of nature. Apollo peers down coldly
from many a pediment—or rather today from many a museum

wall—but close by there may be vase paintings of maenads, Dionysus' handmaidens, swaying in ecstatic dance, their bodies possessed by some irrational power. One block of marble results in a sublimely composed Athena; another in a grotesque Gorgon's head, her tongue stuck out in a primeval grimace, recalling earlier earth powers or demons. The center relief on the pediment of one of the earliest major Greek temples, that of Artemis on the island of Corcyra—modern Corfu—dating from the early sixth century, is a gigantic representation not of an Olympian god but of such a weird Gorgon, grimacing and writhing. Naturalistic or "story-telling" representation of the incidental and anecdotal belongs, for the most part, to a much later day; but the appetites and joys of earth are celebrated even from early Greek time in drinking cups figured with prancing satyrs, in the posts raised before householders' doors as votives to Hermes, protector of the home, and each fronted with a phallus, and in vase paintings displaying sexual activity in so explicit a way that many museums turn them to the wall or keep them in rooms reserved for scholars.

When the arts of form in Greece began to revive in the late eleventh or early tenth century after generations of silence following the death of Mycenae, it was with pottery and pottery-painting that they commenced. The clay jug served as both a religious and a domestic vessel, bearing libations to the gods and the dead, as well as water and wine to the household, and to it the early Greek designer-artists devoted the best of their invention. They made long-necked ceremonial jars, often more than four feet high, which were turned on the wheel in sections and then joined before firing. It was as if in these outsized shapes of fragile material, which required perfect balance and stability, they were already exploring those major questions of proportion and scale that were to absorb the Greek mind. They decorated their work with figures in brown glaze—and what they put there were not images of man or beast or god, but a great variety of abstract and geometric patterns: parallel lines, triangles, concentric circles, semicircles, zigzag lines, and, next, the swastika and the meander line.

Artists went on in this way for perhaps two centuries. Only then does the human figure appear in paint: on the thick rotundities of vases we find rows of silhouetted shapes, schematic and triangular, rhythmic but rigid, and embedded in an over-all geometric scheme of which they are just a part. In their rudimentary appearance these figures bear no comparison with the sophisticated work that had been done by the Minoan painters almost a millennium before, nor are they the equal of the lifelike shapes drawn at an even earlier time on the tomb walls of Egypt. Yet these very modest Greek beginnings or re-beginnings in art presage what was to come; they continued and expanded the emphasis on symmetry and fundamental form—a form moreover determined to a considerable degree by function. The little men banded in a tight, convex procession between the handles of an early amphora are the precursors of the figures sculptured on the rigidly apportioned rectangular panels, or metopes, allotted to decoration along the frieze of a Doric temple, or on the far more difficult triangular space of the pediments at its ends.

Both metope and pediment—the great testing grounds of the Greek ornamental sculptor—were themselves forms created by the geometry of structural engineering, forms in which the practical designer dictated to the artist. The metope was the response to a problem created by intervals between ground supports; the pediment, the result of raising a pitched roof. Egyptian and Mycenaean prototypes had suggested to Greeks the idea of a ceremonial walled chamber fronted by a "porch" consisting of eaves that extended over shafts, or columns. Gradually the idea of carrying these columns around the sides as well as the rear of the building emerged, making of them a structural colonnade carrying much of the weight of the pitched roof, which now extended over them, increasing the dignity and elegance of the structure. A longitudinal beam ran along the tops, or capitals, of these columns to give the roof foursquare support (this became the architrave); but athwart and above it, huge crossbeams were laid at intervals atop each capital, providing the building with rigidity. Proceeding from wood to stone, the Doric designer preserved the memory of his beam ends in the form of projecting stone blocks, or triglyphs, carved to simulate them. But this still left the question of what to do with the successive spaces between them. Simply leave them open, as gaping holes under the eaves? The Greek sense of order and fitness, was not satisfied with that. So the answer was found to fill these spaces with panels (in some early instances of terra cotta) that made a virtue of their freedom from thrust and weight by being decorative. The ornament, however, a design contained within a strictly limited rectangle, had to be in a relief high enough to be clearly distinguishable to the viewer below.

The pediment, in turn, destined to house the splendors of the marbles of Olympia, Aegina, and the Parthenon, appears to have owed its shape in large part to the increasingly common use of roofing tiles in the seventh century. Cretan, Mycenaean, and very early Greek roofs were generally flat (there were some high-pitched roofs of thatch); but when tile, an efficient device for achieving drainage, came into use, it permitted—even dictated—a low-pitched roof and stimulated the shift to gable construction (and because of its weight, to stone construction too). This resulted in a broad and massive triangle above the entablature at either end of a rectangular building. This triangle had extremely acute angles at the base: and how to fill it became the most challenging of problems for the Greek sculptor, since

the figures at its ends had to be low or prone, while those mid-
way under the ascending limb had to be in a crouching or sitting position, leaving only those near or under the apex to
stand tall and free.

Although small cult images and statuettes (mostly of wood
or bronze) had been made previously, large-scale Greek stone
sculpture begins presumably late in the seventh century with
the stiff, ritualistic figure—particularly the life-sized, nude
young male, or *kouros,* derived from Mesopotamian and Egyptian prototypes. With an abstract stare and usually a fixed
archaic smile, he stood foursquare, without any bend or twist,
arms rigidly at his side and left foot advanced slightly forward:
if not a god or a godman, then in any case an ideal. How to
make him bend, or rather unbend? How to make him assume a
more natural—one might say, more functional—human posture,
without losing sight of the ideal? How to express movement,
tension, gesture, individuality, personality, in lasting stone
without at the same time expressing only the fleeting moment?
This was the core of the sculptor's test, and it took generations
to resolve it—a resolution that has left many modern admirers
of the strict and archaic in Greek art wishing that the Greeks
had not gone quite so far.

The sculptor working in relief—chiefly in the relatively small
form of the metope—went at the challenge of motion first and
by the middle of the sixth century was producing some vivid if
crude depictions of action and struggle, using the labors of Heracles in particular as his subjects. In one such metope, from
what is known as Temple C at Selinus in Sicily, the hero is
shown with the two Cercopes, whom he has just vanquished
and is carrying slung upside down from a pole on his shoulders.
The whole design is at the same time a shrewd construction of
verticals, squares, and right angles, to which the metope's
carver evidently gave much thought.

But his problem was relatively simple, since he was dealing with figures carved only frontally or in profile, with a minimum of modeling, and not intended to stand independently in any case. Meanwhile in large and free-standing sculpture the tradition of the rigid *kouros* went on for another half century or so. The form was a departure from Egyptian ones, to be sure, in that the youth was naked: his predecessors had either been robed or at least girt with a loincloth. (While his nakedness told of the emerging Greek cult of the body, his female partner in sculpture, the maiden, or *kove,* remained fully draped throughout the sixth century; it is not until the fifth that her garment begins to slip or become transparent—or in a few rare exceptions, disappear—and not until the fourth that she sheds it it altogether.)

A few harbingers of humanizing change and of relaxation of ritual stance do appear early in the sixth century in large sculpture—none more engaging, perhaps, than the life-sized figure found on the Acropolis of a man bearing a calf on his shoulders. Is he carrying his burden for ritual sacrifice, for home consumption, or just to put out to pasture? One does not know. Some lovingly executed *korai* emerge also, their long tresses elegantly coiffed, their jewels gay, and their raiment rippling down in colorful folds that suggest the height of fashion. Yet these figures, winning as they are, are still highly stylized, impersonal, stiff, a little more than human, and thus somewhat remote. Ages before, the Egyptians and Cretans had been producing images as polished and handsome as these. It is only at the start of the fifth century—the one that was to be Greece's greatest—that there is a basic change, and then it rapidly takes on the scope of a major artistic revolution.

Most of what was built, carved, and painted particularly in and around Athens in those heady first decades of the fifth century was to perish at the hands of the Persian invader. Yet enough survives to tell of marvelous invention breaking out, without the loss of a sense of restraint. Perhaps no single work of art of that period ("transitional," some art historians call it, while others see it as "late archaic" about to go over into "early classical") conveys more of the sense of new perception and feeling astir than the statue of a youth attributed to Critios, and now housed in the Acropolis Museum close by the rubble from which it was unearthed. For here is a man standing not as a ceremonial image but as a man himself stands, some muscles taut, others relaxed, shoulders slightly uneven, head slightly turned, weight more on one foot than on the other—ease and grace in his bearing rather than just stark erectness, yet repose and nobility informing his whole presence. Before, all was strength and schematic simplicity of form; but with the *Ephebe,* or youth, of Critios we have, if you agree with the eminent contemporary critic Sir Kenneth Clark, "the first beautiful nude in art."

Agree or not, here is a figure that stands at the threshold of a new era; the eye of the Greek artist has shifted from the far to the near, from the abstract to the concrete, from the symbolic to the "natural" (in which, however, he seeks to find an embodiment of the perfect). Greek art, in short, has proceeded part of the way to the study of what is of the earth, earthly, whereas Greek philosophy and science proceeded from physical manifestations close at hand to a consideration of what might lie behind or beyond them—that is, some governing rules or principles to be perceived only by the mind. The artist and the philosopher-scientist were both making great leaps of exploration. It took courage for a Critios (if it was he who carved the *Ephebe*) to abandon the tradition of a ceremonial image abstracted from man and replace it by a "real" man, just as it had taken courage for a Pythagoras to identify "reality" with what was most abstract, that is, number. Here, one might argue,

were Apollonian and Dionysian drives at work again and com-
mingling—on one hand the pursuit of the perfect or ideal, and
on the other the desire to be the witness and interpreter of
everyday man, with all his earthly passions.

At about the time the Athenian *Ephebe* was made (say
around the year 480) there was also carved in nearby Eleusis a
figure of a running girl, body leaning as if into the wind, head
turned back over her shoulder, drapery flowing with her current
of passage—her complex motion a complete departure from
convention and her whole air one of bounding grace. Yet she,
too, like the *Ephebe,* is in her way still "transitional": many
problems of form in movement have not yet been solved; the
pose, technically daring as it is, is not quite "natural"; and the
girl still suggests more a generalized presence than any specific
one. At about the same time, also, there were raised on the pediments of the Doric temple sacred to the local goddess Aphaia
on the island of Aegina, just off the Athenian and Eleusinian
coast, the extraordinary marbles found in 1811 by C. R. Cockerell and his party. Here we have "threshold" work in its greatest array: a massive group of warriors, some lunging, some
prone and dying, others kneeling and arching their bows, their
tutelary goddess standing above them—and all together, despite
their battling movements, still inexpressive of individuality,
aloof and cold. The execution of these marbles is rough and
angular, compared with what Phidias was to accomplish when
he designed the flowing figures of the Periclean Parthenon half
a century later, with all their anatomical perfection and emotional finesse. Yet many a modern eye sees some special glory
in such early sculptures as these from Aegina, the work of
artists who had learned much but not yet so much that their
chisels could tell everything—that is to say, perhaps too much.

In the intervening years enormous gains were made in
sculptural mobility, naturalness, and refinement, while little

was lost of the sense of the timeless and universal. The advances were greatly assisted by the use of bronze as a medium, to which artists increasingly turned; they were thereby able to work in malleable materials for molding and casting, instead of having to chip away at resistant rock. Even before the turn of the fifth century an unknown sculptor had cast an over-life-sized figure of a supple and seemingly reflective *kouros* that was recovered only in 1959 at the Piraeus to be acclaimed as both the earliest and one of the finest large Greek bronzes known to us. The decades before mid-fifth century produced two more advanced masterworks in bronze that have survived—the imperious, bearded Zeus or Poseidon, now in Athens' National Museum, superbly balanced in the act of hurling a thunderbolt or a trident, and the elegantly poised and robed charioteer at Delphi.

Though the fifth-century maker of free-standing sculpture preferred bronze to stone and no doubt thought of it as equally durable, it proved singularly vulnerable to the ravages of man. For it was a substance of such value and convertibility that almost all bronze statues of ancient Greek times, as well as Roman ones, were melted down by subsequent generations simply to recover the metal for other uses. (Horace proved to be highly prophetic when he began his famous ode proclaiming the immortality of his poetry with the words *"Exegi monumentum aere perennius"*—"I have finished a memorial more lasting than bronze.") The major Greek bronzes that have survived owe their existence to having been either accidentally or intentionally buried from prying eyes or to having been sunk at sea— presumably on their way to eastern or Roman collectors. Thus the splendid Zeus or Poseidon mentioned above was brought up in fishermen's nets from the sea bottom off the coast of Euboea in 1928, having gone down with some transport in ancient times. The bronze *kouros* found in 1959 came to light with

other bronze trove when workmen repairing a sewer in the
Piraeus hit upon what seemed to be the burned-out remains of
a warehouse for storing loot taken from Athens by the Romans
in the first century B.C.

Three of the greatest Greek sculptors who are known to us
by name, Myron, Phidias, Polycleitus, flourished in the middle
of the fifth century. They worked for the most part in bronze,
though no originals of theirs in metal remain. With these three,
Greek art reaches a brief summit of balance in every sense of
the word. Polycleitus, the measurer and codifier, is profoundly
taken up with the problem of how to combine repose with life-
giving movement, and resolves it in his own intellectual way.
He evolves the figure of a broad-shouldered, massive athlete
who is not quite standing still, nor yet in distinct motion, but
poised as if about to walk—balanced, you could say, in a timeless moment of suspension between rest and action. Though we
know this Polycleitan figure only through Roman copies of two
of its versions, the *Doryphorus* and the *Diadumenus*, the crudity
of the imitations cannot distort the fundamental brilliance of
the conception—one that was to become canonized in western
art.

Myron, on the other hand, whose work we also know only
through replicas, was evidently a sculptor absorbed with rendering strong motion, at the risk of becoming "momentary";
but he solved his problem by subordinating the action to a
strict, geometric pattern. His masterwork, the *Discobolus*, shows
us an athelete at the instant of extreme flection and tension in
the act of twisting about to hurl a discuss; yet, though nothing
could be more fleeting than this, everything in the design is
governed by an idea of equilibrium of lines and forces. As Kenneth Clark remarks, it is "like some Euclidean diagram of
energy."

In Phidias, meanwhile, the master of the Parthenon, we come to a man engaged with both grace and grandeur. We do not know just which sculptures and reliefs mounted on the new structure he himself executed. We do know that by 447 Pericles had made him artistic overseer of the Athenian polis' building program as a whole, and we believe that Phidias' mind and designing hand were present throughout the ornamenting of the great new temple, even though we cannot identify his actual chisel on pediment or frieze. We believe this because we sense a powerful unifying spirit at work throughout the Parthenon, shattered and despoiled and scattered among the world's museums though its relics now are.

It was a spirit dedicated to flowing rhythms, as in the frieze procession of lightly draped maidens now in the Louvre, or in the reliefs of harmoniously seated gods and goddesses, some now seated in the British Museum; to elegance of action, as in the groups of horsemen who once pranced handsomely on the frieze; to naturalism, as in such figures as a surviving horse's head from the east pediment, nostrils distended, veins bulging, as if at the moment of snorting charge; to exuberance of spirit, as in a lively mask or waterspout here and there; to ease of bearing, as in the gracefully reclining male pediment figure sometimes called the *Ilissus*. Above all, it was dedicated to the expressive mood, most expressive and most haunting of all in the reclining pediment group known as the *Three Fates*, headless and armless long before they were shipped away in Lord Elgin's sailing vessels, yet—through the brooding poise of their bodies and the drapery that ripples over them as if touched by some distant air—eloquent now as before of nobility and the mysterious loom of a divine presence.

For, "natural" as he likes to be, Phidias is majestic too. Indeed, he is the most majestic sculptor in all antiquity. Though

his chisel on the Parthenon lintel eludes us, we do know that he
himself did carve (with assistance, surely) three of the mightiest
and most hallowed statues of classical times: first, the colossal
bronze image of Athena, thirty or more feet high, that was
erected about 456 B.C. near the highest point of the Acropolis,
the gleaming tip of her spear visible far out at sea; next, the
equally colossal gold and ivory figure of Athens' patroness
erected within the sanctuary of the Parthenon and dedicated in
the year 438; third, at Olympia, to which Phidias appears to
have removed his studio shortly thereafter, the statue of Zeus,
seven times human size, acclaimed as his culminating masterwork. Ironically, all three have perished, and we know of them
only through travelers' descriptions, representations on ancient
coins, and a few poor scaled-down and hand-me-down later
adaptations and statuettes.

In these immense figures—all difficult to visualize today—
Greek impulses toward order and clarity on one side, and
toward the wild and incommensurable on the other, were inex-
tricably mixed (Apollo and Dionysus again, if you will). Hear
Pausanias, a worldly second-century A.D. traveler, as he confronts the glittering Phidian Athena in her dark Parthenon
sanctuary: "On the middle of her helmet is placed a likeness of
the Sphinx . . . and on either side of the helmet are griffins in
relief. . . . Athena stands erect, with a tunic reaching to the feet,
and on her breast the head of Medusa is worked in ivory. She
holds a statue of Victory about four cubits [some six feet] high,
and in the other hand a spear; at her feet lies a shield and near
the spear is a serpent. . . ."

The statue of Zeus at Olympia—a site until then peopled
chiefly with severe sculptures in the late archaic tradition—must
have been even more overpowering. Pausanias describes the
statue as a magnificent figure in golden robes, holding a
scepter gleaming with precious metals and seated on a mighty

throne adorned with gold and ivory, ebony and precious stones; richly painted screens surrounded the image. To us today this may suggest an image more oriental or Byzantine than Greek, or at least wholly unlike the spare and strict Apollo erected on the west pediment at Olympia less than a generation before. Because time has eroded the painting, we often forget that the Greeks liked to color their sculpture as well as their buildings. Yet, knowing of Phidias' other accomplishments, if only through fragment and echo, we can be fairly certain that even in such a splendid display he never lost a sense of harmony and wholeness.

That sense continues well into the next century, though one could argue that in Praxiteles, who flourished about 350, it begins to become precarious. His glorious Hermes is at the same time a gentle Hermes, a bit exquisite in his sinuous twist and extreme good looks, and almost on the verge of sentimentality in the way he holds the infant Dionysus in his arm. Praxiteles' god, in his perfection, is a very human one. Is he near the point of becoming almost too human to remain a god, too immediate to be an ideal? Subsequent generations, taking Praxiteles rather than his forebears as their model, were to slip swiftly down into the intimate and anecdotal and "naturalistic" in art. The accomplished sculptor of the Hellenistic age knew how to design a figure in every conceivable posture and with any conceivable expression on his face; and at the culmination of that age he delighted in showing his mastery of the moment in such works as the writhing Laocoön group. But the question remained: Between the permanent and the passing, what is "real"?

In architecture, by its very nature inclined to be the most durable and stable of arts, this problem presented no like difficulties to the Greek. Innovator and experimenter though he was in many things, in his formal building the Greek went just so far and no farther. He developed a few basic types; he improved, refined, elaborated on them, and then stuck with them, intent on achieving ideal proportions between all their elements, great and small, rather than reaching for some radical departure in design. From Egyptian prototypes and Mycenaean palace architecture, as we have seen, he derived the idea of a rectangular, porched temple. He developed as well the *tholos*, a circular chamber, perfecting it in the round shrines at Delphi and Epidaurus and the council chamber in the Athenian Agora. From very ancient hillside ceremonies of devotees of Dionysus he may also have conceived the idea of the semicircular out-door theatre, built against the lean of a steep, concave slope, and which led to the masterwork at Epidaurus. Later he added the invention of the long, roofed gallery, or stoa, usually walled on one side, always colonnaded on the other, which served both as a covered market place for stalls, a promenade for citizens, and a particular meeting place for philosophers and their stu-dents—so much so that a whole school became known as the Stoic.

These forms, with their clarity and rhythm, sufficed for the architect. Different areas of the Greek world of course produced their own variations of style. To support their roofs, Ionian designers across the Aegean developed a system of columns culminating in capitals with voluted extensions along the lintel, as against the bluff, square capitals topping the Doric type. These extensions may have encouraged builders to space their columns more widely apart than before. Moreover, Ionic shafts were more slender, and this made them far less obstructive and lent a new sense of airiness to the structure. The effect was heightened by the alternating flutes and smoothly polished ridges that soon appeared on the Ionic column and by the graceful volutes of its capital; it was a winning response to the period's impulse toward greater refinement, and by the mid fifth century it was widely used by mainland architects, especially in Athens. The Corinthian order, with its even more complex capital, was a later variation of the Ionic.

Here were technology and aesthetics in accord; and to this the Greek builder added some shrewd studies in applied psychology. A column with straight vertical lines gave an optical illusion of concavity; this he corrected by enlarging the diameter of the center section of the column (entasis). Then he also learned that to make it seem truly straight and just to the human eye on the ground, he should make a few other small but key corrections: he should have his columns lean inward slightly, and make the whole foundation, along with the entablature above it, rise at the center, dipping imperceptibly at the ends. As the architect Ictinus applied these refinements to the Parthenon, here was supreme calculation at work. (The slight and subtle bend of the building can still be observed by taking a line of sight from one end of its stylobate, or base, to the other: there is a rise and fall of about four inches along the course of 228 feet.)

Yet, though he studied and improved continually, the Greek architect did not revolutionize. Though for instance he created within the Ionic scheme a running frieze that overcame the strict intervals of triglyph and metope, and though he painted his temples richly and piled more and more decoration upon them—from egg-and-dart moldings and dentils to carved rainspouts and figures atop the eaves—he never let this affect or distort the basic rule and reason of his inherited design. He left it almost entirely to the Romans after him to pursue the engineering of the high vault, the arch, the dome, and the grand façade. Indeed, though the Mycenaeans long before him had created an early masterpiece of vaulting in the subterranean "Treasury of Atreus," the Greek himself was content to live for the most part with the post-and-lintel system handed down, with improvements, from old timber-construction days—but he insisted upon striving to perfect the relationship of post to lintel.

Not that the temple and its precinct became just one fixed and rigid symmetry. Its often wild or precipitous site, its winding processional path which followed the course of an earlier one to reach some ancient altar, the accident of a sacred spring—all this kept the geometry from becoming too dry. The Acropolis complex as a whole—like that of the sacred precinct at Olympia, whose construction in large part preceded it—is quite asymmetrical; an accumulation of elements of different origins, styles, and purposes, it is built along no central axis and is collectively beautiful because of the very ease and "naturalness" of the placing of the elements, as against, for example, the parade-ground rigidity of Versailles. At the peak stands the perfect form of the Parthenon, corrected for all illusions or "appearances," and pure in every proportion. Yet obliquely opposite on the cliff, as a sort of counterweight, stands the highly irregular Erechtheum, completed half a century later and built on several levels with three porches of widely differing heights, two gabled and the third and smallest with a flat roof upheld by maiden figures, or caryatids. A profusion of steps leads to several chambers (the temple was dedicated to several gods) and to a crypt or basement below, over the well of Poseidon that was rumored to lie far beneath. For Greece, the Erechtheum is an unbridled building—all impulse and diversity, you could say, whereas the Parthenon is all unity—and it suggests a counterweight to its greater sister not only in its siting but in the Greek mind. Many a student has remarked that the two structures, with all their contrasts or perhaps because of them, together form an admirable composition, or whole.

Recrossing to the south edge of the cliff, you peer down into the semicircular bowl of the theatre sacred to Dionysus—those stones not far below the Parthenon's sunswept eaves that echoed to boundless passion and daemonic outburst. Here Aeschylus' Agamemnon first shouted his terrible death cry; here Sophocles' Aegisthus, thinking a covered corpse before him to be that of Orestes, discovered Clytemnestra slain instead; here the hill resounded to the frenzied shrieks of Euripides' Medea, betrayed by Jason and advancing to kill their children. Here scenes of the natural, the unnatural, and the supernatural piled horror upon horror. There were no ruminating Hamlets here, only the fiercest or most pitiful of men and women driven to their fates. And yet a sense of moral order governed these blood-drenched dramas, as did a sovereign sense of dramatic order, unified theme, and spare rigor in the telling.

Greek drama was an exploration of human faults, passions, and excesses. Yet it presumes the irony of fate, and the justice (or the injustices) of the gods. It tells of heroes overtempted by *hubris,* and yet, like the marble balance above the Dionysian slope, of order, plan, restitution, law. Its very violence is a complement to the immobile grandeur above, yet is part of it. Aristotle, the world's first dramatic critic, was to identify in Attic tragedy the three basic unities of time, place, and action—a way of saying that a great play was built like a temple too. As one of Greece's most searching minds, Aristotle was uniquely qualified to judge between Dionysian extremes and Apollonian restraints, and so to state his doctrine of the Mean.

Greece hardly needed to wait upon great Aristotle to publish this. It had been pursuing this thought all along.

A Greek's man's house was not always his home. He relished drinking evenings with friends, often in the house of a hetaira, where men conversed while flute girls played and danced for them.

VII

LIFE AND LOVE

Health is the best that Heaven sends;
Next, to be comely to look upon;
Third is riches, justly won;
Fourth, to be young among one's friends.

—Simonides of Ceos

While his thinkers and artists wrestled with the questions of the ideal and the real, of harmony and diversity, the typical Greek citizen of the fifth century was chiefly concerned with getting the most out of a life that had become increasingly pleasant for the favored and gradually less austere for those who were not. This easing of existence had the soundest psychological and economic bases, for it rested upon the final breaking of the Persian threat. Vanquished on the peninsula and its close-in waters in the years 480 and 479, Xerxe's retreating warriors were pushed across the Aegean by revolts in the Greek islands; eventually Greek pursuers cleared Cyprus and then liberated the Bosporus region and Byzantium of the invader, establishing strongholds along the wild Thracian coast as they advanced. The rolling-back campaign was not a swift thrust, but a process extending over ten years; finally the remaining Persian army and fleet were broken at the mouth of the Eurymedon River in southern Asia Minor in a land and sea battle brilliantly led by Cimon of Athens in 468 B.C. Minds were now free from fear of a return of the *barbaroi*, while the seas were free for a vast resurgence of commerce, with Athens, at the head of the Delian League, imposing upon the Aegean in effect a *pax athenica* by means of a fleet numbering as many as two hundred galleys.

Many Greek states shared in the vigor and prosperity that resulted from extensive trade. Corinth exported tiles and woolens; Chalcis its bronze utensils and arms; west Peloponnesian ports like Patrae (the modern Patras) their olive oil, wine, and lowland fruit. Athens itself, though drawing on the long hinterland of Attica, had no surplus of food to export; on the contrary, it needed constant and regular supplies of grain from the Black Sea region to feed its teeming populace. In exchange it offered the finished goods of its mines, quarries, tanneries, workshops in abundance—smelted zinc, refined silver, forged ironwork, polished marble, leather fashioned into shoes, harnesses, and saddles, household and ceremonial pottery of every description, furniture, resin and oil for the lamps of northerly coasts, and numberless trinkets to divert the *barbaroi*. Fifth-century Athens, the world's first strong commercial power, bears a marked resemblance to the England of the time of the industrial revolution: both were the leading importers of raw materials and the leading exporters of finished ones, with their naval squadrons cruising between far-flung bases to ensure safe passage.

This traffic above all required a reliable medium of exchange; the Athenians had been among the first to maintain a stable currency. Yet venture capital was still extremely limited: banks were rare, moneylenders usurious; often city temples themselves served as lending agencies, advancing funds from their treasuries to worthy individuals. These men were unlike the later-day merchant adventures of Europe, with their Hanseatic League and East India companies; each was likely to be shipper and skipper all in one, somewhat like the shipowner-captains of early New England, going shares with a few friends to load their vessel with a mixed cargo of whatever might be salable abroad, and then setting off on a long voyage to seek out the best markets and to bargain for what they could most advantageously bring home in return.

Before long a rich variety of cargoes was being unloaded at the Piraeus. A minor playwright, Hermippus, writing in about 429, lists some typical imports: from daughter cities in Italy, sides of beef; from Cyrene, hides; from the Hellespont, dried fish; from Egypt, sails and cord; from Syracuse, hogs and cheese; from Syria, frankincense; from Rhodes, raisins; from Libya, ivory; from Phrygia, slaves. And there was more: rugs from Carthage; linens from Alexandria; dyes from Phoenicia; tin from faraway Britain.

One can reconstruct in imagination Athens' crowded port at that time: its basin no doubt encumbered then as now with flotsam and refuse of every sort; a flotilla of triremes of the Athenian-Delian fleet moored nearby, prepared for quick action in case of alarm; and the heavier merchant ships of burthen (broad-beamed, single-masted, carrying one immense sail to catch a favoring wind) tied up at dockside. Greek crews and polylingual sailors from the Levant, Africa, or as far away as Spain mingle with gangs of stevedores unloading a consignment of wheat from the Crimea or packing an outgoing shipment of amphorae in straw from dusty drays; municipal checkers are weighing incoming grain into the public warehouse (precautions are taken to prevent any middle-man from cornering the supply); owner's agents are scurrying about the chandleries to provision a laden ship for sea; buyers, sellers, people with messages to send by the hand of the captain to a foreign port, are all milling along the waterfront with its creaking cordage, its fish smells, its pumpers flushing out casks and bilges; and, behind all this, fly-ridden little taverns are serving up wine-and-water and goat's cheese, while, in the farther alleys for which the Piraeus was already famous, prostitutes from many lands, in cheap paint and trinketry, are working their trade. Almost every kind of person and chattel of the ancient world passed through this entry port on the way to the great mart of Athens, so that Pericles in the pride and dignity of his famous funeral oration could justly say, "The magnitude of our city draws the produce of the world to our harbor, so that to the Athenian the fruits of other countries are as familiar a luxury as those of his own."

Yet all these incoming products, along with those made at home, still did not endow the Athenian household with a visible air of abundance. Fortunes were made, but throughout the fifth century, at least, ostentation in one's domestic arrangements was frowned upon. Pericles reportedly owned a profitable *ergasteria,* or workshop, and became affluent, but so far as we know he remained modest in his house and appurtenances. In the next century the public orator Demosthenes (who owned a furniture workshop with twenty slaves) lamented the passing of frugality when he remarked: "The great men of old built splendid edifices for the use of the State, and set up noble works of art which later ages can never match. But in private life they were severe and simple, and the dwelling of an Aristides or a Miltiades was no more sumptuous than that of an ordinary Athenian citizien." (Aristides, well-born, wealthy, and talented both as statesman and a soldier, played a leading role at Marathon and Salamis and commanded the Athenian forces at the victory of Plataea; renowned for his rectitude, he appears to have died in poverty.) The self-indulgent, mercurial leader Alcibiades—protégé of Pericles, leader in the war against Sparta, and owner of a manufactory as well—marked the change at the end of the fifth century when he had the interior of his house decorated with wall paintings, an extravagance for which he was widely criticized.

One reason why the fifth-century Athenian—and, one can

say, the town-living Greek citizen in general—kept a simple
house was that he spent so little time in it. It was his dormitory,
his seat for occasional attendance on his wife and for an
evening meal with male companions—not much more. His
sunny climate invited him to live as much as possible outdoors.
His gregarious disposition led him to spend the better part of
the day in the busy market place and under the eaves of its
stoa, walking, talking, doing business with friends; his propensities for male company and for exercise led him to frequent his
public gymnasiums and baths in afternoon; his other male
propensities, to seek out the company of a female friend for the
evening, before returning home.

The structure and furnishing of the Greek house reflect its
master's lack of preoccupation with it. It is built of the simplest
materials—sun-dried brick, hardened clay—and usually consists
of a low, dun-colored oblong cluster backing away from street-
side without any conspicuous portal to mark it, save that a
stone Herm, with its head of Hermes and its phallus, is posted
outside the door as a good-luck and fertility symbol. Inside, a
number of small rooms front upon a central court dedicated to
domestic pursuits; the women's quarters are at the rear, or if the
house is large, under the low rafters of an upper story. Its floor-
ing may consist simply of hard-packed earth covered by rush
mats; then cement begins to be used, and before long, wealthier
families indulge themselves in tile mosaics and a few rugs from
Asia Minor or Carthage. Walls are stucco and whitewashed;
interior doorways are often just curtained apertures; window
glass is unknown. Cooking is done on an open fire, though
some houses possess baking ovens; winter heating is achieved
not by a hearth, but by movable braziers; lighting, by small and
somewhat perfunctory oil lamps; sanitation, by terra-cotta
bathtubs and latrines sometimes flushed by a jug of water
sluiced down a drain. Toward the end of the century some

wealthy families build into their houses a paved bathroom, with
water piped in; but for the most part flowing water is a luxury,
and personal cleanliness consists in an oil rubdown, followed
by a jug of cooling water from the rain-catch or the public well.

In the rooms a functional simplicity of furniture reigns. The
chief articles are wood-frame couches, with a webbed seat of
cords or leather thongs, that do the double duty of serving as
beds at night and as reclining seats for men at meals. (The custom
of eating and drinking in a longitudinal posture is restricted to
men; the women of the house sit upright on chairs and do not
take their meals with the men if guests are present.) Small, low
three-legged tables called *trapezai*—remote precursors of the
modern coffee table—are set individually before each couch for
the service of food and drink: the huge, groaning banquet board
mentioned in Olympian and Homeric myths, and later to figure
again in the history of conviviality, seems in fifth-century Greece
to have disappeared. In one of the rooms there is often something
resembling what Americans of former generations called a
"Grandfather's chair"—one big armchair of honor for the patriarch of the family, appropriately called the *thronos*. There are a
few other armless chairs and stools, gracefully turned, as we
know from numberless representations of them on vases and
reliefs, but with these—apart from a storage chest here and there—
the furnishing of the Greek citizen's house is virtually complete.

Occasionally there is a decorated mirror or a painted wall like
the one in rich Alcibiades' house; but only one form of ornament
is pervasive in the Greek house—figures painted on the sides of
the everyday bowl, jug, pot, or vase. The craft of vase painting
had evolved into a considerable art, and into a diverting portrai-
ture of daily life as well. Nameless artists had both refined the
shapes of pottery and, letting their imaginations run free, peopled the pottery with scenes of verve and exuberance far
removed from the geometric patterns and the little stylized fig-

ures of centuries before. Reversing their technical process along the way (in the sixth century they painted black figures on a clay that turned reddish or orange when fired, and in the fifth they blacked out the background, leaving silhouetted figures to stand forth in the warm color of the clay) and displaying increasing mastery of drawing, they depicted not only the familiar mythic figures in action—gods disputing, heroes battling, satyrs indecently prancing—but also contemporaries going about their work and play, harvesting, hunting, spinning, cooking, bathing, sporting, fighting, marrying, worshiping, begetting, dallying, and dying. Each house, otherwise so bare, contained some share of this social autobiography on jugs, and the vase painters were restrained by no limits as to what they might represent.

These artists tell of a society that is male-centered in most respects—lean, naked youths out exercising, adult men sharing in their sports, sometimes caressing their favorites, or reclining and bibbing at male drinking-parties, or *symposia*, while women go about the household duties of weaving, minding the children, and directing the servants. Yet they tell of strong heterosexuality too, with scenes of amorous pursuit, youths embracing their mistresses, and flute girls and dancers regaling their middle-aged hosts. They tell us also, and with more homely detail than sculpture can do, of the nature of Greek dress—or rather the limitations of it—a topic most pertinent to Greek mores.

A millennium and more before, the elegant court women of Crete had worn multicolored robes with flounces and a tightfitting bodice that left their entire breasts provocatively exposed. But this had long been forgotten; now man and woman alike wore one basic garment, shapeless in itself except insofar as it was pinned together and girdled—the *chiton*, or tunic, which was nothing more than a rectangular piece of material, often linen, brooched at the shoulders and sewn down part of the side, and then, in the case of women, taken up at the waist and left to hang down to the ankles, while men wore it to the knee. The girdle, apart from being the garment's one concession to revealing form and causing a pleasant scheme of folds or pleats, also had its erotic meaning as a symbol of virginity: Homer and other Greek poets speak often of "loosing the maiden's girdle." Yet the girdle and the ankle-length chiton were sometimes worn by men, too.

Men wore no underclothing, while many women did wear a slip and a breastband, or primordial brassiere; their bare feet stood in sandals, their head was covered only when on dusty travel by a felt hood of sorts; and, since the chiton left the fore-arms bare, the woman of good position generally tossed about her shoulders a light cloak, or *himation,* when she ventured from her house. The man often donned such a himation too, sometimes even dispensing with the chiton underneath—a departure that caused some scandal, particularly when the cloak stopped well above the knee and led, especially in a reclining posture, say at a banquet, to what Greek guardians of morals considered indecent exposure.

In general, while Greek men felt a minimum of clothing to be best—for men—and while they stripped for games and baths whenever opportunity offered and made a cult of the beautiful young male over the centuries, they were equivocal about the showing of the female body. We have seen with what diffidence the Greek sculptor proceeded to render the nude female, long after he had portrayed the virile *kouros* in full anatomical detail. A sense of restraint—even a sort of puritanism, if you will—came over the Greeks at the thought of bared breasts or the all too specific revelation of the womanly form. Few things caused greater scandal among right-thinking men or served more to alienate Sparta morally from many a community to the north of it than its girls' practice of wearing their version of the chiton (the Dorian *peplos*) quite unsewn and open on the side where its ends met, with the result that when walking, their whole left thigh would come into view—and then, as if this were not enough, of dropping their peplos altogether to go into the arena to engage naked in contests with men. Critics assailed these girls as "thigh-showers" (we would say "exhibitionists") and accused them of sexual profligacy, in which charge the critics were generally right; and one of the sharpest of them, Euripides, in his *Andromache,* written in Athens during the struggle with Sparta, snorts in disdain: "Wish as you might, a Spartan girl never could be virtuous. They gad abroad with young men with naked thighs, and with clothes discarded, they race with 'em, wrestle with 'em, Intolerable!"

The daily vesture and appearance of the proper Greek was not necessarily severe and drab. Far from it. Having laid a foundation of generally subdued good taste, the Greek then proceeded to embroider it, very much in the way he painted and ornamented his temples (and the relationship of the simple, flowing lines of the chiton to the fluted column has often been pointed out). Thus the tunic did not have to be a bleached white; it could be, and often was, a brilliant saffron or red or purple. Though women adhered to its basic form, they burst out over it with bracelets, amulets, necklaces, earrings, diadems, lockets, and chains, and hung jewels and ribbons in their dressed hair. Men, too, affected ornaments and rings (Aristotle wore several) and went each morning to the barber to be groomed and to have their locks braided or curled. Scented unguents, dyes, depilatories, perfumes, were all in daily use among women and testify that the supposedly "natural" Greeks were not so different from other breeds in wishing to put on their best face. In a text fragment that survives, Aristophanes gives a long and sardonic list of some specific aids to Athenian beauty, ranging from clippers, scissors, grease paint, hair nets, seaweed paint, and pumice stone to beauty plasters and false hair.

The women who made the most elaborate recourse to these aids were, to be sure, those who did so for sound professional reasons—the higher courtesans, or *hetairai* (meaning "companions"), often as gifted as they were seductive and altogether the most interesting (and sometimes the most dangerous) women of Greece. These were the unconventional females in a society in which the position of woman generally was limited—as was man's relationship with her. Demosthenes is said to have expressed the accepted male attitude of his time when he remarked in a matter-of-fact way: "We have courtesans for the sake of pleasure, concubines for the daily health of our bodies, and wives to bear us lawful offspring and be the faithful guardians of our homes"—not a word about love, romantic or other, nor about passion either. The poet Hesiod long before him had been equally matter-of-fact when he said: "A house, a wife, and an ox to plow with are the first needs of life"—in that order. (Aristotle, who liked the order of Hesiod's listing, picked it up and made it central to the theory of the good life he set forth in his *Politics*.) Pindar in his odes and Plato in his dialogues, both of whom saw in women chiefly a source of sensual gratification, celebrated the ardor of young men for one another as being both more noble and more natural than that between male and female. Yet enlightened companionship, headstrong passion, and on occasion a complete love did occur between Greek man and woman, though most of this took place outside of marriage. Its chief beneficiaries on the female side could range from a clever dancing girl of the demimonde to a woman who was the precursor of a Marquise de Montespan, cultivated, dashing, skillful, and a great lady in all but reputation.

In the period of the Persian invasions, the Ionian courtesan Thargelia—"a great beauty, extremely charming, and at the same time sagacious," as Plutarch describes her—had affairs with many a Greek leader while herself beholden to the court of Xerxes, and in so doing is thought to have forwarded many secrets from her bed to his at the Bosporus. Later, the brilliant libertine Aspasia of Miletus so entranced Pericles both by her body and her wit that soon she held the greatest public figure of Greece in thralldom, and his enemies came near destroying him by accusing him of being in her power. The stunning Phryne of Thespiae posed for, loved, and inspired Praxiteles and the painter Apelles as well, and became somewhat of a patroness of arts in her own right when she offered Delphi a statue of Aphrodite for which she had sat for her lover. Leontis of Boeotia is recalled as having helped the elderly thinker Epicurus to a practical understanding of the philosophy of pleasure. A wry comment has it that Lais of Corinth kept pompous Demosthenes virtuous by demanding 10,000 drachmas for an evening with him, though, liking the company of philosophers, she gave herself gratis to indigent Diogenes, the inhabitant of a barrel. Thais of Athens, believed to have been mistress of Alexander the Great, was not only to exert great influence upon his political affairs but to become, after his death, the wife of Ptolemy I of Egypt, and thus a queen.

The history of social customs presents problems to those wishing to draw clear borderlines between the vocations of the courtesan, the concubine, and the prostitute—and nowhere more than in ancient Greece did these roles meet and mingle with innumerable shadings. Prostitution in the ordinary, indiscriminate sense was not only recognized but regularized, the common women, or *pornai*, who filled the brothels of the Piraeus for instance being taxed on their receipts. Sacred, or temple, prostitution came to be accepted and appreciated, but only in Corinth, as an aspect of that robust city's cult of its patroness, the love goddess Aphrodite. Her cult had come to Corinth in the eighth century from the island of Cyprus, near which she had supposedly first risen from the sea and where every Cypriote girl of whatever class was required to give her-

self once in her life to a stranger in the temple precinct, in obei-
sance to the goddess and the fertility principle. By the time the
cult reached Corinth, hundreds of female devotees of Aphrodite
were ready to offer themselves not just once but continually, as
career priestesses of her order, so to speak—a dedication for
which they won considerable respect among Greeks. Some were
free citizens of good birth; others were slaves who could win
citizen status simply by being manumitted by their owners to
the priests of the goddess' temple on Acrocorinth.

One fifth-century Corinthian citizen named Xenophon (not
to be confused with the Athenian Xenophon, the author of the
Anabasis) pledged twenty-five such girls to the temple should
he win two contests at the Olympic games—which he thereupon
did. The proceeds of his "fillies"—so Pindar called them in an
ode—went, we are told, into the collection plate. Enhanced by
such generous endowments as Xenophon's, the number of
Aphrodite's handmaidens at Corinth eventually exceeded one
thousand, if the historian Strabo is to be believed, and the rich
trading city became the bawdiest in Greek antiquity. A proverb
soon arose to warn the visitor: "A journey to Corinth does not
profit every man," meaning that its costs and vices might ruin
both his purse and health.

Several steps above the waterfront *pornai* and the devoted
temple girls—though how many steps, it is difficult to judge—
stood such a popular *hetaira* as Metiche of Athens, who was
engaging enough to become the heroine of a comedy (since
lost) by the minor playwright Eubulus, and who acquired the
nickname "Clepsydra" (meaning "water clock") because she
received her lovers on the hour. What was she—a stylish courtesan or just another harlot? Her history is unclear: perhaps she
was both. And what of the woman in Greece who carried on
another very ancient tradition, that of the concubine, or "minor
wife," more or less permanently attached to an otherwise mar-

ried male? Here we are on even more uncertain ground. According to *Iliad,* in that early time most men of rank kept in their households one or more assistant consorts. In classical times in Attica it appears this was no longer socially accepted—though there is a puzzling reference in an oration of Demosthenes that lumps mother, wife, sister, daughter, and concubine together in one breath. In Sparta, always apart and on its own, a special form of concubinage was allowed in that men could acquire other women to supplement their own progeny in the interests of the state, while wives could also roam afield for the same purpose: the lending or borrowing of helpmeets among Spartan males for this or other aims was quite common.

Among such irregular mates of many categories, Pericles' own Aspasia stands out as the most talented, the most highly placed, yet also the most mixed in her roles. Coming from her Milesian home to Athens at mid fifth century, at a time when the education of girls was confined to elementary reading and writing along with domestic crafts and some music, she emerged as a proponent of more education and freedom of movement of women—an early feminist, no less. To this end she opened a school in which she taught the arts of discourse and rudiments of philosophy, inviting citizen wives to attend along with their husbands, and to bring along their daughters too. From her lecture courses there appears to have developed the world's first salon, frequented by Pericles and Socrates and probably also by Euripides, Phidias, Anaxagoras, and Alcibiades, and many other prominent men of the time. Yet she may also have added to her school an establishment of girls gifted in other arts; at least so Plutarch, the favorite gossip of antiquity, suggests when he writes that "her occupation was anything but creditable, her house being a home for young courtesans."

Just what the truth of this is, remains conjectural. What is known is that Pericles became infatuated with her, abandoned his wife for her, and openly lived with her in what Plutarch describes as "wonderful affection." Yet Aspasia, though the statesmen and philosophers of Athens flocked around her as she became the glass of fashion and the embodiment of the New Woman, was regarded by many as a menace to the state and an offense to its morals. It was widely said that Pericles had been enticed into making war against hitherto friendly Samos at the behest of his foreign paramour, her home city of Miletus having had a long-standing feud against the Samians. He was accused of squandering public funds, and hostility reached the point where he was traduced on the stage as a whorekeeper in such lines as these:

> To find him a Hera the goddess of lust
> Bore that harlot beyond shame,
> Aspasia by name.

In the end, the conservative faction in Athens brought in a charge of impiety and indecency against her. Pericles eloquently defended her before the city's massed jurors and won her acquittal, but his reputation as peerless leader was damaged.

Compared to the life of Aspasia, that of the well-born, respectable women of Greece whose sights she had sought to raise was dull and confined. Or so a long consensus of information and opinion has taught us, though modern scholars have raised searching questions as to whether, as the fifth century wore on, it was always quite as confined as has been represented. In legal status, to be sure, the Greek woman was hardly more than a chattel, as women had long been in the oriental world; it was only through the variety and imagination of Greek experience that she gradually became "interesting." The main social unit, before and after, was the family. Its basic function was to provide continuity through the production of legitimate children and, through them, the orderly handing on of property.

In a day of small population and of much loss by death, the production of such children was the first necessity, if polis and
order were to survive. Marriage, then, was an obligation, a fulfillment of duty to the gods: in Greece celibacy was forbidden
by law in some cities and condemned by custom in all, and not
to have children was not only a misfortune but an impiety.

It followed that marriage was a function not of love but of
social economics. Matches were arranged by contract, the bride
and her dowry passing from her father's into her husband's keeping to do with as he saw fit. If she failed him in any way—particularly in the production of children—the husband could divorce
her without so much as stating his reasons. She could neither
hold property nor claim to inherit it from him nor bring suit
against him or anyone else, nor make a contract of any kind. She
remained throughout her life in the charge of some male; if wid-
owed, she returned into the guardianship of her father or next of
male kin. Her husband could maintain concubines without giving her cause for redress; but adultery on her part, under the
Greek double standard of morality, was a grave offense against
him. If a man in turn committed adultery, his offense was not
against his victim, but against the man who was her guardian.

The place of the good Greek child-bearing wife was not only
the home, but particularly the women's quarters of the home; she
should not mix with the public affairs of men, nor even appear
frequently in the streets (shopping being done by her husband or
the family servants in any case). Xenophon, friend of Socrates
and author of the *Anabasis,* declares sententiously in an essay
entitled *Oeconomicus,* or *Economics:* "The god has ordained and
the law approves that each should follow his own capacity. It is
not so good for a woman to be out of doors as in, and it is more
dishonorable for a man to stay in than to attend to his affairs
outside." Yet he also gives an engaging glimpse of Greek domes-
ticity in this portrait, cast in form of a dialogue between Socrates

and a country squire, Ischomachus, who has taken a young bride. The author Xenophon—a soldier returned from the wars, who disdained the pleasures of Athens while cultivating his lands—no doubt patterned Ischomachus after himself.

Socrates, who in the dialogue has gone into the country to explore for himself the question of whether it may not afford more of the good life than do the jaded cities, delivers himself of a panegyric on the virtues of husbandry and the blessings of the soil as the mother of occupations and of kindly qualities in man as well. Ischomachus tells Socrates how he arranges the life of his country wife and manages his estates. He tells how his wife was not yet fifteen when he married her, and had spent her girlhood in strict seclusion, knowing "no more than how, when given wool, to turn out a cloak, and had seen only how the spinning is given out to the maids." He had told her when taking her to wife that he wanted her to be the best possible superintendent of his household and the begetter with him of creditable children. Finding her "docile and sufficiently domesticated to carry on conversations," he proceeded with her practical education, instructing her in the importance of arranging furniture and utensils in an orderly fashion, of keeping the flour dry and the wine cool, of supervising work at the loom, of making inventories, and of maintaining accounts of income and expense—and gave her some advice, as well, as to how healthy, natural color in the cheeks is superior to cosmetics, when he found her applying paint too thickly. All this, apparently, his girl-wife accepted with dutiful grace. He himself rode out each morning to manage his field hands, put his horse through its paces on a cross-country canter, and possibly visited with neighbors before returning for his first meal of the day.

Housebound as she was, a wife so active, shouldering so many responsibilities, bears little resemblance to an odalisque on a divan. She stands somewhere in that long vale between primordial times when woman was exalted as earth mother, life-giver, and matriatch and a later day when she was to emerge to be recognized freely as man's full partner if not his full equal—the day that Aspasia in her way sought to herald. The wedding ceremony that the Greek bride underwent tells of her position: it was simply an act of property conveyance, with an evening procession from her father's house to her bridegroom's (the scene of a ceremonial meal at which men and women were segregated in separate rooms or at separate tables) and the groom's gesture of carrying her bodily over his doorstep (a symbol of sexual seizure preserved even now in the West). But gradually, late in the classical period, Greek woman began to rise and to be regarded as something more than either chattel or diversion or the object of sudden passion—notwithstanding the lingering opinions of Plato in the fourth century to the contrary.

It remained the rule that a wife could not attend her husband's banquetings (and we have from the same Xenophon an account of one of the most exuberant of these stag affairs, Socrates and eight other male guests being regaled by jesters, flute girls, acrobats, and quantities of wine), but she found herself, like Penelope in the legendary past, managing a great household. Though no unmarried woman, save one resident priestess, was permitted to attend the Olympic games, women were eventually allowed to have their own Olympics. Spartan girls, of course, had long since been parading bare in the stadiums, and the lusty commentator Athenaeus writes, ignoring the moral objections that had been raised. "The Spartan custom of displaying the young girls naked before strangers is highly praised; and in the island of Chios it is delightful just to walk to the gymnasiums and running tracks to see the young men wrestling naked with the young girls, who are also naked.") The young girls of Athens too were allowed to come out from under their wraps, at least figuratively and occasionally: the greatest of the city's processions, at the opening of the quadrennial Panathenaic games—with young athletes forming up at the city gates with their chariots and javelins to march across the Agora and up the steep incline—was led by a bevy of maidens.

The Greek woman of the fifth century could not participate as an actress in the emerging theatre of her time (any more than a woman of Shakespeare's time was permitted to participate in that of his, all parts being taken by men or youths), but she was allowed and encouraged to attend it, and there she found much of it to be written about herself and her relations with man, sometimes tragic, sometimes comic, on occasion ribald. She saw portrayals of such tender heroines of the mythic past as Antigone, Alcestis, Iphigenia, and of such tormented, brutal ones as Hecuba and Medea. She also saw jocular portraits of herself and her fellow women in her own time—none more pungent than in Aristophanes celebrated satire *Lysistrata,* written during the long-drawnout war between Athens and Sparta, and in which the heroine proposes to her fellow wives that the way to end it would be for them to deny themselves to their husbands until they stopped fighting. The farce of the situation develops around the anguish in the minds of Lysistrata's friends concerning such extreme self-denial for so worthy a cause.

Nothing could better demonstrate a brilliant playwright's recognition of the power of woman and of man's abiding weakness for her. Nothing, in short, could be more human, adult, and witty. But while Aristophanes is mocking women, he is also mocking their dense, war-driven men, who would be far better off savoring home pleasures than marching about. And Aristophanes, for all his laughter, is not antifeminist either: on the contrary, in 411, the year that saw the premiere of *Lysistrata* at the Lenaean, or winter, festival in Athens, he also brought forth the comedy entitled *Thesmophoriazusae* (sometimes translated as *The Festival Women*), which was a direct personal attack on the tragedian Euripides for the unfavorable portraits of women given in *his* plays. In its first act Athenian women assemble to vow to punish the tragedian for his insults to their sex. After hearing a chorus leader deliver a speech prizing the virtues of women over those of men, Euripides disguises himself in the costume of a woman—in specific, that of an old bawd—in order to escape retribution; and on this note, complicated by the intervention of the police and the presence of a transvestite father-in-law, the farce ends.

At the outset of *Lysistrata* Aristophanes has one of the wives who has been summoned to the heroine's sexual protest meeting complain, "but it's not easy, you know, for women to leave the house. One is busy pottering about her husband; another is getting the servant up; a third is putting her child asleep or washing the brat or feeding it." Later he has her ask what sensible thing she could possibly do, dwelling as she does "in the retirement of the household." Yet the very fact that a playwright could present such protest and complaint—and that the Greek theatre audience thought it plausible—tells us that women of position were coming forth from their limited world behind the courtyard and the stairs. We have already seen the gradual emergence of the female nude in Greek art; what is more significant is the gradual emergence of Greek woman as a complete personality.

The exquisite marble relief known as the *Birth of Aphrodite*, carved in the fifth century and exhumed in the nineteenth A.D. in Rome, tells of an artist as preoccupied with feminine spirit as form. The goddess, fully shaped, yet very young and delicately and discreetly draped, rises from the sea assisted by supporting maids or goddesses, to one of whom she looks up in an almost diffident way, aware of her own beauty but perhaps not yet quite certain of how to use it—a sensitive image of woman on the threshold, but seen without the slightest sentimentality. Just as expressive in their way are the numerous memorial tablets, or steles, that begin appearing in the fifth century to mourn the passing of a beloved woman. These shafts, carved in low relief, generally show the departed (she may be mature wife or young girl; in at least one instance a slave girl is memorialized) seated in the presence of those who love her or clasping hands with them as she leaves for the world of the shades; and often an inscription recalling her name and circumstance is still legible. Thus on one stele Damasistrate and her husband join hands at parting; they are attended by a child and a kinswoman but have eyes only for each other. An epitaph surviving in *The Greek Anthology* reads: "In this stone Marathonis laid Nicopolis, and bedewed the marble chest with tear. But it was of no avail. What profit hath a man whose wife is gone, and who is left solitary on earth?" Men who could know and remember women in this fashion had obviously learned both to understand and prize them.

Yet, despite all this, Greek attitudes toward the opposite sex remained ambivalent—as did their attitudes toward sex in general. To discover this has sometimes come as a shock to philhellenes of later centuries, who were anxious to erect an image of a culture so much sunnier and presumably freer than that of the constricted Christian West. Many a man, repelled by the frost that descended upon sexuality when Saint Paul so effectively linked it to sin, and by the alternate seizures of prudery, smuttiness, shame, and compulsive ostentation that have come over it since, has looked back nostalgically to a warm-blooded people apparently free from all obsession with the subject one way or the other, and to whom sex was just a healthy natural function, as everyday as eating, and to be enjoyed very much as one enjoys eating. Or so the myth goes. It was strengthened by knowledge of Spartan girls publicly wrestling their males in the nude, of erotic scenes painted like any others on household pottery, or of Aristophanes being as broad and funny about sexual functions as he was about other functions of the body. But while the Hellenes widely savored all this as much as the phil-hellenes, it was only one side of their view of a subject that for them had its troubling obverse. What could be more frank than the spectacle of maidens carrying a huge phallus in procession, often accompanied by a symbol of their pudenda too? But such processions were religious, dating back to prehistoric times, and combined a worship of the miracle and joy of procreation with a sense of awe and mystery concerning the process. And though the fifth-century educated Greek felt he was sophisti-cated about the biological facts of life, there stayed with him an awareness of the generative power as being something larger than his life—a gift of the gods or of nature that could be benef-icent and yet potentially dangerous too. It could provide stal-wart sons as the ancient corn goddess had provided ample fields, yet it could also bring forth demons and disasters, and the Greek had only to look back through his tales and dramas to the Mycenaean Helen or Clytemnestra to remind himself how fatal the sexual lure could be. Dionysian and priapic rites, sacred prostitution along with sacred virgins, excesses here, taboos there, and the pursuit of the cult of male *paiderasteia* in particular, all speak of a people beset as much by sexual uncer-tainty as by attraction.

Physically intimate friendship among men, it should be said, was so far as we know primarily concentrated in the upper class of citizens (in Sparta, the pioneer in this respect, the warrior class), while the lesser orders remained conventionally hetero-sexual. It should also be said that the homosexual, as the man whose erotic impulses are directed only toward males, was uni-versally scorned: what was accepted and practiced in the lead-ing circles was bisexuality—a man siring possibly a large number of offspring and heading the family while engaged with a male lover as well.

In this equivocal area of Greek life, so difficult to comprehend in a modern age unaccustomed, at least publicly, to such a
mixture, the sorriest figure was often the handsome youth from
abroad who had fallen into this or that city's hands by capture
and then into those of some citizen by purchase, and who, as his
attraction waned, declined from the role of companion or male
concubine into that of a common slave. The loftiest figure in it
was none other than Plato himself, after Socrates the most illustrious mind of Greece, intent on exploring the farthest reaches
of the human psyche; he was evidently wedded to male relationships with only a shadowy interest in the female.

Plato in his *Symposium*—perhaps the most absorbing of the
twenty-five dialogues on which his lasting fame as a thinker
chiefly rests—suggests his predilections and those of the highly
cultivated Athenian elite in which he moved and taught. The
work is a remarkable tour de force altogether, full of surprises,
lively exchanges, and poetic ascents. Set down in about the
year 384, when Plato was in his mid-forties and had just taken
to lecturing outside the city's walls in the grove of Academus
(from which arose the name of his Academy), it purports to
recall a convivial evening's talk of almost a generation earlier,
supposedly in 416, when a group of bright spirits had forgath-
ered with Socrates to eat, drink, and discuss the subject of Love.
Those present included the playwright Aristophanes, the two
young literary men Phaedrus and Pausanias, and the physician
Erixymachus; later in the evening, long after the guests have
agreed to dismiss the flute girls and to drink sparingly in order
to pursue their talk in good order, the wine-flushed Alcibiades
breaks in with a band of revelers and disrupts the proceedings.
But before this happens each of the guests reclining about
Socrates has delivered himself of an encomium on *eros,* by
which, it rapidly becomes apparent, he means primarily friendship or love among men.

Then Socrates takes over with a brilliant discourse that lifts the evening to another level. He proposes that Love exists not for the sake of the self but for that of an object; that Love is higher as the object is higher; and that at best, Love lifts man from the passions of earth to a vision of absolute beauty, or God.

At least such are the thoughts that Plato puts into the mouth of the master who died a decade and a half earlier, representing them as having been uttered about a decade and a half before that at a party at which Plato himself was not present in any case (he would have been thirteen at the time). To try to unravel the problem of what the aging, earthy Socrates himself may have said on this or any other topic as against what his pupil in his dialogues said he did, has long frustrated students. In any event the two remain what might be called the Siamese twins of philosophy, since the first never wrote and the second professed, even long after his master's death, that he chiefly listened. In the case of the *Symposium* there is hardly a doubt that the Socrates speaking is not Socrates at all, but the Plato who wishes to be identified with him. What is all the more puzzling, then, is that Plato-as-Socrates, in the great argument that takes the dialogue to its peak, claims that his full insight into Love came not from manly wisdom but from a woman, one Diotima of Mantinea, "who was deeply versed in this and many other fields of knowledge . . . and it was she who taught me the philosophy of Love." What was a woman doing instructing Plato particularly in this subject, especially since he appears to have disdained the sex or at least to have been highly equivocal in his feelings toward it. True, in the *Republic*—his scheme for an ideal society—he argues that some women are superior and, as wives and helpmeets of the Guardians of the state, should receive the same education as men. Yet he seems to feel that the female mind is weaker; in his *Laws* there is reference to woman's "disposition" as being "inferior to man's."

Students will go on, no doubt, investigating and debating the identity of this mysterious Diotima. Did she indeed ever exist outside Plato's own imagination? We shall probably never know the answer to this. What we do know is that in the *Symposium* she exists as a kind of sybil confounding Socrates (or rather Plato-Socrates) with leading questions, seeming to turn the tables of argument on him, and on occasion making open fun of him: "Don't you know that holding an opinion which is in fact correct, without being able to give a reason for it, is neither true knowledge ... nor ignorance?" ("Yes," is the lame response of Plato-Socrates, "that's perfectly true.") And then this curious high priestess of Love seems to turn into Plato himself when she says, in a passage that marks the summit of the evening. "And now, Socrates, there bursts upon [man] that wondrous vision which is the very soul of the beauty he has toiled so long for. It is an everlasting loveliness which neither comes nor goes, which neither flowers nor fades, for such beauty is the same on every hand, the same then as now, here as there. ... Nor will his vision of the beautiful take the form of a face, or of hands, or of anything that is of the flesh. It will be neither words, nor knowledge, nor a something that exists in something else, such as a living creature, or the earth, or the heavens, or anything that is—but subsisting by itself in an eternal oneness. ... And so, when his prescribed devotion to boyish beauties has carried our candidate so far that the universal beauty dawns upon his inward sight, he is almost within reach of the final revelation. And this is the way, the only way, he must approach, or be led toward the sanctuary of Love."

Plato's Diotima, however, hung somewhat in the rarified air above and beyond the sights of the everyday intelligent Greek, whatever his aspirations. The Athenian himself was largely taken up with the everyday pursuit of what we would call the ideal of the all-round man. The ascetic or the specialist or the man of intellect who was exclusively an intellectual was generally not to his liking. Just as in the polis there was no priestly caste and no civil service, there were few other specialized professions either. There were schoolmasters, there were professional reciters of poetry to music, and, most prominently, there were physicians. Late in the fifth century these men began to emerge from their role as quasi-priestly healers working in the name of Asclepius (considered by some to be Apollo's son), with a secret lore of herbs, potions, and ointments; now they became scientific practitioners, followers of Hippocrates, the first Greek man of medicine who was not at the same time a medicine man. Many doctors, in addition to learning from Hippocrates' careful study of bodily symptoms, appear also to have abided by the famous oath of ethical conduct ascribed to the physician of Cos, which marks what could be called the beginning of the professional outlook.

But meanwhile a building engineer was likely to be his own architect, civic organizer, arranger of sculpture and decoration as well. The playwright or historian might find himself commanding troops: Sophocles led Athenian infantry during the Samian revolt, as Thucydides did in the Peloponnesian War. Toward the end of the century, a group of full-time specialist instructors in higher education emerged, coaching aspiring young men for a fee in the arts of rhetoric and oratory—skills most valuable in the highly vocal society of the agora. Yet these teachers, though they let themselves be called *sophistai,* meaning "men of wisdom," and though they included such brilliant masters of persuasion as Protagoras, Gorgias, and Isocrates, were far removed from Socrates, who was never a professional man of wisdom himself, never accepted so much as an obol for his teaching, and rather despised these Sophists for making a business of showing how to influence people. His own area was simply talk—good talk—and he once remarked that his possessions did not exceed five drachmas in value (say ten dollars in today's equivalent).

Unlike the professionals, this robust and earthy individual—in his day a soldier, a president of the Athenian Assembly, and at all times the irreverent gadfly about all that was going on in the polis—was not interested in smoothing anyone's way to fortune but rather in sharpening wits by inquiry. You joined Socrates at the colonnade or under some friend's roof, not to hear a magisterial brain hold forth ex cathedra, but because, in either a serious or a lighthearted mood, he had invited you as one whom he liked. There might be flute girls and wine, or there might not; the old fellow might be slightly awash and full of jokes, or quite sober; but in either state he was likely to be bent on drawing you out, on hearing every argument, and then on bringing you to discover their difficulties or contradictions and to attain the truth yourself. He would start a conversation that was far less a debate or a dispute from prepared positions than it was a joint probing among friends, testing ideas by questioning them—one could say, a dialogue of the mind with itself. What was the nature of virtue? friendship? beauty? Socrates was ready to listen to any line of thought almost endlessly, coaching it along by a searching question here and there, until the persons about him sometimes found themselves still talking at the approach of dawn. If the outcome of so many hours exchange was not agreement, it was at least illumination. Even the hours of Socrates' last day and evening—spent with friends while in prison awaiting the fatal potion of hemlock that was to be administered to him for his offenses against the state—are full of good-humored discourse, Socrates weighing with Phaedo and other young men devoted to him the subject of the soul and immortality. The soul is immortal, he gets his followers to agree, because it can perceive and partake of a truth, a goodness, and a beauty that are eternal. Man knows God to the extent that he has in himself some inkling of these eternals. Then Plato's curtain descends upon this marvelous dialogue and life with Socrates saying in high irony to Crito, another pupil, as he takes the poison, "Crito, we ought to offer a cock to Asclepius"—that is, a thank-offering to the god of healing.

The kind of young man able to converse with Socrates had to be educated and ready of wit. Yet the formal schooling of an Athenian was, at least by modern lights, quite limited. Indeed, outside Sparta, where all teaching was a state prerogative, there appears to have existed nowhere in Greece what we would call an educational system. There were no public schools or colleges. While Greek states other than Sparta prided themselves on being the patrons of their people's arts, they felt that schooling itself should be left almost entirely in private hands. A girl in any case, as we have seen, received household training and the rudiments of reading and writing at home. A boy citizen, once he had been "accepted" by his family in a religious rite ten days after his birth (in Athens no less than in Sparta, a parent had the right to expose a faulty infant upon a hillside to slow death or a speedy one by wild animals), might have an attendant slave or *paedagogus* to oversee him during his school days. At the age of six he was likely to be placed in a private school where a *grammatistes* drilled him in elementary language and arithmetic, while a *kitharistes,* or harpist, taught music and recitation of poetry.

At about the age of fourteen this basic fifth-century schooling ceased, save for the fortunate few whose parents could afford to pay a *sophistes* to carry them on or to find some other advanced school or tutor able to inculcate geometry and philosophy. The curriculum seems brief and sparse when compared with today's—there was no teaching of Civics, Social Studies, or General Science, any more than of Home Economics, or Mass Communications Techniques. Vocational training of any sort was avoided: the Greek evidently felt that just as manners should be taught at home by parental precept, trades should be taught under a tradesman's roof by apprenticeship. Limited as his schools were, they were there to inculcate the fundamental disciplines of word and number. If you mastered these, you could probably move ahead on your own to mastering others. In short, the school was thought of as an early preparation for life, not for a livelihood.

Yet while his schoolrooms remained under private auspices, the Greek delighted in spending large sums of public money on the building of stadiums, gymnasiums, and theatres—the games, festivals, and performances that took place in them being thought of not as recreation but as exercises deeply tied to ethical precept and religion. So, in the broadest sense, in Greece education was public after all; one might even say that it has never been more public. The nude wrestler in palaestra, the chanter on the hillside stage reciting from Homer, the thousand or so men and boys who sometimes took part in a single Athenian festival or drama, the girls who led the solemn Panathenaic procession—all were figures in a scheme of communal participation in cultural experience. And throughout this, from the bout in the local palaestra to the exalted contests at Olympia and the rivalry of playwrights for the prize in the Theatre of Dionysus, runs the strong Greek sense of peaceable competition as a way of proving one's excellence, or *arete*.

The very concept of athletics—from *athlos,* meaning "contest" and signifying the idea of training, testing, and perfecting the body as a unity with the mind—is a Greek one. Organized contests, as distinguished from death-dealing duels, go far back in Greek consciousness—to Heracles, regarded as the first athlete and the founder of sports; to Homer, who in the *Iliad* describes the ceremonial contests that were held following the funeral of Patroclus before Troy, and which included boxing and chariot and foot races. (In the *Odyssey,* in a lighter mood he

has the princess Nausicaa and her maidens play a game of ball
and subsequently the hospitable Phaeacians regale their visitor
with a feast and a meet that includes wrestling, dancing, and
heaving a great stone—precursor of the discus.) Martial Sparta
overdid the cult of the body—or rather distorted it by giving little heed to the mind—but Athens and other Greek cities
regarded physical training as a vital branch of education.

It was one that could best be served by erecting public facil-
ities open to all, comprising athletic grounds, baths, and possibly a lecture hall or colonnade for relaxation and talk as
well—something beyond the means of a private school. Thus
there were three large gymnasiums in fifth-century Athens
alone, and their layout provided pleasant centers for philosophers too. Plato frequented one of them in the grove of Academus before he withdrew to his own garden nearby. His pupil
Aristotle was to meet his students, often fresh from workout
and rubdown, in another called the Lyceum.

Such public establishments, to be sure, were not on the scale
of those at Olympia and Delphi, the chief shrines of what were
in effect sports-pilgrimages. Every few years visitors from all
over Greece arrived to perform in or attend championship
matches, to worship particular gods, to witness spectacles and
parades, and to enjoy something of the excitement of a fair-
ground as well, with local and foreign products and souvenirs
being hawked along the approaches to the precinct. Boisterous
Corinth biennially celebrated its Isthmian games in honor of
Poseidon, and mountainous Delphi staged its quadrennial
Pythian games in honor of Apollo in a rock-strewn enclave
almost in the clouds above its temples.

But the greatest of these assemblies was the quadrennial one
at Olympia—so meaningful a meet that heralds went forth to
every town and to the countryside to announce it, proclaiming
a general truce among all Greek states so that their young men

could join to compete in the pentathlon of jumping, discus throwing, javelin hurling, wrestling, and running; in boxing, chariot racing, and other events. The scene at Olympia—in its prime a vast religious-athletic camp crowded with temples, memorial steles, columns, fountains, statues, dormitories, hostels, individual city treasuries, practice grounds, and shaded paths leading to the grass-banked arena—seized the general Greek imagination. Processions, public prayers, sacrifices, orations, receptions of dignitaries opened the festival, along with the swearing-in of contestants, each youth emerging from his training tent to attest to the judges that he was of proper Greek birth, properly trained, and as such would not cheat in the contests. The award of a crown of olive leaves to the victor culminated it, followed by more religious observances and a banquet to Greece's new heroes in the Prytaneum, the sanctuary in which the sacred fire was kept.

Not everyone in Greece was wholly in accord with the immense adulation bestowed upon the winners of the Panhellenic games, many of whom, after receiving their wreaths, became the subjects of hymns and public statuary and recipients of large donations besides. Euripides, for instance, in deploring what he feared to be a trend toward cult and professionalism, remarked that athletic prowess alone does not fit a man for leadership in war any more than in peace, and that "It is the wise and good man who should be crowned with leaves, the temperate and just ruler of the city who frees it from evils." In Athens itself, that most festive of cities, the basis of competition—and adulation—was broader. Observing some sixty holidays a year in honor of this god or that victory, the Athenians took many days and evenings off to celebrate every form of contest. No less than four major annual festivals were staged honoring Dionysus, and these were exceeded in splendor only by the great quadrennial feasts. One honored Demeter; the other, honoring the patron goddess Athena, was marked by musical competitions, torchlit ceremonies, and boat races.

Yet of all these, the most unique were the spring Dionysian contests or "games" at which the competitors were not athletes, but dramatists, each one chosen by the city's archon to enter the rivalry with a new script, and among whom the chief heroes were Aeschylus (with thirteen annual prizes), Sophocles (with twenty), and Euripides (with four). Fifteen thousand or more persons sat on the slope of the Acropolis to look down at the bare circular platform, or *orchestra,* on which choruses in robes and players in masks moved to the long lines of strophe and antistrophe, interrupted by quick, hard exchanges in everyday speech. The plays they saw, in broad daylight, with a minimum of scenery, were ancestral and religious (in the case of Aeschylus), polished and formal (Sophocles), or highly emotional and critical (Euripides); but in any case, whether invoking old memory and morality or exploring the new, the plays were smashing good theatre—as the people of the polis showed by flocking to them. The squire, the ordinary citizen, the educated slave of Athens, all attended them as the highest voice of competition and imagination as well. Here were stories of dark destinies overtaking the all-too-proud or the unfortunate; yet here also, amid the mirror of fate and adversity, was the recognition of man's strength, his passing joy, his urge to fulfillment, his delight at having friends, and his sorrows at having lost them. "If a man is good, he is happy; if he is happy, he is good," so runs an old Greek saying. This was not necessarily true; but at least it was said and believed.

The tragic hero Oedipus ponders the riddle of the Sphinx: "What walks on four legs in the morning, two at noon, and three in the evening?" Oedipus' correct guess, that it referred to man in successive stages of life, saved Thebes from the scourge of the man-devouring Sphinx.

VIII

TRIUMPH AND TRAGEDY

Thucydides, an Athenian, wrote the history of the war between the Peloponnesians and the Athenians, beginning at the moment that it broke out, and believing that it would be a great war, and more worthy of relation than any that had preceded it.

—Thucydides, opening lines of his *History*

The year 431 B.C. found Athens at its zenith, though no Athenian would have recognized it as such, since a zenith implies a descent to follow. He was aware that year, as in years before, of brilliant advances in his arts, of mastery in his statecraft, and of a general sense of civic well-being around him. Why should all this not lead to even greater achievements and rewards?

In his physical setting he had much to look upon with pride. The shining new Parthenon, Pericles' magnificent memorial to his city's victory over the Persians, had just been completed even to its last pediment sculptures, after barely fifteen years of intensive effort. Phidias' great gold and ivory statue of Athena had been dedicated several years earlier. The Propylaea, that awesome new gateway raised on the Acropolis from the rubble of past assault, had also been constructed to serve as the ceremonial entrance for long processions winding up the Sacred Way. Pericles' building program was so rousing that centuries later Plutarch was to recall it in these words: "As the buildings rose stately in size and unsurpassed in form and grace, the workmen vied with each other that the quality of their work might be enhanced by its artistic beauty. Most wonderful of all was the rapidity of construction. Each one of them, men thought, would require many successive generations to complete it, but all of them were fully completed in the heyday of a single administration."

The Long Walls, built to replace those razed by the Persians, stood secure against any new threat of siege. Such neighboring maritime rivals as Megara and Aegina had been brought under Athenian sway; the Delian League had been converted into what was in effect an organization of tributary states. All this, coupled with the making of a final peace with a frustrated Persia in 448 B.C., left Athens the undisputed mistress of the Aegean. By the year 431 B.C. no ship of whatever homeland could safely traverse the waters from Egypt to Thrace, from Crete to the Crimea, without the benevolence of the lords of trade and admiralty ensconced at Athens, and few captains were of a mind to challenge them.

Pericles had also been striving to surmount another obstacle to the growth and mastery of Athens. The most dubious gift of the gods and nature to the men of Attica was the narrow isthmus, controlled by Corinth, that connected them with the Peloponnesus—a fine overland communications route, to be sure, but also a causeway for any land army from the peninsula bent on taking maritime Athens from the side or rear, as well as a barrier to the entry of Athens' ships into the westward-facing Gulf of Corinth, unless the land approaches to it could be secured. To win command not only of these approaches but of the whole gulf had become Pericles' master plan. In this he had almost—but not quite—prevailed.

The extraordinary Corinthian sea corridor, which runs westward for about eighty miles between the mainland and the peninsula before it opens onto the Ionian Sea under the lee of offshore islands, had long tantalized Athenian sailors. It was the natural, direct avenue for traffic to Greek settlements on the Adriatic and in Italy, Sicily, and beyond. Yet the Athenians, being harbored northeast of the forbidding isthmus, had had no recourse when setting sail for, say, Acragas or Syracuse, other than to strike far south and double around the capes of the Peloponnesus, as Odysseus' men had done, before making their westing. (Light coastal vessels, it is true, were portaged across the isthmus, at its narrowest point, Corinth permitting; but what was needed was a safe landing area at the head of the gulf so that Athenian ships could take on cargo that had been hauled across the isthmus and thus avoid returning home for it.) The gulf was also strategic internally: whoever controlled it could control much of the traffic between states of the mainland and those of the Peloponnesus. Since rich Corinth, sitting comfortably at its apex, was of no mind to share control of it with anyone, Pericles felt he must flank and isolate the troublesome city. In a series of brilliant strokes in the early 450's he had brought the entire northern coast of the gulf under Athenian dominion, including the outpost of Naupactus, which guarded the gulf's narrow western entrance—a Gibraltar if held by a strong power. Moreover, Pericles had built ties of friendship with provincial Achaea, far out along the gulf's southern shore, with its port of Patrae just across the strait from Naupactus. Now Corinthian craft could pass the strait only upon the say-so of Athens and its friends. On the other hand, Athenian or allied vessels could fairly safely traverse the length of the gulf, which seemed to be on its way to becoming another Athenian lake, like the Aegean to the east.

It was never fully to become that—or if indeed it was that for a few years, the condition was not to remain. Athens' extension, and the vigor and imagination that went into it, had stirred men of nearly every Greek state and tribe, some to throw themselves under its protection, others to gather around its foes. An uneasy balance of power prevailed while the rival leagues—the Delian of Athens and the Peloponnesian headed by Sparta—jockeyed and maneuvered to win a new confederate here or gain a further foothold there. Corinth, humiliated and embittered by Athenian encirclement, drew close to its ally Sparta with thoughts of a war of revenge against Pericles' empire—for that was what his demesne now was. Although during the decades following the Persian wars an uneasy balance had existed between the leagues, averting major collision, the 450's saw an increasing number of border clashes, struggles at the periphery, and defections of subject states from one camp to the other. Local revolts among Athens' new-found subjects in particular showed that Pericles had spread himself too far too fast to be able to consolidate his gains; finally the door which he thought he had slammed shut on the Corinthian corridor swung ajar, and out streamed the Corinthian fleet.

The occasion that took these galleys out into the Adriatic in 435 was a colonial conflict that soon threatened to become a general one. The actual quarrel was between Corinth and its own daughter city of Corcyta on what today is known in the West as the island of Corfu. The settlers of Corcyra, arriving from Corinth in the eighth century, had built themselves a hardy island stronghold and then decided to sunder ties with the mother city and preserve "complete political isolation" (so Thucydides describes it, citing their spokesmen) while girding themselves with a fleet second only to that of Athens (Thucydides credits them with 120 galleys in the year 435). About the year 625—such was the complexity of the Greek colonial system—the cities of Corinth and Corcyra jointly had spun off a settlement farther up the Adriatic at a place called Epidamnus, the present-day Durazzo on the Albanian coast; and it was over this remote spot that "mother" and "daughter" now went to war. The Corcyraeans beat off the Corinthians in a first round of battle, but wondered if they could do so if the men of Corinth were to return in greater force, with allies. So they abandoned their proud isolation and sought an ally—Athens.

The reporter-historian Thucydides, fated to be not only a witness of the vast struggle but also a participant in it, records the succinct arguments made by Corcyraean envoys when they arrived before Pericles and the Assembly asking for support. They apologized, in effect, for their past policy of isolation. They warned of the warlike designs of Sparta and Corinth upon Athens. They described their own naval strength and emphasized how great a help this would be to Athens in the event of a general conflagration. Finally they warned that if it should unfortunately happen that Corcyra were overrun in a second attack from Corinth, its fleet and bases would, of course, become part of the Peloponnesian power, which would then far outweigh that of Athens.

The envoys from opposing Corinth, also present in Athens, appeared before the Assembly with a warning against heeding the Corcyraean appeal. To enter into an alliance with the ungrateful Corcyraeans, they declared, would violate the treaty guaranteeing peace that had been signed by the two leagues in 445 B.C. and threaten the balance of power. Pericles was more impressed by Corcyraean naval power than by the Corinthian threat, and persuaded the Assembly to make a pact with the island state. The agreement was to be one for mutual defense only, against the attack of a third power, but its meaning was to tie Greece's two strongest fleets together, which unquestionably did shake the balance.

This was an ominous moment for all of Greece. One thinks by distant analogy of the world of Europe in the years just before 1914: the rival Great Power camps hardening, outlying "incidents" occurring with increasing frequency from Morocco to the Balkans, ministers initialing secret treaties (for "mutual

defense" only), recurrent crises causing the lights of Downing
Street, Quai d'Orsay, Wilhelmstrasse, and Ballhausplatz to burn
late at night, armies growing and dreadnoughts deploying
while daily life went on in a summer of security and content-
ment.

The Athenian world, as the fateful year 431 B.C. neared, had
no glitter comparable to that of Europe of 1914, yet it was astir
with a sense of fulfillment and promise. Its diversity, like its luxury, was limited; yet its intellectual range and richness were
unprecedented. A spirit of originality, of readiness to re-examine
all things past—myth, custom, ancestral order and belief—and
to arrive at new values and insights, coursed not only through
its artists and its scientists but through its public spokesmen as
well. And in a real sense the dramatists and scientists of these
years were themselves also public spokesmen, or at least public
critics, voicing new views about society and taking issue with
past ones in the theatre or agora. Pericles, significantly, was a
particular friend of Sophocles, the great humanizer of Greek
drama, of whom it was said that he "brought Tragedy down
from the clouds." Pericles was also a patron and one-time pupil
of Anaxagoras, a religious skeptic and an extraordinary
prophet of new science.

Anaxagoras—born about the year 500 B.C. in Clazomenae,
near present-day Izmir in Asia Minor—was only one of many of
a school of thinkers bent on pursuing the quest begun back in
the time of Thales of Miletus, to find rational principles or laws
governing the physical world, thus pushing back superstition
and ignorance. Empedocles of Acragas in Sicily, a combination
poet, visionary, magician, and student of nature in the
Pythagorean tradition, had come forth with hints of an evolutionary idea of growth and had also hit upon the thought that
light requires a given time to travel from one point to another.
Parmenides of Elea in southern Italy, who probably was an eld-

erly man at mid-century when he visited Athens, had declared the earth to be round and observed that the moon always had its bright portion turned toward the sun. Leucippus of Miletus, who flourished about 440 B.C., had speculated on the origin of stars and suggested that they had sprung from some central source or vortex. Democritus of Abdera in Thrace, who lived probably from about 460 B.C. to 370 B.C., set forth the theory that everything in the universe was made up of combinations of a basic physical unit that he called the atom. But of all these, Anaxagoras of Clazomenae was undoubtedly the most brilliant in his generation; at the age of twenty he came to Athens and began a splendid career. As many-sided as Pythagoras in the century preceding, he was astronomer, biologist, meteorologist, and philosophical pioneer alike. He correctly explained eclipses; he came forth with a rational hypothesis of planetary origin; he declared that the sun was an incandescent rock (somewhat larger than the Peloponnesus, he thought) from which the moon received its light. He studied tides and weather to the advantage of Greek mariners. He set up, to the distress of the materialists among Greek thinkers, the idea that Mind (*nous*) was the primal cause of all being and held power "over all things that have life." Turning to the study of man, he produced an astonishing evolutionary insight when he argued that the reason man had advanced beyond animals was that his erect posture had freed his hands for grasping and manipulating objects.

This was an amazing and precocious notion. Suggestions had long come from Ionian philosophers that all life—human and animal—could be traced back to a common origin, and that the Olympian stories of creation were just fables. But here a speculative thinker (not wholly speculative, though; he appears to have made some anatomical studies of animal brains) was hitting upon a very specific anthropological truth. It was not the whole truth, to be sure. He had probably never seen or even heard of the apes, and so was unaware of all that anthropology was to learn about human development from studying them. But the fact that Anaxagoras, in a time when propitiatory magic was still generally practiced, sensed a line of man's ascent or, if you will, of descent, makes him a startling Greek precursor of Darwin—just as in astronomy he was a precursor of Copernicus. He was accused of atheism for saying that the sun was not a god, but just a white, hot rock. One thinks of Galileo.

While Greek science forged ahead so daringly, Greek drama was not to be left behind. Nearly sixteen years lay between the triumph in the Athenian theatre of Aeschylus' sombre trilogy, the *Oresteia,* on the theme of the family of the god-cursed Orestes, and the flowering of a different sort of playwright, the polished Sophocles of the *Antigone* of about 441 B.C., forerunner of a long line of increasingly humane and poignant dramatizations that were to culminate in his masterly *Electra* and *Oedipus the King.* Euripides—younger than Aeschylus and Sophocles, a critic of Olympian religion and a brooding romantic to boot—entered the lists in 438 B.C. with his *Alcestis,* a haunting drama based on an old tale in which Apollo, having brought down upon himself the wrath of his father, Zeus, is condemned to serve for a while under a mortal master, King Admetus of Thessaly. He finds the king to be a model of human decency—only to learn that Admetus is doomed to an early death. Apollo prevails upon the Fates to spare the king. They agree, but only on condition that someone else die in Admetus' place. This his noble wife Alcestis agrees to do—she is both the heroine of the play and an exemplar of human character superior to that of the unconscionable deities.

In 431 B.C. Euripides, always critical, always turbulent, presented the *Medea*—his stormy adaptation of the story of the wife betrayed for another woman by the Argonaut Jason. Her vengeance upon this god-favored hero was to culminate in the murder of the children she had borne him. Yet, in this relentless drama of a human alone, bereft of protection, and without prospect of godly justice in sight, there appears an extraordinary interlude which is no less than a paean of the chorus to the high dignity of man—and to the proud and confident city of Athens:

> From of old the children of Erechtheus are
> Splendid, the sons of blessed gods. They dwell
> In Athens' holy and unconquered land,
> Where famous Wisdom feeds them and they pass gaily
> Always through that most brilliant air where once, they say,
> That golden Harmony gave birth to the nine
> Pure Muses of Pieria.

This was spoken, or rather chanted, in 431 B.C. to admiring listeners in a city on the verge of disaster. For in that same year commenced the suicidal struggle between Athens and Sparta that was to leave Attica a shambles and all Greece in disarray. The handsome speech of Euripides in his *Medea* was to be almost the last in this vein. What came next, whether in Greek drama, Greek art, Greek politics or thought, though it still spoke with greatness, was to display the anguish of something lost. Less than thirty years divide Anaxagoras or the playwrights at their proudest from the reflections of the philosophers at their gloomiest and the behavior of politicians like Alcibiades at their shabbiest.

One great speech did still remain—that noble funeral oration in which Pericles mourns those fallen in the first winter of the war. In tones of exaltation he speaks of the unique gifts of the gods and of man's own intelligence to Athens; he praises the city's high civilizing mission, but he still recognizes its faults. While drawing no untoward comparisons, one is tempted to recall an utterance in a related vein two and a half millennia later; opening his memoirs, another chieftain of a proud and harried state, General Charles de Gaulle of France, speaks of his country as "dedicated to an exalted and exceptional destiny. Instinctively I have the feeling that Providence had created her either for complete successes or exemplary misfortunes." Complete successes and exemplary misfortunes: there could be no more perfect characterization of the triumph and tragedy of the Athenian state.

Historians, beginning with Thucydides himself, the eyewitness, have debated over the centuries the causes of the deadly collision. Had Pericles blindly overreached himself as the Athenian master builder, and so brought the whole structure toppling down? Many contemporary critics thought so, accusing him of waste, foolhardiness and worse—and indeed he was driven from office on a charge of embezzlement shortly after war's outbreak, to be reinstated for a brief period before his death. "Pericles made the war," Aristophanes was to say quite flatly, blaming him for having failed to rescind a harsh embargo against the people of Megara, an incident that had added flames to the crisis. Plutarch introduces a yarn that Pericles "kindled the war" with Sparta to distract the public from the accusation of embezzling public funds that had been made against him and his friend Phidias.

The slanders by Plutarch and by Pericles' contemporary enemies do not stand up under the general verdict of history, which finds no reason to doubt Pericles' probity, high dedication, and *arete*. Some doubts remain, though, as to his ultimate perspicacity. Was there in him a tragic flaw that led him from balanced judgment, or *sophrosyne*, in the direction of overweening pride, or *hubris*—that flaw which lies at the heart of so much

Greek drama? Were there, more deeply, some flaws of character
and behavior among the proud Athenians he led?

The Athenians on the eve of the war seemed to possess
everything that mattered—political hegemony, adequate security, immense reputation, sovereign style, intellectual leadership, and a free and inquiring spirit. What went wrong? One
primal danger lay in the jealousy aroused in other Greek states
when they saw one of their number growing so great. Although
the year 431 B.C. figures, so to speak, as the 1914 of the Hellenic
world—the day the lights went out, not to be rekindled for a
generation—a hardly less decisive date is that of 454 B.C. For
that was the year in which Pericles and his party in power in
Athens, hitherto the chief supporters and guarantors of the
Delian League of defense against Persia, caused the war chest or
treasury that had been kept on the sacred mid-Aegean isle of
Delos to be transferred to Athens itself, to be guarded solely by
Athenian power. This bold action, taken on the ground that
Delos was in an exposed position in the event of a renewed
assault from the east, changed the shape of Aegean affairs
entirely. What had been a confederation now became an Athenian empire. Allied states were no longer asked to contribute
ships, they were asked to contribute money with which Athens
itself would build and man and command the ships. Furthermore, island states within Athens' reach were not just invited to
join and pay; they were compelled to do so. Many that formerly
had been autonomous and regarded as friends were reduced to
tributaries. Only Lesbos, Chios, and Samos retained their independence; Athenian garrisons moved in upon the others, while
Athenian emissaries dictated their constitutions and laws of
trade, to the point where Pericles enforced the use of Athenian
coins, weights, and measures throughout many of them. It was
imperial tribute money—there is no other word for it—that paid

for the building of the Parthenon and many other noble Athenian monuments.

Did Pericles fail to perceive that his rising empire over the seas, coupled with his tenuous one on land, would draw Athens' enemies together for common resistance and counterstroke? Or, if he did perceive it, was he ready to risk a general encounter? As an empire-builder, he in some respects resembles Napoleon, who never did quite comprehend why so much growth and victory on his part could provoke such unquenchable antagonism in others. Yet with this, much of the analogy ends: Napoleon was strong on land, uncertain at sea; Pericles commanded a sea empire. As to character, Pericles, the statesman-philosopher, is hardly to be equated with the Corsican *condottiere* with a genius for brow-beating men and an *arriviste*'s lust for the pompous and grandiose. Pericles was the scion of a cultivated family long devoted to the arts and civic responsibility, and most of his life was given to proposing and carrying through domestic reforms and improvements, promoting trade, or pursuing his beloved building program.

Over three decades, beginning in about 463 B.C., the Athenians had recognized the particular strength and quality of Pericles. After coming into prominence as one of the state prosecutors who succeeded in ostracizing Cimon, a brave Athenian leader who had strong pro-Spartan inclinations, Pericles rapidly became the recognized leader of the popular party, and from the year 443 on was annually re-elected one of the military commanders, or *strategoi*. His reforms and innovations brought down upon him the hatred of the party of landholding squires and other conservatives, very much as the reforms of one of his predecessors, Cleisthenes, half a century earlier, had also aroused the old guard. Many of these men identified Pericles' imperial moves with a dangerous scheme to extend and enforce democracy over all of Greece. Paradoxical as this may sound, in a sense this was what Pericles was out to do, hoping to set up popular governments on the Athenian model (under Athenian guidance, to be sure) as far as his fleets could reach. Many conservatives also thought he should not tangle with Sparta, whose oligarchic system they admired.

Others, living perhaps simply on their estates in Attica, and with mixed sensibilities, were antagonized by Pericles' costly visions of a beautified Athens. "Greece," one such voice said, "is surely suffering sore insult and manifest tyranny, when she sees that with the monies contributed perforce for the war we are gilding and adorning our city like a wanton woman, decking her with costly statues and offerings and thousand-talent temples." The more Pericles heard these objections, though, the more he seems to have been determined to push ahead and make of Athens, as he later declared, "the school of Hellas." The man who walked with Sophocles and Anaxagoras was no demagogue; yet he was a partisan, an expansionist, a believer in what we might call the Manifest Destiny of Athens—and this, while it inspired him and led to glory, invited catastrophe also.

To mention yet another paradox, perhaps this outward show of power would not have become so compulsive and great if Athens' own inner equilibrium had been greater. The glories of the Periclean age were mixed with uncertainties; perhaps there never was a supreme creative period so divided, often against itself. For all the posed perfection of a figure by Phidias, the Athenian mind of his generation seems to have been permeated by an increasing sense of flux. "*Panta rhei ouden menei*," ("All things flow, nothing remains the same"), the early philosopher Heraclitus of Ephesus is reported as saying, meaning that reality was something whose essence lay in "becoming," rather than in "being." This, again, was only a partial vision; all intelligent Greece had long been in search of lasting certainties, ideals, and laws amid the vagaries of change. But where to find them? By the latter half of the fifth century neither Olympian religion nor constituted moral codes seemed to provide them.

Religion? Attacks had been delivered not only upon the Olympian system but upon the very idea of gods in man's image, Xenophanes, a sixth-century Ionian philosopher, having remarked contemptuously that if donkeys had religion, they would no doubt imagine their gods in the shape of donkeys. Creation myths? To Anaxagoras, with his physics and metaphysics, they were a sheer laughingstock. Homeric legends and those of Hesiod and early bards came under sharp scrutiny also, and Euripides at one point was to go so far as to refer to myths and legends generally as "the wretched tales of poets"—as if he were not a poet too.

Ancient rules of tribal fealty and blood brotherhood of a rough chivalric sort had long persisted. Yet these, so often violated, were being brought into increasing question as well. Neighborliness, altruism, assistance to one's fellow man had never been among the particular Greek virtues; philanthropy, though the word is of Greek origin, was hardly practiced, beyond such customs as providing a free education to sons of soldiers killed in the wars. The good Greek was taught to love his friends and hate his enemies; to forgive an enemy was a sign of weakness. And now these old tribal loyalties were breaking down, too, amid the class and political conflicts of growing states. Was personal ambition or personal anger at a rebuff greater than devotion to the welfare of a polis? It often seemed so. Scheming for power, the Spartan chieftain Pausanias, victor at Plataea in 479 B.C., had entered into treasonable relations with the Persians. Themistocles of Athens, no lesser hero of the Persian wars than Pausanias, as well as the chief rebuilder of the city before Pericles, had fallen out with his people and deserted to the Persians, where he rounded out his life as a noble at the court of Artaxerxes. Whom could you trust?

Pericles, it is known, had large sums at his disposal for secret uses, including bribery. "At no time," says the other Pausanias, the Greco-Roman historian, "was Greece wanting in people afflicted with this itch for treason."

So the years of Athens' highest fulfillment were lived under the sign of much uncertainty and an increasingly precarious balance. On one hand stood the man of oligarchic persuasion and guardian of traditional mores; on the other, the man of experiment and venture, exemplified at his best by Pericles and at his worst by Pericles' young friend and protégé, the demagogic and irresponsible Alcibiades (a mixture of genius and fraud, and one day—when he allegedly played a part in smashing the city's sacred Herms—to be quite literally the image breaker of Athens). On one hand Attica, like other areas of Greece, still saw the persistence of primitive cults with their magic rites; supposedly self-reliant leaders still hung upon the latest cryptic sign from Delphi. On the other hand, Athens was the center of the urban sophisticate, the skeptic, the searcher after new lights.

Yet Athens itself was not wholly committed to urbanity and new lights either. So bitter was the strife between religion and science that at the height of the Periclean age, the study of astronomy was forbidden in Athens altogether, as threatening to lead to impiety—and this despite Pericles. Anaxagoras of Clazomenae was hailed before the Assembly on a charge of irreligion; and though Pericles saved his friend from what might well have been doom by arranging his escape, the leading scientific mind in fifth-century Greece had to set up school elsewhere.

Innovation in Athens had a way of leading to counterinnovation. Young Socrates, for instance, though a challenger of old dogmas, was inclined to dismiss science as an inferior concern; and, far from being an admirer of Periclean democracy, he was on his way to becoming one of the chief critics of it. The boisterous writer of comedy, Aristophanes, when setting out in his twenties to satirize all that he saw about him, did not pick tradition as the butt of one of his first important plays, *The Clouds*. Instead, he seized upon the new generation of fashionable doubters of religion, the followers of such men as Anaximander and Anaxagoras, whom he regarded as charlatans. In *The Clouds* he makes his assault all the funnier by presenting as chief charlatan and sophist an impersonation of Socrates, whose disdain of Sophists he blandly ignores. The character Socrates becomes increasingly pompous as he propounds his notions of an in inanimate, godless world. After a "Chorus of Clouds" has entered and the earthling Strepsiades cringes at a clap of thunder, we have this passage:

STREPSIADES
Name of Earth, what a voice! Solemn and holy and awful!
SOCRATES
These are the only gods there are. The rest are but figments.
STREPSIADES
Holy name of Earth! Olympian Zeus is a figment?
SOCRATES
Zeus? What Zeus? Nonsense. There is no Zeus.
STREPSIADES
        No Zeus?
Then who makes it rain? Answer me that.
SOCRATES
        Why, the Clouds,
of course.
        What's more, the proof is incontrovertible.
        For instance,
have you ever yet seen rain when you didn't see a cloud? But if your hypothesis were correct, Zeus could drizzle from an empty sky while the clouds were on vacation.

STREPSIADES

> By Apollo, you're right. A pretty
> proof.

And to think I always used to believe the rain was just Zeus
pissing through a sieve.

> All right, who makes it thunder?

Brrr. I get goosebumps just saying it.

SOCRATES

> The Clouds again,

of course. A simple process of Convection.

STREPSIADES

> I admire you,

but I don't follow you.

SOCRATES

> Listen. The Clouds are a saturate water-solution.

Tumescence in motion, of necessity, produces precipitation.
When these distended masses collide—boom!

> Fulmination.

STREPSIADES

But who makes them move before they collide? Isn't that Zeus?

SOCRATES

Not Zeus, idiot. The Convection-principle!

In his *Ecclesiazusae,* which was written several decades
later, Euripides was to take on the radical democratic leaders,
uplifters and utopians too, asking in effect the question, All
right, who's going to do all the daily work?—and in his *Lysistrata* he was to make his unique sexual argument for achieving
peace. All this was lively, bracing, and wonderfully diverting
for a society so adult as to be openly self-critical—up to a point,
that is. There was worry in Athens about so much criticism.
Aristophanes was held in question no less than Socrates. The
inquirer mixed with the scoffer, the idealist with the adventurer,

the political scientist with the rabblerouser, the poet with the propagandist: and the result, while phenomenal, was also parlous. Athens, although it had grown strong, was not so sure of its ways as to be totally secure, not so rich as to become satisfied. Its very nature, on the contrary, had developed into a most volatile one. So abounding in diverse energies and drives, it had either to proceed or erupt.

If in all this turbulence there was anything around which Athenians could gather in common emotion, irrespective of party or faith, it was undoubtedly the world of the great living dramatists—that of the tragedians, not of the ribald and derisive Aristophanes. You did not have to believe, any more than Euripides himself did, in Olympian religion and all the ancient myths to share in what was said and chanted there under the hillside auspices of Dionysus. Most of the audience shared in drama as a public moral rite, as few playgoers since have done, except for the medieval townsmen attending so-called morality plays, performed before the doors of cathedrals or on platforms set up in the market square. The dramatists were increasingly concerned with human character and its attempts at grace under fateful pressure; but always they remained preoccupied with moral law. Punishment or retribution follows flaw or *hubris,* as the dark follows the day—except when skeptical Euripides helps resolve and relieve a dread situation with a *deux ex machina* (quite literally, a god who descends from above by means of a machine).

The lesson of pride and fate, as illustrated by stories ranging from Aeschylus' *Oresteia* to Sophocles' Oedipus plays, became more and more pertinent and urgent as Athens' own *hubris* grew, though perhaps few in the vast applauding audiences grasped an immediate application. The English philosopher Alfred North Whitehead was one day to remark that the Greek tragedians, because of their belief in immutable law, were themselves, more than the Greek philosophers, the founders of

scientific thought. But their audiences, spellbound on seeing
the self-blinded Oedipus or Medea splotched with the blood of
her brood, were probably not thinking of scientific laws. They
were experiencing the purge of "pity and fear"—the function, as
Aristotle saw it, of tragedy. Presumably they were also being
chastened by the thought of a will greater than their own, when
for instance they heard the chorus in Sophocles' *Oedipus the
King* intone:

> *May destiny ever find me*
> *Pious in word and deed*
> *Prescribed by the law's that live on high:*
> *Laws begotten in the clear air of heaven,*
> *Whose only father is Olympus . . .*
> *Insolence breeds the tyrant, insolence*
> *If it is glutted with a surfeit, unseasonable, unprofitable,*
> *Climbs to the roof-top and plunges*
> *Sheer down to the ruin that must be . . .*

Here, both in the lines and between them, could be heard the
cautionary voice of a playwright who was also tutor and
prophet, counseling restraint and the "holy fear" that runs
through the Greek consciousness, though not calling for abject
submission or passivity. For "I pray that the God may never
abolish the eager ambition that profits the state," the chorus
goes on to say; it is only that a man, like a state, should be pru-
dent, recognizing limitations while exercising strengths:

> *If a man walks with haughtiness*
> *Of hand or word and gives no heed*
> *To Justice and the shrines of Gods*
> *Despises—may an evil doom*
> *Smite him for his ill-starred pride of heart!*

These lines of Sophocles, however, were probably first heard at the Great Dionysia in Athens, several years after the outbreak of the war with Sparta, when the holocaust of pride had already begun.

It is difficult today, in a time when the theatre at its best is an adjunct to life rather than a monitor of it, to think of this most successful and admired of Greek dramatists in a quasi-priestly role. Handsome, dashing, an athlete in his youth, genial and witty in his middle years, a great befriender of young men, twice one of the *strategoi* under Pericles, and the holder of many other public posts as well, author of possibly more than 120 plays, and vigorous enough to console himself in his old age with a *hetaira* by whom he had children, Sophocles seems the model of the highly endowed Athenian in balance. For fully thirty years, between Aeschylus' death in 456 B.C. and the fulfillment of young Euripides' promise by the 420's, he ruled the Athenian stage as splendidly as Pericles ruled the state. Yet he was also the man who saw far ahead, alive with warning, and who lived on, as Pericles did not, to see the collapse of so much pride and hope. As the Peloponnesian War led Athens from defeat to defeat, he wrote his sorrowing sequel to *Oedipus the King.* In *Oedipus at Colonus* he narrates the end of a great man fallen, though ennobled by ordeal; and this play rings to some like a dirge to Athenian greatness. In it the chorus is moved to speak in astonishingly dark and personal tones:

> *Though he has watched a decent age pass by,*
> *A man will sometimes still desire the world.*
> *I swear I see no wisdom in that man,*
> *The endless hours pile up a drift of pain*
> *More unrelieved each day and as for pleasure,*
> *When he is sunken in excessive age,*
> *You will not see his pleasure anywhere.*

The last attendant is the same for all,
Old men and young alike, as in its season
Man's heritage of underworld appears:
There being then no epithalamion,
No music and no dance. Death is the finish.
Not to be born surpasses thought and speech.
The second best is to have seen the light
And then to go back quickly whence we came.

This is a far cry indeed from the exuberant invocation to the promise of Athens that appears in the *Eumenides,* the culminating play of the Orestes trilogy. Aeschylus had written his paean to Athenian greatness and wisdom only fifty years earlier.

Equally dark is the tone of the aging Euripides, who in about 415 B.C. produced *The Trojan Women,* its legendary subject being the utter destruction of Troy and its more immediate theme the mindless ruination of war. He was writing at a parlous moment. Athens, already embroiled with Sparta, was about to send out a punitive expedition to Sicily that was to end ruinously. As if he sensed the outcome, he had Hecuba of Troy symbolically speak:

Ah, wretched me. So this is the unhappy end
And goal of all the sorrows I have lived. I go
Forth from my country and a city lit with flames.
Come, aged feet; make one last weary struggle, that I
May aid my city in its affliction. O Troy, once
So huge over all Asia in the dawn wind of pride,
Your very name of glory shall be stripped away.

For "Troy," read "Athens": the troubled and tormented mind of Euripides was putting out an impassioned plea for peace. He did not live long thereafter, but as a son of Greece's age of anxiety he lived long enough to see the worst of war. Upon his

death in 406, the Athenians gave him a funerary ceremony in
the Theatre of Dionysus, and the aged Sophocles was there to
lead actors in a masque to mourn him. Aristophanes also paid
handsome tribute to this man who had given so much to art
and to the state.

Though there was no Sarajevo to set off the greatest conflict
"yet known in history," as Thucydides called it, there had come
in 432 B.C., just after the Corcyra crisis, a collision over an even
more distant spot that led directly to the assize of arms. Potidaea was a remote outpost on the wild Macedonian coast of the
Aegean. It had been settled by Corinthians and remained much
under their influence, though it had also been made a tributary
ally of Athens. Fearful that Corinth might try to extend its
influence there, the Athenians ordered the Potidaeans to raze
their city walls and dismiss their Corinthian magistrates. This
the provoked men of Potidaea refused to do, and a general
revolt against Athens broke out in the area, to which Athens
responded by placing the city under siege (Socrates and young
Alcibiades both taking part in the attack). Corinthian leaders in
turn responded to this assault upon their colonists by trying to
incite the whole Peloponnesus to war. With disorder fast
spreading throughout the Greek world, Pericles took another
aggressive step: he proclaimed harsh trade decrees against
Corinth's ally Megara, on the nearby isthmus, excluding her
from all the empire's markets. This only increased the tension.
Parleys between Athens and the Peloponnesian League over the
rescinding of those decrees led nowhere, with the result that the
League presented an ultimatum requiring Athens to acknowl-
edge the independence of all Greek cities—that is, dissolve her
empire and thus humble herself.

The twenty-seven-year war that followed was actually a
series of wars interrupted by truces that solved nothing, by
treaties that were soon broken, by seasons of stand-off and

peacemaking efforts that soon gave way to resumption of
unbridled savagery. It was in part a tribal war, in the sense that
the heirs of the age-old contenders for primacy in Greece, the
Dorians and the Ionians, their ancient differences made more
acute by big-state rivalries, now struck at each other with the
ferocity of Teuton and Gaul in later ages. It was also a class war
in the sense that fellow friends of oligarchy often crossed these
tribal lines to help each other bring democracy down. It was in
many of its stages as much a civil war inside Athens and its
dominions as one among Greeks as a whole. It was a war for
commerce and empire, fought with the usual military weapons
of the time. Yet in its method it was also a distinctly psychological war, in which every device of emotional appeal, persuasion,
prejudice, and threat was deployed to sustain morale on one
side and undermine it on the other, and thus to augment iron
blades with mental shafts to determine either side's staying
power. It was the first modern war, and in some of its ramifica-
tions more akin to those of the twentieth century A.D. than
those even, say, of the eighteenth.

It was a dirty war, as civil wars usually are: mass executions
of prisoners, massacres of the disaffected, assassinations of
public leaders who had taken the wrong course, were the order
of the day. The Athenians slaughtered the adult citizens of
Melos and sold their women and children into slavery; later,
when the reviving oligarchic party of Athens routed the polis'
democrats in the time of worst military defeat, perhaps fifteen
hundred heads fell. For all the bravery of the hoplites and
sailors on either side and the particular brilliance of the Spartan
commander Lysander, much of the war's leadership was igno-
ble. Cleon of Athens, a rich and corrupt tanner's son who rose
to power by his part in throwing out Pericles and who then
turned demagogue, cynically warned his fellows against any
softness toward wavering allies on the ground that "your

empire is a despotism and your subjects disaffected conspirators, whose obedience is insured not by your suicidal conces-
sions, but by the superiority given you by your own strength
and not their loyalty." Indeed it had become a despotism,
Cleon's faction having put over the outrageous notion that the
war was not to be paid for by Athens itself, but by taxes
imposed on its tributaries. Even more outrageous was the
behavior of Cleon's rival, Alcibiades, the Periclean favorite—
showman, adventurer, rabble-rouser, roisterer, lady-killer, good
soldier, and traitor all in one—who became as much a menace
to his own city as he ever was to Sparta, his unbridled ambition
and personal instability ruining all of Pericles' designs.

Previous wars in historical times of Greek against Greek had
generally been brief, local encounters—often just a single clash
of arms between individual city-states, each mustering no more
than a few thousand soldiers. The Persian wars of course had
been of another character, with vast Asiatic hordes sent like
dumb beasts against the superior skills of the Hellenes. Now
these blooded Hellenes were out in full force against each other,
league against league, tooth and claw, driven to furious com-
mitment for almost a generation, their theatre of war eventually
extending all the way from Sicily to the Bosporus.

The forces were formidable: Sparta, supported by almost its
entire peninsula and by many states north of the Corinthian
Gulf as well, could muster some 30,000 crack hoplites plus
auxiliaries; Athens, on the other hand, had its strong fleet of
possibly 300 triremes (with additional squadrons from the
islands of Corcyra, Lesbos, Chios, in support) and a land force
of some 13,000 firstline infantry, which were backed by a small
cavalry and reserves of undetermined quality. The military
problem was clear: a great congregation of land forces was
confronting a sovereign sea power. (Among the Peloponnesian
states, only Corinth could muster a fleet of strength, while not

even the proudest Athenian could assume that his foot soldiers would be a match for Sparta's in a showdown.) Pericles, dictating strategy in the short time that remained to him before his death, saw the point entirely: let the Lacedaemonians attack us by land and wear themselves out by overrunning most of it, while we withdraw and stand securely behind our walls and bastions and at all costs preserve our command of the sea, its vital supply routes, its wealth, and in so doing, maintain the idea of an Athenian commonwealth. He had not forgotten Themistocles.

Pericles' strategy was wise, yet he did not live to execute it. In 430 B.C., just after the war's outbreak, an incalculable disaster struck Athens in the form of the plague, which decimated the masses of people drawn back behind the Athenian walls for safety and carried Pericles away too a year later. Athens did hold off Sparta to the point of a truce in the year 421 B.C., which even involved a fifty-year treaty of peace; but in 415 B.C., Alcibiades, taking advantage of this pause, promoted and made himself one of the leaders of a huge expedition to Sicily designed to subjugate strong, independent Syracuse and all the other Dorian settlements there as well. In this way the whole Peloponnesus would be outflanked and the Ionian Sea, between Greece and Sicily, converted into another Athenian lake. This was a complete reversal of Pericles, who had learned enough to know just how much Athens could safely attempt. Alcibiades' frivolous scheme involved, as Thucydides tells us, "by far the most costly and splendid Hellenic force that had ever been sent out by a single city up to that time" (4,000 Athenian heavy infantry, 300 horses, and 100 galleys, accompanied by 50 Lesbian and Chian vessels and many more besides). And it came to utter grief at Syracusan hands, its men—the elite of Athens' soldiery—all being either killed or enslaved. Meanwhile Alcibiades, who was recalled to account for his part in the affair of the

smashed Herms, deserted to the Spartan side and made contact
with the Persians as well, who stood waiting on the eastern
sidelines with revenge in their minds.

This was the most bitter of hours yet for Athens, but worse
was still to come. Sparta, seeing the empire of its enemy in such
disarray, renewed the war. Syracuse joined in, and Persia lent a
helping financial hand from afar. One by one the Athenian
allies, like Alcibiades himself, deserted. The Athenian treasury,
which only a decade before had been drawing close to 500 tal-
ents a year from its Delian tributaries, was all but bankrupt.
Social revolts, both conservative and radical, swept the uncertain system which Pericles had sought to bring into some sort
of equilibrium. Many of the slave workers of the Athenian
mines of Laurium deserted, and the mines were closed. The
reviving oligarchic party of Athens revolted also, abolishing the
Assembly and setting up in 411 B.C. a Council of Four Hundred
to liquidate the democrats and to make peace with Sparta on
collaborationist terms. Soon thereafter a counterrevolution, led
by surviving democrats in Athens, broke out. They in turn liq-
uidated the Four Hundred, substituted a limited assembly of
five thousand citizens—and called back Alcibiades with a promise of full amnesty!

Let Thucydides, who saw and endured all this, have the last
word about its degradation: "Thus every form of iniquity took
root in the Hellenic countries by reason of the troubles. The
ancient simplicity into which honor so largely entered was
laughed down and disappeared; and society became divided
into camps in which no man trusted his fellow. To put an end to
this, there was neither promise to be depended upon, nor oath
that could command respect; but all parties dwelling rather in
their calculation upon the hopelessness of a permanent state of
things, were more intent upon self-defense than capable of
confidence."

What was perhaps most surprising was that in these years of combined onslaught, division, and desertion, Athens held out as long as it did. Nearly ten more years were needed to break its power and spirit. In 407 B.C., after being pardoned, Alcibiades gained a round of victories in the eastern Aegean, but when a fleet under his command had been destroyed by the Peloponnesians, he went into exile. Now the last resources of Athens were mobilized to raise still another fleet to save the vital grain supply routes from the Bosporus. This armament of perhaps 180 vessels, incompetently led and indifferently manned, was caught off guard by Lysander's squadrons at Aegospotami on the Hellespont. Alcibiades, who in this disorder had tried once again to reinstate himself, soon after met a not undeserved death at the hands of the Phrygians.

This was the end. When news of the abject naval defeat reached Athens, Xenophon tells us, a sound of wailing rose along the Long Walls: "That night no one slept." Denuded of fleets, supplies, and allies, Athens behind its walls soon caved in under siege and signed a total surrender. The terms were that its empire be wholly dissolved, its Long Walls be razed, its remaining warships be forfeited (although in the end Athens was permitted to retain twelve galleys), its numerous antidemocratic exiles be allowed to return (with the thought that they would assume power), and that the city become an ally (that is, a subordinate) of Sparta. Pro-Spartan turncoats, we are told, took joyfully to tearing down the walls hand in hand with their conquerors; and a new regime of oligarchs known as the Thirty Tyrants and led by the vindictive Critias declared a virtual holiday of judicial murder of many of the supporters of democracy.

In this turmoil of humiliation and betrayal, surviving Athenian patriots sought to strike back from exile. Led by Thrasybulus, they managed within a year to oust the Thirty (who had further dishonored themselves by calling in a Spartan

garrison to man the Acropolis) and to restore the old constitution. Among the Athenians, filled with a sense of having been
abandoned by their gods, there was also a hunt for scapegoats
in the form of men who had failed them, or misled them.

Alcibiades was dead; cruel Critias had been killed in battle.
The most vulnerable person remaining in the Athens of 400 B.C.
was old Socrates, the perpetual critic and disrespecter of
accepted beliefs—old-line ones on this hand and new democratic ones on the other. It was the returning democrats who
hailed him into the dock on a charge of impiety and corruption
of youth. The legend has long persisted, launched by Plato and
Xenophon (both of them antidemocrats) that the old man was
the victim of a political vendetta. This does not appear to be
true. He was placed before a jury of 501 citizens chosen by lot
from the annual roster of many thousands of talesmen representing the whole voting body politic, following the system
developed by Pericles himself. What is true is that a majority of
this vast people's jury found him guilty as charged, and so tes-
tified to their own fears and doubts and disarray.

So the wisest and shrewdest mind of Athens became the
martyr for its failings, and in taking the hemlock ended its
Golden Age. Still, by no means all was lost to the city. Vengeful
Sparta, having won its victory under the slogans of liberation
from Athenian oppression and self-determination of Greek
states, proved a harder taskmaster than ever Athens was, post-
ing garrisons as far as its arms could reach—and a far less capable one too, being ignorant of trade or of the management of
any men other than soldiers. Athens had grown great partly
through its leadership in the Persian wars and its championship
of the Greeks of Asia Minor. Sparta, having accepted Persian
gold to help vanquish Athens in the final stage, promptly abandoned the Ionian Greeks to the Persian realm. Soon Corinth and
Thebes, its former allies, were to turn against it, as dubious of

its hegemony as they had been fearful of Athens'. Athens, chastened in defeat and trying to revive itself, was to many Greeks a more attractive presence than semiliterate Sparta in triumph. The word must have traveled up and down the peninsula that, as Plato himself remarked in a letter, "In general, the restored democratic party of Athens behaved justly and equitably."

To be sure, shorn of empire, decimated, all but subjugated. Athens was never to be again what it had been. Thebes, Corinth, Sparta, Athens itself, were to contend along with lesser states in a kind of vacuum of which no one could be the master. If there were any victors of the Peloponnesian War, they were the Persians, who saw the Greeks in fratricidal chaos, and the rough Macedonians of the north, who were soon to be heard from in history. But Athens, though it had lost its glory and much of its spirit, still had its incomparable mind. It had Plato, only twenty-three when the war ended, who amid all his disillusionment gave forth over the next generation the most intricate and poetic body of high thought and reflection uttered in any autumnal age. It was next to have Aristotle, born twenty years after war's end, who trudged down from the northern hills to become at seventeen a disciple of Plato, then sixty-one, and who soon became Greece's precentor in logic, political science, general philosophy, biology, grammar, aesthetics, and morals: so versatile and lasting a precentor, in fact, that Dante, eighteen centuries later, spoke of him as "the Master of all we know." Yet Aristotle, born of Plato, who in turn was born of the light of Socrates, was also in his lifetime to become the personal teacher of young Alexander of the mountainous kingdom of Macedonia, who overran all the Greeks and most of the known world—though not according to Aristotelian principles. The Delphic oracle, devious and inscrutable, had foretold much. But it never foretold all that.

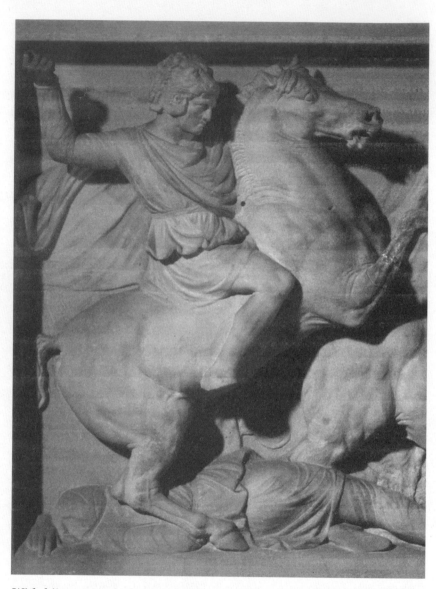

With his conquest of a vast empire, the Macedonian king Alexander the Great, who is shown above, disseminated Hellenic culture throughout the eastern Mediterranean and western Asia.

IX

FINAL HARVEST

Until philosophers are kings, or the kings and princes of this world have the spirit and power of philosophy, and political greatness and wisdom meet in one . . . cities will never have rest from their evils—no, nor the human race, as I believe . . .

—Plato, The Republic

Although few of us read Plato's Laws, yet hundreds of thousands have made use of Alexander's laws and continue to use them.

—Plutarch, On the Fortune of Alexander

Greece, a land in which brilliant, high weather is usually prolonged through the month of September and then gives way abruptly to the coming of the rains and the darkening of the land, does not know the pleasures of autumn, as say, New England knows them. The Greek countryman sees the leaves fall, the vintage brought in, the furrows for winter sowing plowed; but he generally lacks the experience of that season when all the landscape is transfigured into a shimmering haze of final glow, the very weather standing still in a calm that is all the more poignant because everyone knows that any day the wind and frost will come and bring all color down. Yet Greece, without this annual interval of blazing life before the onset of the dark, experienced in its history a long, rich autumn of its own in the fourth century B.C.

It was a time, to be sure, of diminishing vitality. The sap, the essential Greek lifeblood, ran both thinner and slower than it had in the high summer of the fifth century. Until the final quarter of the fourth, it was not yet diluted by the Macedonian strain, but its traditional strength can be seen gradually declining almost decade by decade. This is most apparent in tragic drama and architecture, both of which came almost to a creative standstill, and in public mores, which even in victorious Sparta lost their old rigor. It is least apparent in sculpture and philosophy, which achieved triumphs of increasing refinement, though at the cost of a certain ruggedness of concept and contour. The sciences flourished while traditional religion shriveled, giving way to agnosticism on one hand and to mystery cults on the other. The old polis disintegrated as a viable institution, and there was no working ideal of another kind of community to replace it.

In the tragic drama, there was no successor to Aeschylus, Sophocles, and the ever-troubled Euripides—the latest of whose works, such as the *Iphigenia in Aulis* and the *Bacchae,* had portrayed a chaotic world without a moral order to help man find his way. After them, the fount dried up. In comedy Aristophanes, having exuberantly mocked the philosophers, the warriors, the moralists, and the amoralists alike, declined into rambling farce in his last known play, the *Plutus* of 388 B.C. He was followed by what is known to literary historians as the Middle Comedy; it was not until very late in the century that the New Comedy arose, its most talented playwright being Menander, whose witty commentaries on everyday mores were widely prized and were later adapted for the Roman stage by Plautus and Terence. (Of his plays, only portions of the originals had escaped oblivion until the discovery of an ancient papyrus of a complete comedy, the *Dyskolos,* in 1957.)

As epic poetry and tragic drama had withered away with the passing of the gods, lyric poetry too declined in this mundane era. Skillful versifiers maintained the technique of amatory and reflective form, but there was no Hesiod or Sappho in the fourth century. The writing of history itself, so brilliantly begun by Herodotus and Thucydides, weakened in a time when there was very much to record. True, fourth-century historians were legion in Athens, and Ephorus was probably more widely read in the Hellenistic period than Thucydides; but the only chronicler comparable to the earlier masters was Xenophon, the stirring author of the *Anabasis,* describing the march of the Ten Thousand, which he led across Asia Minor.

In architecture there was no fourth-century successor to the virile Parthenon of the fifth. There were lesser temples in profusion, generally showing an absorption with the graceful Ionic style and its ornaments and motifs, but one would be hard put to single out any of those that have survived as equal in originality to the Ionian Erechtheum of the preceding century or in jewel-like balance to the little shrine of Athena Nike at the edge of the Acropolis. Indeed, apart from developing theatre construction in such superb hillside designs as that at Epidaurus or devising the leafy Corinthian capital, fourth-century Greek architects and engineers showed a marked decline in originality and enterprise.

Yet the face of Greece showed little change in the fourth century from the preceding one. The style of its sculpture, to be sure, did change rapidly in the hands of such masters as Praxiteles, Scopas, and Lysippus, peopling its temples and agoras with figures of increasing individuality and stir. In painting, a master of the first rank arose shortly after mid-century in the person of Apelles, whose portraits of living persons and panels of mythological scenes were considered to be the marvels of the age. Many anecdotes are told of this fashionable and engaging man—none more familiar than that concerning a day when Alexander of Macedonia posed for a portrait with his royal steed Bucephalus. Alexander, apparently not happy with the rendering of his horse, had Bucephalus brought into the studio for a closer look. Bucephalus, the story says, whinnied with approval at the sight of the panel, and the artist turned to Alexander to say, "Your horse seems to know more about painting than you do." Yet, great as Apelles' reputation was, his art suffered the ravages of time, and not one trace of it survives.

To many a man today, fourth-century Greece is more ambiguous and difficult to assess than is Greece of the classical age. Amid its curious declines or lapses in some areas and its high achievements in others, however, several things stand out. Greece, as the century wore on, was a more cosmopolitan and relaxed place to live in than before. Its internecine struggles had not devastated it; they had simply sapped and modified it. Though many of the best men of Athens had been killed or banished, the Greeks had learned not to make a holocaust of civil strife. The Spartans themselves, for all their severity as taskmasters, grew so prosperous from the tributes they exacted from vanquished states that they began to take on many of the worldly ways of their victims; wealthy Spartan families enjoyed creature comforts undreamed of by Lycurgus or the austere Leonidas. The Athenians, for their part, having seen their state battered and shamed, were of a mind to doubt its old virtues. All over Greece the old, strict sense of obligation of each citizen to his polis waned, and men of substance withdrew more and more into private pursuits and pleasures, leaving the conduct of public affairs to professionals.

It was an age of the political manager, the public rhetorician, the intellectual specialist, the hired attorney, the dawning civil servant, and the mercenary soldier as well—all employments which the old Greek polis had either deplored or hardly envisaged in its unique and imaginative notion that all qualified citizens should participate on every level in affairs of state. To be sure, the polis idea had often been nobler in thought than in realization. In Athens, for instance, it had not been helped by

the gradual introduction of daily pay for civic duties that had
originally been regarded as freely given. That scheme, applied
first to jurymen in Pericles' time, had been extended by about
400 to provide a daily fee to any citizen willing to take the
trouble simply to attend the sessions of the Assembly. The
intention of the democratic party, then in command, was
understandable enough: it was to ensure that citizens of small
means, hard put to take time off from their regular employments, would not suffer when joining in public activity, and
that they would appear in such numbers as not to be outvoted
by those of ampler means. Its result, though, was to amass on
the Pnyx and around the law courts hordes of hangers-on and
petty job-seekers, many of them of meager qualifications and
out for a government dole of a drachma or more a day. Such an
environment itself lowered the tone of public life and caused
increasing numbers of better qualified citizens to turn away
from it in disdain. The philosopher Isocrates, a severe critic of
what he felt to be the excesses of democracy in his home city of
Athens, remarked that if the Assembly was to be paid, it ought
to be paid by Athens' enemies, since it made so many blunders.

Yet while Isocrates worried and Plato sought to do away
with popular government entirely, by substituting rule by the
"best," the weaknesses of the polis idea lay much deeper; for the
polis had been overtaken not so much by spoilsmen and incom-
petents as by history. Devised in a simpler age, it was proving
itself no longer adequate to the demands of a far more complex
one, with the increasing intricacies of Greek alliances and
counteralliances that extended over the entire Mediterranean
area. The day called for the amalgamation of small squabbling
Greek states into one great design; but for all the sharpness and
breadth of the Greek mind, no genius arose who could achieve
that, even though Isocrates preached it. On the contrary, Plato
and Aristotle, the leading political philosophers, went on prais-

ing the small, independent polis as the ideal state, while deploring its Athenian democratic form in practice. Many city-states had banded together, intermittently, to resist the Persian invader; but now, a century later, the idea of effective Greek unification was as remote as ever.

Instead, particularism and feuding went on, first Sparta exerting hegemony, then Athens reviving, then Thebes coming to the fore, and faraway Syracuse extending its own sway. The Greek states remained as obstinately divided and parochial as ever, but the traditional pride and patriotism of the individual citizen withered away. During the Peloponnesian War Sparta had accepted Persian aid against Athens; in 393 B.C. or thereabouts a humbled Athens in turn accepted Persian assistance in rebuilding the Long Walls, pulled down by Spartan order. In Athens, moreover, a principle particularly cherished under the constitutions of Cleisthenes and Pericles had been abandoned with ill effects upon the cohesion of the state. Under the old polity, it was assumed that a citizen chosen for office would stand ready to serve in a civilian and military capacity both. But during the long years of the Peloponnesian War, the demand for soldiers had been so great that city-states were forced to recruit mercenaries to augment their citizen armies. The result was a caste of paid warriors whose purpose was more the pursuit of arms than patriotism as such, and the old concept of the citizen-soldier and of the unity of civil and military functions dissolved.

The end of the Peloponnesian War left many of these professionals without employers. They then hired themselves out to foreign states, sometimes taking with them whole contingents of the best hoplites into alien pay. All told, during the first quarter of the fourth century at least 25,000 Greeks were probably in active mercenary service somewhere, and the total may later have reached 50,000. Their achievements in fields abroad added luster to Greek arms, but not stature to their states.

Of these mercenaries, one of the most famous and successful was a young Athenian noble, Xenophon, who in 401 B.C. went into Persian service with the Ten Thousand, an army of Greek soldiers employed to assist one royal side in a dynastic struggle against another. For the Persians, under the line of kings following Cyrus, Darius, and Xerxes, who came to grief at Salamis, were undergoing internal strife too. When Darius II, monarch during the time of the Peloponnesian War, died, he left two sons: the younger was a prince named Cyrus, who was a satrap in Asia Minor and a strong friend of Sparta; the other was an elder brother who took the throne under the name of Artaxerxes II. To help oust Artaxerxes and install the young pretender Cyrus was the mission of these Greek soldiers of fortune. In his *Anabasis* Xenophon vividly described the concentration of the Greek mercenaries in Mesopotamia, their smashing victory over Artaxerxes' forces at Cunaxa, the tragic death of Cyrus in battle, and the collapse of his cause. When the Greek generals were treacherously murdered by their Persian employers, the isolated soldiers elected Xenophon to lead them on the long, hard march homeward across arid, hostile Asia Minor. After weeks of struggle they finally, with unbounded joy, caught sight of the sea, the Black Sea. Thus Xenophon describes the climactic moment of his emaciated men:

"They came to the mountain on the fifth day, the name of the mountain being Thekes. When the men in front reached the summit and caught sight of the sea there was great shouting. Xenophon and the rear guard heard it and thought that there were some more enemies attacking in the front, since there were natives of the country they had ravaged following them up behind. . . . However, when the shouting got louder and drew nearer, and those who were constantly going forward started running towards the men in front who kept on shouting, and the more there were of them the more shouting there was, it looked then as though this was something of considerable importance. So Xenophon mounted his horse and, taking Lycus and the cavalry with him, rode forward to give support, and, quite soon, they heard the soldiers shouting out 'The sea! The sea!' and passing the word down the column."

There are few passages in all the chronicle of struggle and adventure that surpass the graphic force and vividness of this one.

Yet, just what was Xenophon struggling for? He was a restive Athenian attracted to Persia for pay and also, perhaps, because of the lure of the sheer vastness of its realm compared to the smallness of Greece. Like many other Athenians, he was also attracted to Sparta and its authoritarian ways. Later, he joined a Spartan expedition against the Persians and became an honored resident of Sparta, recipient of a rich estate and busied with writing apologetics in succinct prose in defense of his latest adopted city. Athens banished him for his wandering loyalties, as it had condemned his master Socrates for his supposedly subversive teachings. Yet there was a fundamental difference: Socrates, while as disenchanted with Athenian democracy as Xenophon, was wedded to an integrity of his own; Xenophon, for all his individuality and literary gifts, was basically a soldier of fortune—the Greek precursor of the Renaissance *condottierre*.

So able and brave, yet in his way unstable, Xenophon characterizes much of this equivocal age. In it, patriotism mixed with betrayal; hard rationalism, with Orphic cult or with Eleusinian mysteries; ancestral ties, with disdain of them; new science, with disdain of that too; idealism, with gross hedonism or self-interest; learned philosophy, with what one might call anti-philosophy, in the form of the Cynics' mockery of Plato and his school.

The Cynic persuasion arose among thinkers who were dubious of high-flown metaphysical speculations and particularly of Plato's teaching that physical appearances were merely "shadows," and that only the "ideal" was "real." (The Greek term "cynic" had the connotation of "doggishness," not that of over-all doubt and sneering, as we use it today; the school probably took its name from the nickname applied to one of its leaders, Diogenes, "The Dog.") Against the aristocratic Plato's lofty disdain of the material world, the Cynics set forth their own concept: divest yourself of earthly needs and possessions, but do this for the purpose of getting back to nature and its illumination, not away from it. The Cynic school was founded by Antisthenes, an Athenian philosopher, who argued that most pleasures are treacherous and do not contribute to happiness; his goal, which he realized in his own life, was to find self-fulfillment in ascetic poverty. Diogenes, his pupil, took this "back-to-the-natural" doctrine to the extreme, holding that happiness is reached by satisfying only one's natural needs and by doing so in the most natural way, even as animals do. To exemplify this, he himself lived almost literally like a dog in the streets, sheltered only in a cask, or clay storage jug, and relieving himself in public. Repellent as he may have been in person, he was obviously a winning wit. Once, when a threat of war aroused the rich and comfortable Corinthians to drill and train, he took his cask and rolled it back and forth across their agora, explaining, "When everybody is so busy, I thought I should contribute something." Later, in one of the most familiar anecdotes of Greek history, the conquering Alexander of Macedonia paid a call on Diogenes. He found the old shaggy man lying in the gutter near his cask; when he asked if there was any service he could render, Diogenes' curt response was, "Stand out of the sunlight."

This was undoubtedly less philosophy than it was pose—indeed, it was outright exhibitionism. Showmanship, though of a more decorous kind, appeared also in the craft of a new kind of performer—the *rhetor,* or professional public speaker, as trained to his calling as any masked actor of Aeschylus' plays. He was often a skilled lawyer (it was only recently that Athens had accepted the notion of the paid attorney, its old principle having been that any accused man should stand up on his own in court and defend himself in his own words as best he could). Drama being in decline, oratory became a sort of art form and a source of entertainment in itself: rhetors were known on occasion to rehearse their speeches before mirrors in order to gauge gestures and possible effects, and became renowned as they delivered themselves of scathing attacks on their opponents—the more violent the assault and the more pungent the reply, the better the show all around.

The art, or rather craft, of forensic advocacy (which the Greeks were to hand on to the Romans, and the Romans to us) arose in large part from Sophist teachers and their techniques of persuasion and of outpointing opponents. Occasionally it produced a major figure, as in Isocrates, a brilliantly gifted pamphleteer and polemicist who founded his own school of rhetoric in Athens about 392 B.C. Though a critic of Athenian democracy, this forceful and articulate man was sincerely dedicated to the cause of Athenian revival and moreover to Greek unity as a whole. He lived to the age of ninety-eight, always talking, always writing, always summoning his fellow citizens to action. It was perhaps largely under his goading influence that the city aroused itself from a certain lethargy to create a new maritime league designed chiefly to curb further Spartan extension—only to be overtaken by neighboring

Thebes, which under the highly effective general Epaminondas threw the Spartans out of central Greece at the battle of
Leuctra in 371 B.C. This was a decisive victory, which, with
Epaminondas' consequent invasion of Sparta's own home valleys, marked the breaking of Sparta's power for all time. But it
left the whole question of leadership among the Greeks in
abeyance once again.

A second Athenian master of the public mind then came
forth in the person of Demosthenes, the greatest orator to arise
before the Roman Cicero, and one of the most stirring flayers
of public morals to arise before Savonarola, and also one of
the most successful practicing attorneys of all time. He was
brilliant, yet shot through with contradiction; he lived self-
indulgently and collected enormous fees, yet spoke with a stern
tongue of prophecy and died bravely. Born to wealth and
schooled in rhetoric, he early made himself a master in complex
topics of civil suit—estate, inheritance, and the whole area of
what we call the law of torts. A superb trial lawyer (it was said
of him that he could prepare briefs for either party with equal
ease) and a lobbyist in the Assembly for measures in behalf of
his clients, he also served as a strict public prosecutor out to
trap those who had done the state some wrong. Personally
relaxed in morals—he apparently had liaisons with a large number of youths and women alike over the four decades of his
prime—he nevertheless upbraided his fellow citizens for their
laxity and lack of probity. Apparently in foreign pay at one
point (the charge was made and never denied that he had
accepted Persian money to arouse the Athenians against Macedonia), he stood out as the first leading Athenian to recognize
the rising Macedonian threat for what it was.

Philip II, a highly virile, lusty, and shrewd chieftain from
Macedonia, had in 359 B.C. made himself the feudal master of
the rough tribesmen of the mountains and plains of northern

Greece. He then had begun to conceive a scheme of aggran-
dizement against the Greek states themselves, planning to place
his kingdom at their head, as Athens had once led the Delian
League. Soon he also conceived the idea of a joint expedition
against the Persians at the Bosporus and beyond. A bold and
original organizer of fighting men, he improved on the old
Greek system of close-ranked spearmen by devising a more
open and mobile scheme: his phalanxes, bearing long spears,
were supported by well-armored swordsmen, by archers who
shot over the swordsmen's heads, and by cavalry sweeping
around the flanks. Thus armed, he seized several northern
Greek cities but was momentarily blocked by the resistance of
Athens. But soon he was able to take advantage of a war
among Greek states that had broken out over the seizure of the
sanctuary of Apollo at Delphi and its treasury by the Phocians.
Amid the turmoil a number of states called on Philip for help,
and he was swift to respond, descending from the northern
passes to be welcomed by many Greeks as a liberator and protector of the shrine. Not by Demosthenes, however, who as
patriot, democrat, and leader of the resistance party, launched
in 351 B.C. an extraordinary series of trumpet calls to his com-
patriots, warning them that the liberator might well be an
enslaver. What he said, in the ringing orations known as
Philippies, was that the new rising power in Macedonia was a
threat to the Athenians, that Athens should consolidate all its
forces to stand ready to meet it, that the city should seek allies,
but that in any case it might have to bear the brunt of a Macedonian attack itself and thus must stand forth to lead as it had
led in earlier days—if need be, alone. In the midst of his rolling
periods, reminding Athenians of their past greatness, he did not
hesitate to pour obloquy on what he felt to be their latter-day
decay, crying out that the old Athenian courage had given way

to cowardice, discipline to disorder, ancient decency to corruption.

While the Athenians listened to their great tribune thundering against both Philip and their own fallen ways, then also heard other orators arguing that, far from fearing or resisting the Macedonians, the Greeks should accept their leadership. Aged Isocrates in 346 B.C. sent an open letter to Philip encouraging him to unite the quarrelsome city-states of Greece and to lead them against the Persians, still overlords of the Greeks on the Ionian coast. Alternately accommodating and opposing the aggressive hillmen of the north, the Athenians did make a strong military stand against Philip at Chaeronea in Boeotia in 338 B.C. But by now the time was very late. With little support other than that of Thebes, they were soundly trounced by Philip's phalanxes, his eighteen-year-old son Alexander leading the cavalry that helped sweep the field. The dismayed and divided Greeks now stood in the presence of what was in effect the first European nation—that is, a whole people spread over many provinces, but centrally administered—and their leaders accepted victorious Philip's call to meet with him for what could be called a "unity" conference at Corinth. The following year he set forth a plan for a joint expedition against Persia (as Isocrates had counseled); with it he gave an assurance that the individual Greek states' autonomy would be preserved, provided they followed him as their commander in chief. This summons, backed by Macedonian lancers, appealed to many a Greek—though it did not move so stalwart a patriot as Demosthenes, for all the deference Philip voiced to Athens as the torchbearer of Hellenic civilization. He had already paid his respects to it: anxious to acquire an Athenian gloss for his royal house, he had engaged Aristotle as his son Alexander's tutor when the boy was only thirteen.

Events now moved with gathering rapidity. In 336 B.C. Philip was murdered by one of his own retainers in a palace conspiracy, which led to uprisings both among northern tribes and in Greek cities against the suzerainty of his house (Demosthenes again being the chief Athenian agitator). But Alexander, barely twenty, at once seized the throne, although his legitimate claim to it had been disputed, and proclaimed his phenomenal mastery of men by subduing outlying tribes in lightning raids and descending upon the disaffected Greek states like a wolf upon the fold. He knew there had been conspiracy between some Greeks and Persia against Macedonia after his father's death; he razed Thebes as an example, yet spared Athens on receiving its submission. With the allegiance of almost all shaken Greece in hand, he embarked in 334 B.C. on the venture that exceeded the furthest dreams of Philip—not just the reduction of the Persian power, but the subjugation of as much of the eastern world as possible to Hellas, of which this astonishing and possessed spirit now felt himself to be the leader. In this mighty march of empire, many heads had to fall: among them was the brave Demosthenes, whom Athenian collaborationists delivered into Macedonian hands soon after Alexander's death; doomed to the fate usually meted out to resistance leaders, he forestalled his enemies by committing suicide.

During the long period of erosion of Greek faith and pride, and the emergence in its stead of a union of force led by northern chieftains whom the Greeks themselves considered barbarians, the two greatest living minds in Greece itself had been hard at work, building structures of their own—in the abstract. Of the two, one thinks of Plato as the more lofty, the more poetic, the more imaginative, and certainly the more readable; of Aristotle as the more systematic, the more didactic, the more encompassing in the vast range of his investigations, and since he lacked Plato's grace of discourse, as the more forbidding

today. Over the centuries, a special, almost mystical aura has
surrounded Plato, the pupil and interpreter of Socrates, as perhaps the strongest spiritual presence in the Western world
before the coming of Jesus of Nazareth. To many minds Aristotle, Plato's pupil, is, on the other hand, the hard dialectician
who cast a confining spell over an entire Christian era, because
medieval theologians accepted his teachings without question,
at the expense of freedom and advance of thought.

Though Plato at first reading may seem by far the more
palatable of the two, it can be argued (and it has often been
argued, particularly in modern times) that he was one of the
most reactionary, inhibited, and authoritarian minds to arise in
the spaciousness of ancient Greece. For, although highly
revered as the embodiment of Greek humanism, he was also
profoundly at odds with it—alienated, we might say today. The
problem of Plato is not simply that he deplored democracy, as
we have seen, on the basis of its Athenian practice, and pro-
pounded in his *Republic* a utopia of a rigidly hierarchic state
ruled by a specifically trained elite. The problem is much
broader. He frowned not only on Homeric myths but also on the
works of the tragedians and on much of the art and music of
his own day as being unedifying, proposing for his ideal state a
rigid censorship of art and literature to guard against what
might seem to its governors to be unwholesome. This curious
personality, who wrote poems and epigrams in his youth and
was in maturity surely the most accomplished man of letters of
his time, virtually banished poets from his ideal society; he
even deplored reliance on books in Greece's existing society,
fearing that this might weaken man's powers of memory. Moreover, he mistrusted all sciences save those of mathematics,
geometry, and astronomy, fearing that they would place undue
emphasis upon the evidences of the senses as against the ineffable, abstract truth that exists beyond the senses.

Behind all this lies his teaching (for the most part given as if through the voice of Socrates) that all impressions received by our senses are fragmentary and misleading, if not false, and tell us nothing of the true nature of things. Arguing that behind physical appearances and what he calls "the rabble of the senses," with their misshapen, passing images, there lies a realm of ineffable, perfect, eternal order which alone embodies "reality," he is preaching a doctrine of two worlds—one visible and one invisible. He is in effect saying that science, in its efforts to explore physical phenomena, is merely pursuing chimeras or "shadows." More than that, he is rejecting one traditional Greek ideal by arguing that man is in a state of disharmony between an evil, imperfect body and a divine spirit that enters into the body but is not part of it. Man, then, can attain fulfillment not by developing all his faculties of physical grace and intellectual insight together, but by divesting himself of all that is this-worldly and pursuing the transcendental light that lies yonder.

From this, in practical terms, it follows that man's leaders should be an aristocracy of philosophers or philosopher-kings who have clearly perceived such a light—unlike the rest of us who (to cite his famous metaphor) remain mentally imprisoned as if in a cave, seeing only shadows. Only a few elect can attain this illumination, which alone embodies truth and thus the idea of God, and they will give us the inspired Word. Plato was evidently infatuated with his concept of imprisonment in a cave, since it was figuratively such a confinement that he proposed for most of mankind: creative experiment in art, empirical studies of the world, and new movements in social organization were taboo unless specifically sanctioned by his philosopher-policeman. Rarely has a scheme been designed that is so rigid and so regardless of human capacities as this one evolved by the master of the grove of Academus. The inquiring Plato, born of skepticism, hardened into the absolutist who held that each man must fit into a preordained order of things (at top, the guardians, next the soldiers, below them the common people) and who thus projected Greece toward the acceptance of a dictator. In his ideal, the dictator to be accepted was a spiritualizing one, to be sure—which may help explain why so many men have considered Plato, in a distant sense, a prophet of Christ the King. But the dictator whom Greece actually received was of quite another character. He was the imperious, daemonic Alexander of Macedonia, half-wild, half highly cultivated, possessed by the notion that through his mother he was descended from Achilles and must outdo Achilles' deeds, ablaze with the ambition to conquer and unite the entire known world of the eastern Mediterranean and beyond, and ready, as his conquests succeeded, to have himself worshiped as an oriental god-king.

Plato died in 347 B.C.; he could not possibly have forseen the revolutionary changes that Alexander, then only nine years old, would soon make in the Greek world. Plato's pupil Aristotle would live long enough to be able to ponder his own theories of the advantages of small communities over large ones in the light of historical developments; for his death did not come until 322 B.C., one year after the death of *his* pupil Alexander.

The young king who accomplished in a few years the incredible feat of not only uniting all men of Greek language but also of extending Greek influence as far as India did in many ways resemble the legendary Achilles, whom he strove to emulate. Just as Achilles had come from the very fringe of Achaean culture, so Alexander was a half outsider too. And indeed his Macedonia, despite its nationhood, was more akin in daily life to the pastoral, tribal ways of Homeric society than to those of urbane Athens. Like Achilles, he was phenomenal in personal beauty and unpredictable in behavior, one day chivalrous, kind, sunny, generous, and on the next possessed by frenzies of savage rage or withdrawn into brooding darkness. From

his father Philip he no doubt inherited his lordly vitality and
iron skill; from his mother, the fiery princess Olympias of
northerly Epirus, who was rumored to have joined in Dionysian
rites of the wildest sort, his uncontrolled temper and his instability. He loved his friend Hephaestion as dearly as Achilles had
loved Patroclus; he loved women too; he also loved—or said he
loved—philosophy, and he wrote to Aristotle: "For my part, I
assure you, I had rather excel others in the knowledge of what
is excellent, than in the extent of my power and dominion." But
despite this protestation, his chief lust was for glory.

He had, or acquired as he advanced, a vision of cultural and
political union of East and West under Greek, and particularly
Macedonian, hegemony; and he took with him a retinue of
court philosophers, surveyors, chroniclers, and engineers, as
Napoleon was to do when entering Egypt. Yet he burned King
Darius III's capital at Persepolis, killed or tortured the brave
defenders of Gaza to the last man, and in anger at Tyre's resistance had his levies slaughter 8,000 Tyrian soldiers and had the
entire population sold into slavery. He paid gallant court to the
fair kinswomen of beaten Darius, but Alexander's true method
of persuasion was brute force brilliantly deployed: the high-
speed march, sometimes covering forty miles of arid country in
a day, the infantry phalanx tightly massed against superior
numbers, the armored cavalry attacking on the flank, skirmish-
ers fanning out to distract the enemy, and catapults used as
field artillery.

Using such tactics, he was able in 333 B.C. to rout Darius'
army of 100,000 men or more at Issus in the southeastern cor-
ner of Asia Minor, and an even larger host at Gaugamela near
the Tigris River two years later. The most fortunate cities or
states were those that submitted to him without a fight: the
Ionian Greeks welcomed him. Damascus and Sidon bowed to
him, somnolent Egypt not only received him but proclaimed

him Pharaoh, gilded Babylon and Susa in the Persian heartland
opened their gates. It was only when in his insatiate rush he
struck across the wild back country of Bactria to the Hindu
Kush to fight guerrilla actions against mountaineer tribesmen
that he met diminishing returns of victory and loot. By 326 B.C.,
when he had crossed the Indus and decided to press on to the
Ganges, his legionaries (though chroniclers tell us how they
idolized him) had had enough and mutinied, forcing Alexander
to return to Persia. There this possessed man, for all his dreams
of Hellenizing the whole East, became more and more the pris-
oner of Eastern ways: he announced that he wished thenceforth
to be worshiped as the divine son of Zeus, took to wearing Per
sian clothes and sitting on a golden throne, and asked his offi-
cers to prostrate themselves before him. In Babylon, at thirty-two,
surrounded by sycophants and soothsayers, and ridden with
drink and possibly with doubt, he died, leaving a stupendous
empire without a royal heir, and his whole scheme of organiz-
ing and uniting it unrealized.

Apart from feats of arms, he had accomplished some great
deeds. He had set up along his traverses of the Middle East a
whole string of cities modeled along Hellenic lines, complete
with columned temples, council chamber, gymnasium, agora,
and stoa. Of these, great Alexandria in Egypt was to become a
major East-West cultural and commercial meeting-ground (and
Antioch in Syria, founded soon after in its image by one of his
successors, was to be another). In addition, Alexander refur-
bished many existing cities to conform to the Greek model. He
had brought in Greek and Macedonian traders no less than soldiers to intermingle and intermarry with the Eastern peoples,
thus setting in motion a vast new migration in which eventually hundreds of thousands of men from the Hellenic mainland
settled in the Middle East, Egypt, and Asia Minor, many of them
repeopling the Ionian cities that other Greeks had once settled.

Yet while he took with him the forms of Greek culture wherever
he went, he had implanted little of its traditional substance: this
was the tragedy of the conqueror who, for all of Aristotle's tute-
lage, had himself learned only its veneer, and (as his readiness
to change himself into an oriental despot showed) had never
penetrated its heart.

If the spirit of old Athenian Greece eluded him, it was even
more remote to his chief Macedonian generals, who upon his
death at once proceeded to carve up his empire among themselves, each making himself an absolute ruler of a share, some
adopting Eastern god-king notions, setting up or attempting to
set up dynasties, and then proceeding to attack his neighbor for
a greater share, secure in the knowledge that no outside power
remained to interpose itself in this in-fighting. This was an utter
travesty of the unity Alexander had set out to achieve; the
Macedonian had won, only to have his empire sundered and ori-
entalized—the East revenging itself upon an overambitious West.

Three quarreling dynasties emerged: first, that of Alexander's
boyhood friend and favorite general Ptolemy, who took over
Egypt and passed it on to a line of heirs all also named Ptolemy
(numbered II to XV) and most of them incompetent and decadent; second, that of Seleucus, another favorite, who acquired
Mesopotamia, Persia, and eventually Syria and most of Asia
Minor—all told, a dominion of some 1,500,000 square miles—in
which Semitic, Persian, and Anatolian tongues and cultures persisted just under the Hellenized surface; third, that of still
another general, Antigonus, who seized the Macedonian throne
and whose successors exerted varying degrees of control over
the old city-states of mainland Greece and the Aegean islands.
Other kingdoms arose in this welter of imperial order and disorder, notably vigorous Pergamum in Asia Minor, which was to
play a vital part in the eventual dissolution of Macedonian rule.

In commerce, the new lines opened to the East produced rich

rewards. Goods from China and India now arrived fairly safely over the Afghan passes, skirted the Caspian shore to reach Mesopotamia, and so moved on to the coastal cities of the Mediterranean. A sea route brought spices, ivory, and gold from India to Arabian ports, from which they were hauled overland.

Most significant of all was the blaze of scientific study and discovery that was stimulated by Greek contact with the work of early astronomers and mathematicians of Babylon and Egypt (a reverse effect of the Hellenizing process). Indeed, scientific achievement is the culminating splendor of Hellenistic civilization—a sprawling, self-doubting, morally and aesthetically declining but technologically brilliant culture that has been likened to our own. Sweeping theorems, now supported by close physical observations, engaged the minds of many of the ancient world's shrewdest investigators. Aristarchus of Samos in the third century set forth a theory that the earth moved orbitally around the sun, and calculated the length of the solar year. Hipparchus of Nicaea in Bithynia in the next century opposed this, setting forth a geocentric theory which was long to persist; he also—apparently drawing upon Babylonian records—figured out the precession of the equinoxes, made the first known chart of the heavens, and greatly improved instruments for making astronomical observations. Under Ptolemy I, Euclid opened in Alexandria a school at which he taught his theorems of plane and solid geometry that were to remain for two thousand years the bible of the subject. Archimedes of Syracuse studied in third-century Alexandria too, and became the author of many studies, including those on specific gravity, conic sections, and the principle of the lever, that were to make him, next to Pythagoras, the greatest scientist of antiquity.

Alexandria itself, a city laid out on a grid plan, with straight and transverse streets and squares to accommodate a population of perhaps nearly a half million Egyptians, Macedonians,

Greeks, Jews, Syrians, Arabs, Persians, became the center of all this energy. It boasted the celebrated library and museum, a zoological garden, parks, gymnasium, stadium, hippodrome, beach resorts, the great harbor and lighthouse, and was the scene of diverse activities—scientists convening and teaching; doctors of medicine like Erasistratus and Herophilus pursuing studies of physiology and anatomy; scholars galore collecting and collating old papyri; merchants promoting new ventures and watching their ships come in. Wealth, leisure, culture, self-indulgence, reached a point there that caused the writer Herodas to call it "the house of Aphrodite," in which everything was to be found, from playgrounds and philosophers to fine wines and beautiful women.

Yet, amid all this, there could be no doubt that the beliefs and virtues that had once been essential to Greece were fast drying up. Men who thought they had outgrown Olympian religion and the worship of traditional city-gods were now being drawn to rationalism or reverting to old cults and to the occult; sometimes all these impulses combined. Astrology and alchemy—much of them of Eastern origin—and beliefs in chance and magic seized many a mind, undoing much that logical and scientific interpretations of the physical world had tried to bring about.

In the heterogeneous population of the Hellenistic world there was a prevalence of demons such as there had not been since pre-Homeric times. The universalism of Alexander had achieved an unexpected result—a kind of fatalism or quietism in which each subject, no longer an effective member of his own polis, now sought personal means of salvation. Some found it through asceticism, others simply through withdrawal and passivity. The Stoic philosophy, with its emphasis both on the brotherhood of man and on accepting one's station in the scheme of things and not trying to alter it, dominated and symbolized these years, with their pessimism and petrification. Moreover, Greek divinities often became blended with oriental ones. Thus on Delos, so long sacred to Apollo, there flourished the cult of Serapis, who combined some of the attributes of Zeus and other Olympians with those of Osiris, who in Egyptian belief was the representative of the departed Pharaoh and ruler of the dead. Isis, consort of Osiris, became identified in many Greek minds with Aphrodite and, thus assimilated, one of the great deities of the Mediterranean world. The cult of Mithras, a sun god of Indo-Iranian origin and connected with the religion of the Persian Zoroaster, in turn mingled with that of Apollo. Meanwhile Zeus became Zeus Ammon in Egypt and Zeus Hyp-sistos in Asia Minor. This tendency toward worship of a central god above all other gods increasingly exercised the imagination of the ancient world. The Hebrews had borne witness to Yahweh from the beginning; the new trend prepared the way for reception of a divine spirit such as man had not known before.

Politically, the Greeks were now near the end. The rising empire of Rome, blooded amid its duel with African Carthage, in which Greek Sicily had played an equivocal part, was not of a mind to suffer Greek opposition as its eyes turned from the western Mediterranean to the eastern. Macedonia, fearful of the Roman threat, had allied itself with Carthage—a poor decision, as it turned out, since after their victory over Hannibal the Roman legions descended upon Greece, in part in response to an appeal by Pergamum and Rhodes, which were being threatened by Macedonian ambitions. At first most Greeks received the Romans as liberators, especially upon receiving assurances from them that Greek independence would be restored. Later, particularly in 146 when the Roman general Mummius destroyed Corinth, they began to hate the Roman "liberators" as they had once hated the Macedonians. In 86 B.C., after feeble opposition, Athens submitted to Roman occupation and all was over. Or so it seemed.

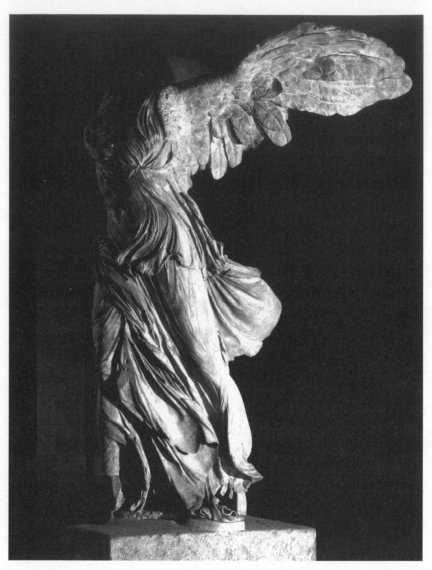

A winged figure of Victory, carved in the second century and discovered in the Aegean island of Samothrace, was designed to appear as if it stood on the prow of a ship heading into a strong wind.

X

THE LASTING LIGHT

The teachings of Plato are not alien to those of Christ.

—Justin Martyr

We are all Greeks.

—Percy Bysshe Shelley

In the year one of the Christian era, once-great Athens was only a run-down provincial seat in the wake of Roman advance, politically silent ever since Sulla's seizure of it in 86 B.C.. Its academies were stultified. The great library which Aristotle had gathered and which the minor philosopher Apellicon had preserved, along with scrolls of Aristotle's own writings, had been carried off to Rome. So had innumerable treasures of art. The warehouses of the Piraeus, which once received goods from all the eastern Mediterranean and beyond, had become a transshipment center for old bronze and marble works to adorn the villas of wealthy Romans. The march of empire had virtually passed the city by. As Romans reached out, like Alexander before them, to grasp Asia Minor, Egypt, and the vast eastern interior beyond, apathetic Athens was little more than a well-looted mausoleum.

Yet the final decay of Athens as well as of its Hellenic sister states did not mean the extinction of Greek influence. On the contrary: even while most of them lay stunned and prostrate, a remarkable emanation from them continued—one might say, like that of some departed hero of an ancient tale who exerted

extraordinary powers from the grave. In their prime of life the
Greeks had possessed the quality of making their presence and
ways felt vividly wherever they went, from the philosophers of
Ionia, who puzzled over the nature of the universe, to the
traders and settlers who took the culture of the vine and the
olive to southern France and primitive Spain. In their later
years the Greeks brought their influence to bear in large part
upon those who had subjugated them, and through them, upon
other cultures far and wide.

Before all-conquering Alexander struck deep into Asia, no
artist of India had presumed to represent the image of the sub-
lime Buddha. But Alexander's men carried images of Greek
gods with them, and some centuries after their arrival the first
sculptured figures of Buddha appeared in Gandhara, a region at
the eastern foot of the Hindu Kush range—a type of figure,
moreover, that appears to be modeled on the lineaments of
Apollo and wears flowing Greek raiment (though with a third
"eye" of Eastern insight implanted in the brow). Thus, Greek
influence at its periphery gave shape to the image of the teacher
of the East and thereby left a deep impress upon Buddhist religion.

Meanwhile, under Alexander's successor kings in the Near
East a fusion took place in art. Ancient, hieratic Egypt had
made the power of its monumental art strongly felt throughout
archaic Greece; now the expressive forms of Greek art in its late
flowering mingled with traditional Eastern ones; this in turn
was to serve in forming the art of Byzantium. Traces of Greek
influence are also to be found in the arts of the Egyptian Copts
and the remote Ethiopians. It was great Alexandria itself, however, with its intermingling of Greek and Roman, of Egyptian
and Jew, that became the leading transmission center of Greek
impulses. There the vast library assembled in the centuries after
the death of the city's founder provided what one might term

the first international meeting ground for scholars. (Before the despoliations it underwent at the hands of the emperors Aurelian and Diocletian in the third century A.D. and of Theodosius I in the fourth, it may have contained a half million rolls of parchment or papyrus.) For more than half a millennium, virtually every scientist of renown either studied or taught there, as did innumerable annotators and interpreters of ancient literary texts.

In the interplay of West and East, no movement was more profound than that which brought together the world of Greek philosophy—especially Plato's—and the body of Hebraic devotional tradition. The outcome was the Christian revolution. Though Christianity sprang from provincial Judea and claimed continuity from Judaism, surely it would not have grown into the sovereign faith it was soon to become throughout the Mediterranean world had it not included a powerful admixture of Greek ideas. The Jewish philosopher Philo of Alexandria, born some two decades before Christ, and a close student of the Pythagoreans, Platonists, and Stoics, was to be a major transmitter of Plato, and the mysticism derived from his thought, to the early Church. Saint John and Saint Paul were particularly influenced by Platonic thinking; and later, Saint Augustine was to remark that "only a few words and phrases" need be altered to bring Platonism into full accord with Christianity. Jesus himself taught in Aramaic, but it has been remarked by so distinguished an authority as the late Dean Inge that "the early Church spoke in Greek and thought in Greek."

Before this confluence, though, another had occurred that demonstrated surviving Greek influence in different fashion. This was the spell that moribund Hellas cast upon its master, all-conquering Rome. From the outset of their contacts with Greece, the Romans, uncertain as to their own origins, had felt a deep impulse to relate themselves and their background to this people across the sea, so senior to them in history, culture, and accomplishment. The Greeks in their time had pursued a hunt for high lineage too, producing their tales of godly ancestors and primordial heroes. Among the ambitious, status-seeking Romans the urge to establish a worthy genealogy was particularly strong.

Tradition had it that Rome had been founded by the brothers Romulus and Remus, reared by a simple herdsman but themselves descended from a king. Late in the third century B.C. a tale arose linking Roman origins to Troy through the person of Aeneas of the Trojan royal house, who was represented as having become the ancestor, after his city's fall, of Rome's founder-brothers. Such a legend showed, for one thing, the Romans' increasing absorption with Greece and its literature. Very many educated Romans in the second century read Greek (and as Rome achieved supremacy in the eastern Mediterranean, knowledge of Greek became increasingly important as a means of communication between the masters and their Hellenized subjects). The playwrights Terence and Plautus adapted and imitated Menander and other writers of Greek New Comedy. Above all, the Romans read Homer. This we know from the innumerable uses to which Homer was put in Rome for purposes of citation and show of learning. No one read him more closely than a man who was born in northern Italy, near what is Mantua, and named Publius Vergilius Maro, the arch-poet of the Romans known to history as Vergil. Highly schooled, a friend of the poet Horace and the patron Maecenas, he set out in his later years to compose a vast epic poem that would ennoble the Roman presence. In the *Aeneid* he created the Roman *Odyssey*—and more.

To his patriotic and imaginative mind, the old story centering on Romulus and Remus was meager. The thought of an ancient connection with the Trojans, equal in valor to their Greek attackers, was prouder; and he found a way of making the Trojan-Roman lineage seem to outshine even that of the Greeks. A clue appeared in a passage in the *Iliad* about a child of Zeus named Dardanus, who had fathered the line of kings of Troy. Where had Dardanus come from? Vergil has it that he came from Italy, and had led his people to Troy, but with the thought of later returning to their homeland. Upon this idea Vergil, taking the side of what he termed "Priam's guiltless race," against Agamemnon's Greeks, constructs an elaborate tale. Aeneas, who is a son of Anchises (a descendant of Dardanus) and Venus (the Greek Aphrodite), is the one Trojan leader to survive the holocaust and is divinely appointed to return his folk to their Italian patrimony, where a great fate awaits them. After many voyagings and his affair with the Carthaginian queen Dido, Aeneas does find his way to Italy, there to become the progenitor of the Roman race.

There are vivid parallels between Vergil's epic and Homer's. Aeneas, like Odysseus, has fabulous adventures, including a descent into the underworld; Romans and Rutulians fight very much as Homer's Achaeans and Trojans did in the *Iliad*; gods intervene; and the long speeches of heroes and the tumultuous similes beloved by Homer are adopted almost as a canonical device. Yet while paying literary respect to Homer and thus to the Greeks. Vergil's tone and message depart from that of his great predecessor. Homer celebrated individual valor and *arete*; Vergil, although honoring *pietas,* or traditional Roman civic virtue, produces what is essentially a political poem, prophesying the power of the Roman state. The Romans, Jupiter promises at the very outset of the *Aeneid,* will enjoy a dominion without limits; they will be *rerum dominos*–"rulers of the world":

. . . An age shall come, as the years glide by,
When the children of Troy shall enslave the children of
    Agamemnon,
Of Diomed and Achilles, and rule in conquered Argos.
From the fair seed of Troy there shall be born a Caesar—
Julius, his name derived from the great Iulus—whose empire
Shall reach to the ocean's limits, whose fame shall end in
    the stars.

Vergil's work is only one example of the ambivalent attitude of Romans toward Greeks. The ever-loquacious historian Livy is intent on proving to his readers in instance after instance that the Romans are the world's elect. Yet the popular biographer Plutarch—a Greek writing for a Roman audience—makes a veritable cult of the Greeks in his *Lives,* where he pairs off Greek and Roman statesmen (Demosthenes with Cicero, Pericles with Fabius) in such a way as to make the point that leading Greeks had qualities every Roman should respect.

The homage Romans paid to Greece was shown not only by their thefts of works of art but by their continuing urge to copy Greek styles. Thus the Roman Forum was built in the Corinthian and Ionic architectural orders; while in the first centuries after Christ the remote Hellenized city of Aphrodisias in Caria in Asia Minor became by reason of its excellent marble and skilled craftsmen a veritable factory for the making of reproductions of classical Greek sculpture for export via Ephesus or Miletus on a thousand-mile trip to Rome's port of Ostia. The Romans conquered; but as their most stylish poet, Horace, himself remarked, "Captive Greece made captive her rude conqueror."

Vergil, for all his pride in Rome, did sense the glimmer of some era of finer feelings ahead; thus he dreamed in his celebrated fourth *Eclogue* of a time when "Our iron breed shall

come to an end, and a golden race rise throughout the world."
But in general the Romans—those ambitious climbers or *novi
homines* of the ancient world—with their shrewd, materialistic
approach, were not ready for such intimations. They looked
upon the Greeks as a race of engaging artists and philosophers,
patronized them, used them, but in their own stirrings of
thought moved little beyond them. They adopted and adapted
from Greek city-states many civil statutes, and, more impor-
tantly, from Greek society as a whole the idea of law as an
accumulated body of ancestral precept, divine in origin, that
should be binding upon all; upon this they built their own great
structure of law. But they never seemed to penetrate to the core
of Greek thought at its most advanced.

Early in their history they identified the Olympian gods with
their own pantheon, at a time when many intelligent Greeks
were looking elsewhere for truth. They were taken up with the
powers of Mars and the charms of Venus when Greek thinkers
were increasingly absorbed with the idea of *logos,* meaning the
presence of an immanent reason governing the entire world,
visible and invisible. Plato himself, in making his sharp distinction between the physical or sensory world and the ideal world,
had taught that *nous,* or abstract mind, dominated the latter,
while it was not concerned with the former. But with the Stoics,
who came after him, the idea of *logos* as an everyday ethical
principle came to the fore; and in Philo, the Hellenized Jew of
Alexandria, *logos* is the divine designer who seeks to realize in
the physical world the ideas long in his mind. Here Hebraic
ideas of an all-knowing Creator intermix with Stoic and Platonic metaphysics; and soon the combination came to Rome.
With it came ideas of abstinence, purification, mystical revelation, redemption—all derived from the mystery religions so
prevalent in the Hellenistic world.

While these ideas remained distant or incomprehensible to

many Romans, Plutarch in a flash of insight saw the approaching marriage of beliefs when he wrote, "There are not different
gods in different nations, barbarians and Greeks, southerners
and northerners. Just as the sun and moon and sky and earth
and sea are common to all though named differently by different people, so the one Reason ordering this world, the one
Providence governing it ... have different honors and titles
among different peoples according to their customs." Newer
thoughts were to come, as when Saint John, at the outset of his
Gospel, wrote, "In the beginning was the Word [in the Greek
text, ;α';γο ;γλ;αα;γο;γγ;γο;γ8 λογοσ], and the Word was with
God, and the Word was God." And it was Paul, son of a Roman
citizen in Tarsus, of Jewish descent and raised in the strict
Hebraic faith in an area where Hellenic and Eastern influences
particularly met, who set forth in his Epistles such transcendental phrases, Platonic in character, as "Now we see through a
glass, darkly" and "The things which are seen are temporal; but
the things which are not seen are eternal." Paul, converted to
Christianity in about A.D. 35 after his early years of persecuting
it, preached such doctrine to the early Christian believers in
Antioch, to the Galatians, to the Corinthians, to the Athenians
in their own Agora, and carried the burden and passion of his
message of Christ the King to Rome as well—where he was
imprisoned in A.D. 60, later to die a martyr's death. Wherever he
went, Paul bore not only the witness of Jesus but also the heritage of Plato.

While Christianity invaded Rome's wavering mind with its
Platonic mysticism and Hebraic rigor, restive Teutons, Goths,
and tribesmen of eastern origin soon turned against Rome itself
with sheer force. They sensed the weakness of an overextended
civil structure ridden with rivalry and strife. By the third century A.D. the centralized machinery of heterogeneous Rome had
become so creaky that the emperor Diocletian divided his vast

state into two parts, East and West, and the center of power moved east. In the fourth century Constantine, a man of Balkan birth and the first emperor to give official sanction to Christianity, abandoned Rome, in his effort to bring the pieces of his empire together, and established his own seat at Byzantium. There, in what had hitherto been hardly more than a small port town, he built himself the glittering capital he called Constantinople, rifling art treasures from East and West to do so.

The eastern half of the Roman Empire came increasingly under the influence of Greek culture. Though Latin remained the official tongue of Constantinople through its age of splendor under Justinian in the sixth century, it was superseded by Greek in the seventh. And there Hellenic, Roman, and Eastern canons of art were combined to form that rigid and hieratic style known—to some with disdain, to others with admiration—as Byzantine.

Yet Greek influence did not remain confined to encrusted Byzantium, once Rome had been sacked by Alaric and other barbarian invaders. Though by now the Hellenic stream had been far diverted from its origins, it went on flowing into many lands, even through darkest times and often by roundabout ways. Aristotle, whose works had long been known in Rome, was first translated in part into Latin by the Roman scholar Boethius in the fifth century and was to exert a commanding influence on Christian schoolmen in centuries to come. Greek was carried as far west as Ireland and was studied there until the eighth century. At that time in Byzantium a controversy over the representation and worship of images was stultifying art. Yet Greco-Byzantine models had already spread to Europe—witness the mosaics at Ravenna that were to help set a style for the early Middle Ages.

Meanwhile another stream of ancient Greek emanation passed to Europe through a quite different channel—the Arabs.

Striking out from their ancient deserts to overrun Egypt, and inspired under the banners of Mohammed to sweep across all North Africa and into Spain as well, they preserved far more than they destroyed, and passed their finds on to the West. Thus the thirteen books of Euclid's *Elements* became one of their prized possessions, first recorded Arabic in the eighth century (a later manuscript is illustrated on this page). Similarly the vast studies of the second-century A.D. Alexandrian astronomer, mathematician, and geographer Ptolemy (unrelated to the line of Macedonian monarchs of the same name in Egypt) were translated and disseminated by Arab scholars. This extraordinary man, creator of a brilliant mathematical theory of planetary motion about the earth, represented the culmination of classical science, and it was in large part through Arab transmission and commentary that his work exerted such a profound influence upon Europe. Finally, in the seventeenth century, the astronomer Copernicus was able to prove his geocentric theory wrong. Even then, however, Copernicus left the mathematical basis of Ptolemy's thinking all but intact. And Euclid, saved during the Dark Ages by Moslems, was to remain the god of Western geometry until far into the nineteenth century.

But primary to the medieval world was the transmission of Aristotle, much of whose work was also passed through either Arab or Byzantine hands. What the early Boethius had translated into Latin were only fragments. The great bulk of Aristotle's writings entered Europe by means of Arab scholars who put the original into their own tongue and glossed it, at such advanced seats of their learning as Córdoba and Toledo. From Spain, chiefly in the twelfth century, knowledge of Aristotle spread northward—either across the Pyrenees or via Palermo, the half-Arab, half-Western capital of Sicily. At the same time his texts were also coming from Constantinople through Eastern Church scholars who had translated from Greek to Latin.

Aristotle became the subject of intense study and controversy at European universities, which were fast becoming major collecting points of ancient learning and centers of new instruction. Some of his work was banned at Paris in 1210 as inconsistent with Christian doctrine. But the mighty power of his logic and knowledge led theologians—Thomas Aquinas in particular—to see in his work a great encyclopedia of ancient learning and to seek to reconcile his systematic wisdom with Christian revelation. As Plato's mysticism inspired the Church Fathers, Aristotle's rigor shaped Saint Thomas' *Summa Theologica*—the vast metaphysical treatise that directed the thought of those in the Middle Ages who could read Latin manuscripts.

Many, of course, could not read at all—certainly not Latin. After convulsions caused by the invasions of Visigoth and Ostrogoth, Hun and Vandal, Europe slowly became literate again and found itself with many vernacular tongues, and with numerous classical tales transmitted into them. Thus a French troubadour fable based on distant legends of the Trojan War, *Le Roman de Troie*, by Benoît de Sainte-Maure, became popular. In the thirteenth century another French tale of chivalry and romance, permeated with classical allusions, *Le Roman de la Rose*, came into being at the hands of Guillaume de Lorris and Jean de Meun; it grew to be probably the most widely read story in the late Middle Ages. This long-drawn-out yarn, in effect an *ars amatoria*, or commentary on elegant seduction, shows that its authors were familiar with Vergil, with Greek legends as retold by Ovid, and very likely with Byzantine influences that had transmitted a certain polish to Western courts. England's first major poet, Geoffrey Chaucer, at the outset of his career was to try his hand at translating part of *Le Roman de la Rose;* and so we find him retelling his version of the very ancient story of the beautiful youth Narcissus, who was desired by all the girls but who would not give himself to them:

Narcisus was a bachelere,
That Love had caught in his daungere,
And in his net gan him so streyne,
And dide him so to wepe and pleyne,
That nede him muste his lyf forgo,
For a fair lady, hight Echo,
Him loved over any creature . . .

Chaucer himself, like Shakespeare after him, very likely had
"small Latin and less Greek." Dante Alighieri, whose greatest work
preceded the beginning of Chaucer's by half a century, is also
thought to have had almost no knowledge of Greek. Yet he had so
acquainted himself with classical lore as to find in it the inspiration for his *Divine Comedy*—that incomparable achievement
which both revived the epic form and sought a reconciliation
between Christian and ancient ideals. In the *Inferno,* the most
admired part of the work, Dante makes an imaginary visit to an
underworld of memorable spirits—very much as Homer's
Odysseus and Vergil's Aeneas had made their great descent. Dante
chooses Vergil as his guide to this realm because he sees in him a
prophet of Christianity, warm in his humaneness and prized for
his premonition of a better world to come. At the same time, references to Aristotle and Greek history and myth abound in the
Comedy—evidence that literary and philosophical knowledge of
the Greeks was much alive in Western minds again. And, though
cast in the vernacular, his nobility of speech harks far back:

Per me si va nolle città dolente;
per me si va noll' eterno dolore;
per me si va tra la perduta gente.

I am the way into the city of woe.
I am the way to a forsaken people,
I am the way into eternal sorrow.

Soon after Dante's time, when direct acquaintance with Greek and Roman models still remained rare, a veritable hunger to rediscover them arose. The Italian poet Petrarch recommended that new authors copy ancient ones and tried (though without much success) to master Greek. His young friend Boccaccio in 1360 arranged to have a Byzantine scholar, Leontius Pilatus, appointed professor of Greek at Florence, and together with him made the first complete translation of Homer into Latin prose. Subsequent generations saw an immense increase in the work of rediscovery, translation, and adaptation, stimulated in part by the westward emigration of Byzantine scholars as the threatening Turks drew near, and then by the invention of printing. Herodotus and Thucydides were put into Latin in the mid fifteenth century; the scholar Ficino, employed by the Medici family, began his full rendering of Plato into Latin in 1462, completing it twenty years later; by 1475 the Vatican Library had on its shelves nine copies of the *Iliad* and four of the *Odyssey*, and translations of these works into modern languages were made during the following century.

Erasmus of Rotterdam, the leader in northern Europe of what was taking shape as a classical revival, proposed that every student should make the effort of reading the whole body of ancient literature, taking notes as he went. But well before this—in 1423, in fact—the Italian scholar Vittorino da Feltre had opened in Mantua a school dedicated in great part to such pursuit, seeking to combine in his pupils a harmonious blend of thorough classical knowledge and a devotion to Christian virtues. For Vittorino, the medieval tradition of training youths primarily in jousting, hunting, and prayer was not enough: he sought to build strong bodies, but in consort with searching minds, very much as Plato himself had done. So the pupil at Vittorino's school, while being taught to wrestle, throw javelins, and climb mountains, was also made to begin his study of Latin and Greek at the age of six. As a result of such thinking as Vittorino's, Renaissance men emerged, vigorous, well schooled, bold in action and yet conscious of the past.

The Renaissance, though, did far more than exhume antiquity. It returned to it (first to Rome, and then to the Greece that lay behind it) in search of ideals of thought and behavior that would impart fresh values in a day when the spiritual power of the Church, grown both rigid and decadent, had lost its hold on many minds. Classical subject matter, in art or tale, had long been used in innumerable borrowings, some far removed from the meaning of the originals. It remained for Renaissance man not only to dig out the treasures of antiquity directly, but to relish their beauties for their own sake and to apply to himself the ideals of human grace, valor, and independence that he felt they embodied.

No movement in the Renaissance better illustrates this than the school of Neoplatonic thinking that flowered particularly at the court of the Florentine Medici, the most princely patrons of art and letters since the days of Roman emperors and aristocrats. Neoplatonism, owing much of its impetus to such scholar-translators and philosophers as Ficino and Pico della Mirandola, combined the ideals of bodily perfection with those of the purity and freedom of the soul. The Neoplatonists developed the language of men like Vittorino, who had tried to achieve a unity of the classical and Christian spirits. The perfect body in itself was, as the Greeks had felt, the image or mirror of a lofty spirit. Yet life was or should be (and here we come to Platonism and Christianity mixed) an advance from service of the material body to emancipation of the mind. Art, dedicated to beauty, the Neoplatonists believed, could serve to advance man toward the spiritual realm by bridging the divide between what was physically present in everyday man and what was divine in him.

This ideal was complicated in practice by the increasing lure of the pagan world, the more it came to light. Ghiberti, Brunelleschi, Donatello, all delighted in rummaging about ancient ruins for relics they could use as models. Greco-Roman mythological figures were found in great numbers, to be adapted as noble allegories; the educated gentry of Florence and all the other Italian cities loved to identify themselves with classical forebears, in paint, marble, or poetry. In his *Primavera* (shown at right) Botticelli adapted a classical theme to Neoplatonic sensitivity with ineffable delicacy and restraint. Michelangelo, though also strongly influenced by Neoplatonism, was one of the first to admire the violent, late Hellenistic Laocoön group after its discovery in 1506; and he celebrated in his statuary the noble form at its most virile, and in his sonnets the beauties of naked young men. The direct study, or rather restudy, of the nude may have begun early in the fifteenth century, related both to classical finds and the particular Florentine interest in anatomy. The peak was reached by Michelangelo himself, the greatest of whose brooding, anatomically detailed, undraped figures recall not so much the Laocoön group as the sculptures on the Parthenon pediment.

Well before this, Greek plays were being acted in translation in Italy, to commence a gradual revival of the theatre arts. As Gilbert Highet remarks in *The Classical Tradition,* the very basis of Western drama derives from the Greeks and Romans: the recognition of the play as potentially a form of high art, its use of complex plot, its division into acts, and the physical structure of the theatre. Attempts to write afresh in dramatic form, leaning on classics for substance yet using the language of the day, may have begun with a pastoral play, half-spoken and half-sung, on the ancient Orpheus theme written by the young scholar Politian for the court of Mantua in 1471. Opera, introduced as a new art form just at the end of the sixteenth century by such experimenters as Peri and Caccini, was an effort to incorporate music into spoken drama as the Greeks had once done—though precisely what the role of music had been in Greek drama, no one was certain, save that it had been pervasive. Renaissance plays and masques had contained what we would call "incidental" music or interludes of songs (and of course Shakespeare's plays include a multitude of lyrics); the new thought was to combine words and music throughout. The first attempts, with declaimed solo speeches, or recitatives, accompanied by instruments, seem clumsy; but very soon, in his *Orfeo* of 1607 and his *Combattimento di Tancredi e Clorinda* of 1624, the masterly Claudio Monteverdi achieved a union of word and tone of amazingly heightened emotional power. From here the line passes through the courtly, baroque operas of France (again, frequently on classical subjects) and Handel's vigorous oratoriolike ones (chiefly on biblical themes) to its first culmination in the works of Gluck, a major revolutionary in the art and a remarkable embodiment of later eighteenth-century neoclassicism. He abandons the declamatory style; his actor-singers (in his *Orfeo ed Euridice,* reduced to three) sing long arias of sustained and pensive beauty; choruses of Furies and Sacred Spirits hover in the background or come forth with turbulent or statuesque sound.

Shakespeare, though six of his plays and longer poems are based on Greek subjects, was quite clearly far more influenced by the Romans—particularly the dramatist Seneca, the poet Ovid, the historian Livy, and the biographer Plutarch. As everyone knows, even his plays dealing with nonclassical subjects abound in ancient allusions and images, but these appear to have come to him through Roman transmission. As for the Greek tragedians' canon of unity of time, place, and action, it is rarely reflected in his far moving and multitudinous scenes. Messengers, as in Greek drama, do bring reports of what has occurred away from the central scene, and there are tellings of what happened anterior to the action, but generally Shakespeare likes to pack the entire complex story on the stage itself—battles, duels, marches, countermarches, in many a month and place.

It is with John Milton that we come to a man far more directly influenced by the Greeks—by Homer, father of the epic, whom he tried to emulate in a vast poem that would outdo Dante's and Vergil's ("While it pursues/Things unattempted yet in prose or rhyme"), and also by Athenian tragedians. His *Samson Agonistes,* stark, extremely concentrated, is highly reminiscent of Sophocles or Euripides. *Paradise Lost* and *Paradise Regained,* on the other hand, may seem endless to the modern reader, but it is a Homeric kind of endlessness, absorbed with noble speeches, spirits, marvels, and rolling similes, such as this, following Mammon's speech in revolt against the Almighty:

> *He scarce had finished, when such murmur filled*
> *The assembly as when hollow rocks retain*
> *The sound of blustering winds, which all night long*
> *Had roused the sea, now with hoarse cadence lull*
> *Seafaring men o'erwatched, whose barke by chance*
> *Or pinnace anchors in a craggy bay . . .*

Yet Milton could also write in a gentler, elegiac mood, coupling the pastoral style made fashionable in the Renaissance with a great mass of mythology, as when in his *Lycidas,* of less than 200 lines, he calls upon nymphs, dryads, muses, and "Sisters of the Sacred well" to help him commemorate his lost young friend Edward King: "Look homeward, angel, now, and melt with ruth. . . ." Here he is close in spirit to Poussin, that other master of classical evocation, whose vast landscapes with

their calm figures breathe a sense of melancholy over something loved and lost.

In the courtly French theatre of the day, classical subjects
were revived with stately magnificence but also often with
somber power—nowhere more stirring than in Racine's great
Phèdre of 1667, retelling the tale of Theseus' bride Phaedra.
Tragically she falls in love with Theseus' stepson; with dark fate
approaching she prepares to kill herself, facing death in a noble
speech whose Alexandrine cadences represent the height of
classical French: *"Jusqu'an dernier soupir de malheurs pour-
suivie, / Je rends dans les tourments une pénible vie."*

Against such nobility, the eruption at Versailles of ceiling
paintings by Le Brun of gods and muses allegorically celebrating the glories of the French Jupiter, Louis XIV, was gilded vul-
garity. It was not until the latter half of the eighteenth century
that another, stronger classical revival occurred. Again, as during the Renaissance, minds first turned to thoughts of Rome,
stimulated particularly by the remarkable excavations at Pom-
peii. Yet an obscure German scholar, Joachim Winckelmann,
was instrumental in attracting fresh attention to Greek art when
he became infatuated with the study of it and in 1755 wrote his
eloquent *Thoughts on the Imitation of Greek Works.* This essay,
coming at a time when many men were surfeited with baroque
extravagance and rococo frivolity, emphasized the "noble simplicity and serene greatness" of Greek art and likened it to the
highest Greek literature. Soon another German, the dramatist
Gotthold Ephraim Lessing, wrote *Laokoon,* a treatise that was to
have enormous influence; in this essay he took that famous
sculpture group as a model of dignity and restraint and proposed that new art emulate it.

No one today (the cycle of taste having revolved again)
would call the Laocoön group "restrained." But the high seri-
ousness of Lessing's subject and the eloquence of his argument

drew many an artist directly back to Greece. "I want to work in a pure Greek style," wrote the painter Jacques-Louis David, turning against his own rococo background to become in a few years, with his lofty themes and severe line, the leader of French neoclassicism, favored both by the revolutionaries and the court of Napoleon. Meanwhile, diverse political overtones enlarged the revival. Revolution and the impulse toward republicanism made many men look back to Athens as a state near to their ideal, and the Hellenes' own war for independence from the Turks in the 1820's reinforced this attachment to them as the symbol and embodiment of man's dauntless mind and free spirit.

When in his "Ode on a Grecian Urn" John Keats exclaimed "O Attic shape! Fair attitude!" what he may well have been gazing at was a Wedgwood adaptation of a Greco-Roman vase, not Attic at all. That hardly matters; he was voicing a belief, shared by other romantic poets, in the liberating power of Greek beauty. Their romanticism also led them back to Plato, with his vision of a world of true Being of which ours is only the reflection. Plato's spirit pervades Wordsworth's "Ode on Immortality"—the poet being haunted with the sense of having had childhood glimpses of that perfect world, now lost to his sight. Goethe too was under Platonic spell when in *Faust* he wrote of our life being but a "colored refraction" (*"Am farbigen Abglanz / haben wir das Leben"*)—a close parallel to Shelley's mystical lines: *"Life, like a dome of many-colored glass, / Stains the white radiance of Eternity."*

Romanticism pursued both the "natural" and the ideal; its enemy was artifice; perhaps that explains why it found its spiritual home both in the wild moors of England and in the ruins of Athens. How to reconcile the two? Goethe in his later years, concerned with the contrast between the "storm and stress" of Western man and the classical ideal of perfection, tried to resolve it symbolically in the second part of *Faust* by having his turbulent hero mate with the most beautiful woman of antiquity, Helen of Troy. This was romantic imagination at its extreme. Yet, in a longer view, it was only another instance of the effort Western man has been making for centuries, turning to the Greeks not only for an image of the ideal but also for deeper light upon man's own nature and the powers around him.

Thus Western man has been drawn repeatedly to the Oedipus legend, a favorite subject to Renaissance humanists who discussed it, to Corneille, Dryden, and Voltaire who built plays on it, and to Sigmund Freud, who found in its tale of parricide and incest a clue to profound unconscious drives—the son's unacknowledged urge to replace the father and possess the mother. Igor Stravinsky and André Gide have made their own terse, brutal settings of the tale for our time, preferring it to such idyllic themes as that of Orpheus, beloved by Gluck.

Nineteenth-century Americans, romantically attracted, gave new cities in their countryside such names as Troy, Athens, Ithaca, and erected gleaming Greek Revival mansions. The twentieth-century dramatist Eugene O'Neill, drawing on Greek substance rather than outward form, interpreted a New England ancestral story in terms reminiscent of the tragic house of Agamemnon. The French Jean Giraudoux wrote *Amphitryon 38*—its title meaning that it was the thirty-eighth attempt over the centuries to retell the ancient Greek tale of Alcmene's husband, cuckolded by Zeus. T. S. Eliot's polished verse play *The Cocktail Party* harks back in theme directly to Euripides' *Alcestis*. One of the most revolutionary of contemporary artists, Pablo Picasso, has gone back repeatedly to the Greeks for both subject and style.

We are always going back to them—each in our own way, every generation in its way—because we sense that their gifts were incomparable. Democracy goes back to them. The cultivation of the body, of sports, of Western good taste and manners goes back to them. The idea of free scientific inquiry and philosophic speculation derives from them. Our pursuit of shapeliness and grace in the arts—insofar as we pursue it—was theirs also. Above all, when we speak of the ideal of all-around excellence in man, we are thinking as Greeks did, though we do not use their word for it. We are thinking of *arete*.

Extended Captions for Reconstructed Ancient Greece

MILETUS: North Agora

Of the three agoras of ancient Miletus excavated thus far, the so-called North Agora is probably the oldest, as its construction began with the rebuilding of the city following its destruction by the Persians in the fifth century B.C. It occupied the space of several building plots of the city's Hippodameian grid, on the west side of the Sacred Way. In its initial phase, the North Agora consisted of a Doric, L-shaped stoa, the Harbor Stoa, which faced the Harbor of Lions. Connected to its rear side (west) was a smaller, square building, a peripteral atrium, surrounded by four stoas. To the south, loosely connected to the North Agora, was the Prytaneion. During the second and third centuries B.C. a new Doric stoa surrounding the Agora was constructed on all but the eastern side. As well as creating the outline for the market square, this new addition served to connect the Prytaneion to the Harbor Stoa. A temple-like edifice, most probably dedicated to the worship of the Seleucid kings, was built at the very center of its west wing. During the first century B.C. and the first century A.D. a wall parallel to the eastern stoa of the market square was built, while numerous votive monuments were erected along the facade of the Prytaneion. Passageways between the market square and the surrounding public areas were possible through an elegant Ionic gate (propylon) across from the temple and through numerous passages located at various points in the encircling stoas. At the same time, the passage between the Harbor Stoa and the Delphinion Sanctuary was transformed by the erection of the Harbor Gate, which consisted of two Ionic colonnades, with horizontal entablatures, leaving a narrow passageway. Two circular votive monuments were erected in front of the west wing of the Harbor Stoa. In the final building phase, a double-faced stoa with shops was built on the east side of the market square. Meanwhile, a second floor was added to the colonnade at the south wing of the North Agora. In the very last phase, a Jewish synagogue was built off the west end of the Harbor Stoa.

ASSOS: Temple of Athena

At Troas in Asia Minor, across the north coastline of Lesbos, at the highest point on the acropolis of ancient Assos, an archaic Doric temple dedicated to the goddess Athena was built around the middle of the sixth century B.C. It was the only notable temple of the Doric order to appear at that time in Asia Minor. This temple is a unique case in ancient architecture where elements of the Ionic order are introduced with such an experimental boldness in an edifice of the Doric order.

The temple follows the Doric standards in its overall disposition: It is a normal hexastyle peripteral temple (6 columns on the front and back and 13 = 2×6+1 on the flanks) with a rectangular cella with pronaos. The columns are quite slender, and they have only 16 flutings (18 in the pronaos) and widely spreading capitals. There is no angle contraction on the front, and the column spacing on the flanks is reduced.

The most important peculiarity of the temple is the continuous frieze that was carved on its architrave. The frieze covered the entire length of the front architrave, and part of the flanks. It is an obvious and unique Ionic influence, rarely repeated since. Also, the apparent lack of sculptures in the pediments could be attributed to an Ionic custom.

The building is oriented east-west and has a slight southeastern inclination. The entrance to the temple was at the east. No remains of an altar survive, although this was probably situated at the eastern side of the temple.

KITION: Inner Harbor Ship Sheds

Kition in Cyprus (modern Larnaka) is one of the oldest cities of Cyprus, inhabited continuously from 6000 B.C. to our days. It was a very important commerce station of the east Mediterranean.

Excavations of the French Mission of Kition brought to light a row of seven *neosoikoi* (ship sheds) of a military harbor dated at the end of the fifth century B.C. in the middle of Larnaka. The harbor lied in the city at quite a big distance from the seashore (present distance 400 m), and it was connected with the open sea through a channel. In the *neosoikoi* the war vessels were kept in safety and maintained when not in use. Rows of ashlar walls separated the sheds and supported the timber roofs, covered with red terracotta roof tiles. In the middle of every shed there was a timber slipway on which the ships, stripped of their movable parts (oars, sails, masts, etc.), were hauled up with the help of pulling devices.

KNIDUS: The Gate of the Military Harbor

According to every archaeological indication, the construction of ancient Knidus on a grid plan of the type invented by Hippodamus in the contemporary Turkish site of Tekir, dates from around 330-340 B.C. Its walls aimed at protecting three areas crucial for the city: the Triopian peninsula, the mainland region of the city and of course, its military harbor. On the contrary, the commercial harbor remained outside of the walls that skirted its shores, perhaps because its mouth was too wide to be protected.

The land relief demanded different solutions for each position. The basic defensive system is that of the wall with round or square towers at intervals. Both the thickness of the wall and the density of the towers depend on the vulnerability of the position. Although the city has not been thoroughly excavated or studied, it is calculated that the whole distance of the wall comprised about sixty towers of different dimensions and shapes and at least ten gates. The walls and the towers were built with limestone and tufa in pseudo-isodomic and isodomic ashlar masonry. However, in certain sites the polygonal masonry was also used.

The mouth of the military harbor was protected by a pair of towers, between which a sliding chain controled the passage of the ships. The graphic restoration by F. Krischen, on which the construction of the digital model was based, is modelled on the few surviving ruins and on the best knowledge about fortifications of the time.

On the left, as seen from the harbor, descended a part of the wall ending in a square, three-storied tower, with saddleback roof and embrasures protected by wooden shutters. A narrow pier—also protected by a wall with embrasures—protruded into the sea, narrowing the available passage for defensive reasons. Right across there was a two-storied square tower with a flat roof. Between the two towers hung a sliding chain controlling the passage. Also on the right side rose an oblong part of the high sea wall of the city with embrasures, ending in a large, three-storied, round tower.

OLYMPIA: Zeus Temple

The Zeus temple in Olympia is one of the most famous Greek temples, especially because of the gold and ivory statue of Zeus made by Phidias. The construction of the temple started in 468 B.C. and it was finished some ten years later. The architect, Libon from Elis, produced a design based on simple proportions, round multiples of the Doric foot, and clear constructional details. It is not without reason that the temple is regarded as the *canon*, the standard of Doric temple architecture. It was a hexastyle building (six columns on the front and thirteen on the flanks) built with local shelly limestone covered with a thin layer of stucco, except for the cornice, the roof tiles, the sculptured metopes and the sculptures of the pediment, which were made of fine white Parian marble. The corners of the twelve metopes of the front and back inner entablature depicted the Labors of Hercules. The sculptures of the east pediment, a work of the sculpture Paionios, commemorate the preparation for the mythical chariot race between Pelops and Oinomaos, while the sculptures of the west pediment, probably the work of Alkamenes, depict a battle between Lapiths and Centaurs.

In 438 B.C. Phidias was called from Athens to Olympia, after finishing the gold and ivory statue of Athena at the Parthenon, to undertake an even more ambitious project: the gold and ivory statue of Zeus, which was bound to become one of the most famous statues of the antiquity, one of the Seven Wonders of the Ancient World.

MILETUS: Gate at the Harbor of Lions

The Lion Harbor was situated between the Theatre hill and the north part of the Humei Tepe hill, and penetrated deep into the north part of the Miletus peninsula. It was the main military port of the city. Its southwest side was, from Geometric times on, a center for the cult of Delphinios Apollo.

The North Agora, the main agora of Miletus, developed on the south side of the harbor after the Persian Wars. On the pier there were long Doric stoas with shops and depots.

An imposing gate with two double rows of three Ionic columns supporting an Ionic entablature with coffered ceilings, the Harbor Gate was built in front of the Delphinion during the rule of Augustus (A.D. 31-14). There, the Sacred Way started and then crossed the whole length of the North Agora.

MILETUS: The Delphinion

The open-air sanctuary of Delphinios Apollo was built during Archaic times (sixth century B.C.), and was used without interruption until the Late Imperial period (third century A.D.). In Hellenistic times, the sanctuary was surrounded on three sides by a two aisled stoa of the Doric order. In Early Hellenistic times a single aisled stoa was added on the western side, which used to be the sanctuary's entrance. During Roman times a circular monopteral building was erected in the central area of the open-air sanctuary. All the stoas were made single aisled, with Corinthian colonnades. Only gray-white marble was used in the construction of the buildings. There were altars from the Archaic period inside the sanctuary, whereas semicircular votive stands, a circular pedestal, bases for statues, and inscribed stelae were added later. These columns, as well as a large number of the inscriptions covering the internal side of the stoa's wall, present information on the political and religious life of the city, for example indicating the use of the sanctuary as the Public Archive of Miletus. The annual pilgrims' procession, which started at the Delphinion, passed through the Sacred Way towards the sanctuary of Apollo at Didyma.

MILETUS: Theater

The Theater of Miletus was erected in the fourth century B.C. on the southwest side of the hill of Kaletepe (which was the citadel of the city, during Classical and Hellenistic times at least). The Theatre's koilon faced the sea and the part of the city across the bay from the Stadium. Part of the Archaic and Hellenistic walls of the city was incorporated into the rear stage wall of the Theater.

Six building phases have been distinguished in the Theater: four in the Hellenistic period, and two in the Roman period. The remains surviving today date to the last phase of the building, from the second century A.D. It was then that the Theater acquired its largest size, 140 meters long, and its capacity 15,000 spectators.

In the Hellenistic period, the Theater had a capacity of 5,300 spectators and looked like a typical Greek theatre. It consisted of the koilon, the slightly lower orchestra with its encircling corridor, and the stage. There were two entrances for spectators on the east and west sides, the one on the west having steps down to the sloping ground.

During its first Hellenistic phase, it was a small theater with two 20-row sections of seats each, and a 15 meter-long stage.

In the second Hellenistic phase (third century B.C.), the Theater was expanded. The stage reached the length of 28 meters, a third section was added to the koilon, and the lateral buttresses were moved slightly towards it. The total height of the Theater reached 40 meters. Arched corridors below the koilon and between the middle and higher sections ensured the movement of spectators without any inconvenience to the seated ones. The relief sculptures with images of weapons probably belong to this phase.

During the Roman period, the Hellenistic koilon was maintained, but partial alterations were implemented to the orchestra and the stage. The level of the orchestra was lowered in order for it to be two meters lower than the first row of seats of the lower section. There, a corridor was added to facilitate spectators' movement. The stage acquired a second floor (69-79 A.D.) consisting of consecutive, free colonnades, and a pulpitum was added at the level of the koilon's lower row of seats. Two apses connected the 40 meter-long stage with the chorus entry walls.

During the second Roman phase, the stage acquired a third floor (161-180 A.D.), and its width was significantly increased. An inscription of the Antonini era indicates that the expansion of the stage finished at the end of the second century A.D. Also during this phase, the imperial gallery was added in the middle of the lower section, its roof resting on four columns.

The facades of both Roman stages were formed by monolithic columns and were distinguished by rich decoration. Scenes of hunting in relief probably decorated the frieze of the third floor of the stage. Two statues of Apollo found in the area of the Theatre, one of which is a copy of the statue made by Canachus for the Apollo temple at Didyma, also came from the stage.

MILETUS: Grattius Monument at the Harbor of Lions

The Monument of Grattius was located on the western coast of the Harbor of Lions, near the North Agora. It most probably was a votive monument offered by the Miletians in honor of a Roman civil servant or civilian who contributed significantly to the city. An inscription on its side reading C. GRATTIO C. F. GAL(ERIA), as well as its architectural style date it to the period of the Roman Flavian Dynasty (first century A.D.).

It was a solid marble monument, typical of its time. The overall structure, whose total height reached 5.32 meters, was vertically divided into three successive sections: base, shaft and crown. The base consisted of a single-step crepis with a marble bench. The solid shaft was formed like a triangular prism with concave sides, whose edges were integrated into pilasters topped by Corinthian capitals supporting a continuous Ionic entablature. The roof was most likely shaped like a triangular pyramid with slightly bevelled edges. Following the style of the times, the structure was probably crowned by a marble vase.